Writing Erotic Romance

by Alison Kent

ALPHA
A member of Penguin Group (USA) Inc.

To the aspiring author who writes, revises, edits, polishes, queries, and submits—and then goes back to the beginning as many times as it takes.

ALPHA BOOKS

Published by the Penguin Group

Penguin Group (USA) Inc., 375 Hudson Street, New York, New York 10014, U.S.A.

Penguin Group (Canada), 10 Alcorn Avenue, Toronto, Ontario, Canada M4V 3B2 (a division of Pearson Penguin Canada Inc.)

Penguin Books Ltd, 80 Strand, London WC2R 0RL, England

Penguin Ireland, 25 St Stephen's Green, Dublin 2, Ireland (a division of Penguin Books Ltd)

Penguin Group (Australia), 250 Camberwell Road, Camberwell, Victoria 3124, Australia (a division of Pearson Australia Group Pty Ltd)

Penguin Books India Pvt Ltd, 11 Community Centre, Panchsheel Park, New Delhi—10 017, India

Penguin Group (NZ), cnr Airborne and Rosedale Roads, Albany, Auckland 1310, New Zealand (a division of Pearson New Zealand Ltd)

Penguin Books (South Africa) (Pty) Ltd, 24 Sturdee Avenue, Rosebank, Johannesburg 2196, South Africa

Penguin Books Ltd, Registered Offices: 80 Strand, London WC2R 0RL, England

International Standard Book Number: 1-59257-546-3
Library of Congress Catalog Card Number: 2006924291

08 07 06 8 7 6 5 4 3 2

Interpretation of the printing code: The rightmost number of the first series of numbers is the year of the book's printing; the rightmost number of the second series of numbers is the number of the book's printing. For example, a printing code of 06-1 shows that the first printing occurred in 2006.

Printed in the United States of America

Publisher: *Marie Butler-Knight*
Editorial Director: *Mike Sanders*
Managing Editor: *Billy Fields*
Senior Acquisitions Editor: *Paul Dinas*
Development Editor: *Christy Wagner*
Production Editor: *Megan Douglass*
Copy Editor: *Emily Garner*
Cartoonist: *Richard King*
Book Designers: *Trina Wurst/Kurt Owens*
Cover Designer: *Bill Thomas*
Indexer: *Angie Bess*
Layout: *Brian Massey*
Proofreader: *Mary Hunt*

Contents at a Glance

Contents

Foreword

My name is Kate Duffy, and I edit erotic romance. (*Hi, Kate.*)

Some years back, it occurred to some of us who labor in editorial offices that wonderful romances with lots of great sex were fun to read and profitable to publish. In other words, sex sells. And sex and romance sell a lot. With that, the amazingly popular new genre of erotic romance was born.

As this part of the romance market was developing, I was asked to define exactly what I, as an editor, was looking for. I had to develop a new language in some cases because while I knew it when I saw it, I hadn't analyzed why one book worked for me but another didn't.

The book you're reading now would have saved me some time. In these pages, Alison Kent has given us all—editors, writers, and readers—a language for discussing and creating erotic romances. And she is uniquely qualified to write this book. She is talented and analytical, practical, and imaginative. The characters in her erotic romance novels are smart, brave, attractive (to put it mildly), witty, and truly heroic. Her stories are true page-turners that make the reader eager to see not only what the characters will do next but what they will say next.

The Complete Idiot's Guide to Writing Erotic Romance is one of the most enjoyable and informative books on writing I have ever read. From the creative process to the publishing marketplace, there is not one aspect of our business that Alison Kent has overlooked, and the anecdotal information she includes illustrates just how personally invested in these books we all are.

If you are interested in publishing a romance, erotic or otherwise, you should read this book. Alison has furnished a Master's class in writing between these covers, and while the emphasis is on erotic romance, she shows us that at the core of these books is storytelling. Alison Kent helps you fashion your plot, characters, and dialogue in such a way as to make your story more accessible to readers and more commercial to publishers.

Compulsively readable and undeniably insightful, as are her novels, Alison Kent's *The Complete Idiot's Guide to Writing Erotic Romance* is money remarkably well spent.

Kate Duffy
editorial director
Kensington Publishing Corporation

Kate Duffy has worked in publishing for a very, very long time. She has worked at Dell, Pocket Books, and Paddington Press (London) as a senior editor. She was the first editor-in-chief of Silhouette Books, as well as editor-in-chief of Tudor Publishing and Meteor Publishing. She is currently an editorial director at Kensington Publishing Corporation in New York and founder of the Brava imprint. In 1991, she became the first individual to receive the Romance Writers of America Industry Award. And in November 2000, she was honored at the Romantic Times' convention for her contributions to the romance book publishing industry.

Introduction

The first romance novel I ever read was Kathleen Woodiwiss's *The Flame and the Flower*. I read it in 1977. I remember specifically reading the last chapters while sitting on the end of my bed in an apartment where I only lived for 6 months. My ironing board was up, my iron plugged in, a dress waiting to be pressed. Wherever it was I was going, I didn't make it. I had to finish the book.

Strangely enough, that was the only romance I read for a long time. I read Colleen McCullough and Phyllis Whitney and Sidney Sheldon and Jackie Collins … but no more romance—not until 10 years later when a bookstore owner in Dallas introduced me to Sandra Brown, Linda Howard, Diana Palmer, and Elizabeth Lowell. From the get-go, I was hooked on authors who wrote the hot stuff. I couldn't get enough. I was in line for their every new release.

Is it any wonder my own writing traveled the same path? Or that one of the first writing contests I won was for sexual tension? I sold my first book in 1993, and during the editing process I was asked to cut a shower scene. That same scene would be considered tame by today's standards, but my editor at the time (who just happens to be one of my editors now) felt it was too risqué. My, how far we've come!

I've now written more than 30 novels and novellas, almost all of them published under an imprint showcasing steamy stories. There are those who contend that certain authors are predisposed to writing with an erotic voice, style, tone, whatever. In other words, we can't help it. We're born that way. All I know is that this is how I write. And if you've picked up this book, then you know the same about yourself.

In this book, I'm going to guide you through taking that natural talent you have and combining it with your love for reading erotic romance so you come out on the other side with a novel a publisher can't wait to snap up. To get in as much information as I can, I've divided this text into six separate sections discussing the craft of fiction, the erotic component, and giving readers what they want.

In **Part 1, "What Is a Romance, and How Do I Know If It's Erotic?"** I show you ways to implement storytelling fundamentals within your erotic romance.

In **Part 2, "Lust at First Sight: The External Journey,"** I walk you through several methods of plotting a novel and give you information on how to look for erotic potential.

In **Part 3, "Who Do You Love? The Emotional Journey,"** I concentrate on your erotic romance's love story.

In **Part 4, "Tangled Sheets: The Physical Journey,"** I cover the intimate and sexual components of romance.

Part 5, "Talk Dirty to Me: Writing Explicit Sex," is where we get down and dirty with body parts, toys, and games.

And you won't want to miss **Part 6, "Satisfy Me: Meeting Your Reader's Expectations."** This is the section where we look at what a reader wants and figure out how to give it to her!

At the end of the book, I've included several appendixes. One is a glossary of specific words defined throughout the text. There is also a comprehensive list of publishers looking for erotica and erotic romance, as well as several resources to help you on your writing journey. I also picked the brains of a few published authors and put together a roundtable discussion on the genre. I hope you enjoy what the experts have to say!

A Few Extras

In addition to the appendixes, you'll find extra nuggets of advice in the form of sidebars sprinkled throughout the pages. These little jewels offer tips, definitions, and words of wisdom from pros in the writing field. Here's what to look for:

Scorchers

You'll want to check out these hot tips guaranteed to keep you on track and help you add the sizzle readers want to your erotic romance.

def•i•ni•tion

This sidebar offers definitions and explanations for terms and expressions that will help you understand more about writing erotic romance.

Naughty, Naughty

These mistakes are ones you'll want to avoid so you write the best erotic romance you possibly can—one readers will be clamoring for.

Slip of the Tongue

In this sidebar, you find comments, advice, insights, and anecdotes from a number of authors.

A Word of Warning

Many of the resources listed throughout this book as well as the actual content itself address sexually explicit material—which shouldn't be a surprise based on the subject matter. Also, several of the online sources (publisher websites, author websites, etc.) provide external links to sexually oriented websites or include sexually graphic advertising banners on their pages.

Acknowledgments

A huge thank you to my editor, Paul Dinas, not only for offering me the project, but for so patiently dealing with my never-ending questions. An equally huge thank you to my agent, Karen Solem. And one more huge thank you to Kate Duffy for thinking of me.

My family. Ever so patient. From the bottom of my heart, thank you Walt, Casey, Megan, Holly, and Mike for supporting me. And extra kisses to Walt for bouncing around my ideas and tossing back more than I ever expected. I don't know what I would do without you.

Jolie, Bekke, Larissa, and Stephanie read chapters when I begged, no matter how busy they were with their own lives, and brainstormed any time I asked, correcting my mistakes and giving me extra food for thought. True friends. I love you all.

I would also like to acknowledge the generosity of the authors and editors whose words of advice are sprinkled throughout this book. I asked. You gave. Willingly, openly. You went above and beyond, allowing me to offer readers more insight than I could have managed alone. I thank you one and all.

Trademarks

Part 1

What Is a Romance, and How Do I Know If It's Erotic?

The promise a romance author makes to a romance reader is to deliver a love story with a happy ending. In an erotic romance, she also promises to imbue the love story with a highly charged sexual component.

However, no erotic romance will work if the basic story elements aren't in place. Part 1 contains information on how to be sure they are and gives you tips on implementing the fundamentals of storytelling within your erotic romance.

Chapter 1

Focus, Focus, Focus: It's All About the Love Story

In This Chapter

- Crafting characters who bring your story to life
- Plotting the framework of your novel
- Creating conflict that keeps readers reading
- Understanding the push and pull of sexual tension
- Keeping sight of the romance

Let's start at the very beginning. It's impossible to talk about writing erotic romance without first taking a look at what makes the *romance genre* tick. Are you wondering whether or not what you've written is a true romance? Take this simple test: if you can remove your love story and come away with a book that works as a complete, whole, and viable novel, then the answer is no, you don't have a romance. There, that was easy, wasn't it?

In a romance novel, the events that occur must be fueled—or at least be impacted—by the interactions of your male and female *protagonists* on their journey to falling in love. Your novel's couple and their impending romance is the reason your story exists. Got it? Okay!

Now, what elements does a genre romance novel require? Another simple answer: a romance novel contains the same elements found in any good work of fiction—with a few add-ons specific to the genre. I start here with the foundation, because once that's in place, you're on your way to having at your disposal all the necessary tools for building a great—and sexy—erotic romance.

I Need a Hero

Boy, don't we all! A knight in shining armor to sweep us off our feet. Or at least to sweep the floors when we're too sick or have deadlines to meet. Ask a romance reader why she reads romance, and 9 times out of 10 she'll tell you for the hero. (If I spend a lot of time on this subject, this is why!) Not only does your hero have to be a man worthy of your heroine's love; he also has to be a man your reader can fall in love with.

def•i•ni•tion

A *genre novel* is one with distinctive content designed to meet specific reader expectations. A novel in the **romance genre,** for example, always has characters who fall in love by the last page, leaving the reader with a satisfying ending and a romantic commitment made by the story's couple. The **protagonists** are the main characters in a literary work. Because a romance novel is the story of a couple falling in love, both your hero and heroine share this billing.

One thing your hero doesn't have to be is perfect. At the beginning of your story, he can even be unlikable. Readers love heroes who need to be redeemed … especially when that redemption comes at the hands of a heroine he can't live without.

So what are the characteristics romance readers (and heroines) most want in their heroes? The *2004 Romance Fiction Sales Statistics, Reader Demographics and Book-Buying Habits* report compiled by the Romance Writers of America, Inc., reveals readers' top three favorite traits to be muscles, handsomeness, and intelligence. Here are a few more most of us can't live without:

- Sense of humor
- Sense of honor
- Honesty
- Integrity
- Confidence
- Protective nature
- Adventurous streak

Basically, beneath whatever his veneer, he's got to be an admirable man with heroic qualities. And way sexy to boot!

Slip of the Tongue

On the subject of writing believable heroes, author Lynn Viehl says, "As writers, we women need to be aware of the differences between the genders, and get them on the page. Men and women are biologically programmed to look, act and speak differently, and that's made our species successful. This is not something to mourn or homogenize; I think we should celebrate our differences. If you find your *heroes* are *sheroes,* then you need to do some research into writing more realistic male characters."

Order Up!

Romance novel heroes are as varied in their occupations as their real-life counterparts, but there are career choices which, by definition, lend themselves to the genre's *larger-than-life* male roles.

def•i•ni•tion

A **larger-than-life** character is one of the sort from which legends are born. He is imposing, impressive, memorable. Think Wolf Mackenzie from *Mackenzie's Mountain* by Linda Howard or Jamie Fraser from Diana Gabaldon's *Outlander.* Think Rhett Butler or Jane Austen's Mr. Fitzwilliam Darcy. When put into a challenging situation, a larger-than-life hero rises to the occasion and meets every obstacle thrown his way head-on.

These professions tend to be thought of as sexy and are often accompanied by elements of risk and danger that put the hero in a truly heroic situation. Here are a few examples:

- Cowboys
- Law enforcement
- Firefighters
- Doctors, paramedics
- Spies, secret agents
- Military, special forces
- Pirates, warriors
- Astronauts, pilots
- Bounty hunters
- Fortune hunters
- Bodyguards

The Greek Alphabet

Alpha heroes, *beta heroes*, and now *gamma heroes*. Anyone familiar with the romance genre has probably heard these terms used to describe our story men. But what exactly do they mean?

- An *alpha hero* is domineering, the leader of a pack, a man of action. He doesn't back down from confrontation. He is, of course, an amazing lover, and readers adore him! Why? Because a true alpha is *not* a jerk or an abusive brute. He is the epitome of heroic—not only in how he fits into your plot, but in how he treats his heroine.
- A *beta hero* is no less heroic than an alpha. He is simply more likely to employ brains before brawn. What a beta is not is a man with female qualities. His prowess is simply more mental than physical. Think Tom Hanks in almost any of his roles.
- A *gamma hero* possesses the best traits of both the alpha and beta. He is strong, a leader, a protector. He is thoughtful and sensitive enough to consider other's feelings and to look before he leaps.

Slip of the Tongue

One of my favorite romance heroes from 2005 was Reece Sheridan from Pamela Clare's fantastic romantic suspense *Extreme Exposure*. Pamela says about writing Reece, "For me, Reece Sheridan represents an updated version of the alpha male. He's strong, confident, protective, courageous—all of the qualities we love in traditional alpha males—but he's living in a post-feminist world. He's sensitive while still being very much a man. He's not threatened by an equally strong woman with her own career, ambitions, and sexual needs. I felt he was the perfect hero for a modern career woman, someone the heroine could rely on no matter what the situation."

The Complete Package

Your hero does not exist in a vacuum. There is more to his life than the heroine. If he is an attorney taking a deposition and the heroine is across the table as opposing counsel, his mind had better be on the case. He can get his hands on her later after their business is done.

A romance hero does not turn into a bumbling idiot the minute the heroine comes onto the scene. Neither does he turn into a walking, talking, erection. His life may never be the same, but he is still a man in control. He can lose it in the bedroom, yes. At the bargaining table, no.

Who's That Lady?

She's your heroine. She's the female character your reader either wants to be or wants for a best friend—at least by the end of your book! She doesn't have to be any more perfect than does your hero.

What she does have to be is a woman to whom your female readers can relate. They need to understand who she is now and where she's come from to identify with and respect the choices she makes—especially her sexual choices. This is paramount in an erotic romance.

Naughty, Naughty

You don't want your sexually active heroine to come across as a slut!

The Real Deal

Many readers complain that romance heroines seem to have no life outside their interaction with the hero. That the minute he enters her world, everything else—her interests and hobbies, her friends and family—cease to exist.

Give your heroine a life, including girlfriends to bond with, co-workers to share work issues, and neighbors to pick up her mail and feed her Rottweiler while she's out of town. Heroines in today's romances are not reclusive orphans whose only companions are cats!

A Perfect Match

A romance heroine is capable of bringing home the bacon, frying it up in a pan, and has BOB—her battery-operated boyfriend—to send her to sleep with a smile. She doesn't *need* a man to solve her problems *for* her; she *wants* him to solve her problems *with* her. If there is a rescue involved, she's an active participant—not a dishrag.

A romance heroine has to be just as worthy of a hero's love as he does of hers. No hero is going to want to spend his life drying tears of weakness or ordering from a menu for his wishy-washy, whiny mate. A romance heroine needs to be as strong as the man she leans on. Together they make an unbeatable team.

Slip of the Tongue

On the difference between strong heroes and strong heroines, *Silhouette Bombshell* author Sandra K. Moore says, "I saw a clip from an old Chinese kung fu movie in which a woman warrior, when challenged by a sword-wielding man, said she would allow him to pass into the house if he could cut the tofu she'd made. He slashed, hacked, jumped, etc. and the woman simply moved the big wooden flat of tofu up, down, behind her back, over her head, under the table, etc. until he gave up and left in defeat. That, for me, epitomizes a strong heroine."

All Woman

Being strong does not make your heroine a man in woman's clothing. What it makes her is the ideal mate, the yin to the hero's yang. Whether your heroine is a corporate CEO, a shop clerk, a fighter pilot, a portrait artist, or a soon-to-be stay-at-home mom, she is a woman who is able to meet the challenges life throws her way in her own inimitable style—while well aware that she, the supposed weaker sex, is the one capable of bringing the bigger, stronger, and more powerful male to his knees with no more than the crook of a finger and an honest, interested smile.

Once Upon a Time There Was a Plot ...

Even though the focus of a romance novel is the love story, there needs to be an external framework of rising dramatic tension that brings your hero and heroine together. In other words, something besides sex has to be going on! In the arena of erotic romance, a number of situations can lend themselves to believable forced proximity and in turn, to believable sexual situations. For example:

- Marriage of convenience
- Stranded together
- On the run
- Hostage situation
- Road trip
- Competition
- Close working conditions
- Bodyguard scenario

Scorchers

Don't ignore the importance of plot and action in your writing—action *outside* the bedroom, I mean! If you do, you're liable to end up with a lot of talking heads and navel gazing—and one boring book!

This isn't to say you must use a similar plot device. The plots of successful romance novels run the gamut from high seas adventures to high country round-ups to high-stakes corporate mergers. Just be sure you have something happening.

It Was a Dark and Stormy Night

It wasn't until I read Tami Hoag's 1995 release *Night Sins* that I realized how powerful a tool setting can be. The story took place in Minnesota in the middle of winter, and I was cold the entire time I spent reading the book. It was a lesson I will never forget on using setting to enhance a reading experience.

How you use setting will, of course, depend on the story you tell. But don't underuse it or ignore it when location, environment, and ambiance can all serve to draw a visceral response from your reader—whether she experiences warm fuzzies, desert dry-mouth, or a frightening chill!

Love Is a Battlefield

A story without conflict is a snoozefest. Readers want to see characters fight for what they want and believe in. They want to see them work and suffer and come out on top, triumphant in the end. Conflict is basically what keeps your couple apart.

It can be a case of different beliefs and opposing goals requiring compromise, sacrifice, growth, and change. It can be a villainous *antagonist*. It can be a series of unfortunate external events they have to overcome. Whatever it is, conflict must be believable and sustainable.

def•i•ni•tion

An **antagonist** is a fictional character in opposition to your protagonist. He is an adversary, nemesis, or enemy, and he stands in the way of your protagonist reaching his goals. An antagonist is a fully developed character with his own fully motivated objectives. He needs to be connected to the story as intimately as the rest of the characters—not just thrown into the mix as a bit player or throwaway member of the cast.

Remember, if your characters work through their problems on page 1, you'll have an awfully short book! Conflict needs to be present in every scene, carried from page 1 to "The End." It cannot be entirely external. Romance is about characters, so internal conflict is vital. I talk about conflict in more detail soon. For now, when considering conflict, here are a few things you should avoid at all costs:

- Big misunderstandings easily solved with a simple conversation. Mature people talk.
- Three hundred pages of bickering settled in one page of kissing and making up.
- *Deus ex machina* as a resolution. Solutions to problems need to stem from the characters, not from out of the blue.

> **def•i•ni•tion**
>
> *Deus ex machina* is Latin for "god from the machine." The term refers to an improbable or unbelievable person or event dropped into a fictional story to resolve a situation or plot point. It originated with Greek and Roman theater where a crane or machine lowered actors portraying gods onto the stage to solve unsolvable circumstances.

Motivation and Goals—Understanding the Why

The why of your book is tied into your plot, your romance, your characters, and your conflict. The why is what enables a true *suspension of disbelief* by your reader. The why is all about believability and plausibility. The why will get you over bumps and humps and writing blocks. The why will propel your story from one scene to the next.

What is the why? Motivation. Every action taken must be motivated. Whether as simple as choosing a fancy restaurant over fast food, or as complex as performing surgery to save a child at a great personal risk, or as emotionally charged as unprotected sex with a stranger, the choices your characters make must have sufficient motivation or your reader may very well give up on your book because the characters' actions don't ring true.

> **def•i•ni•tion**
>
> **Suspension of disbelief** is the reader's willingness to set aside her skepticism and ignore a story's faults, accepting the author's telling to be a true version of events so she can enjoy the experience of reading.

What is motivation? Simply put, motivation is the impetus or catalyst—whether conscious or buried deep within a character's psyche—that pushes him or her into action. Motivation is always based on the past events in a character's life, even those a reader never sees, even those a character may not consciously acknowledge. This is why it's so important to know your characters inside and out.

Motivation looks beneath the surface of a character's behavior and digs into who she is at the most basic level, exploring where she came from and what made her the person she is today. That exploration gives your character true depth and prevents her from being a cardboard cut-out. You want your reader to see your character as a real person, to sympathize and empathize, to relate to her situation, and to understand the reasons for her actions and the choices she makes. So when you're writing those choices? Think, *motive*, *motive*, *motive* every time!

Naughty, Naughty

No element of a story will work if it reads as if the author is the one controlling the outcome. Everything must stem from the characters—who they are, what they want, how they get beyond the obstacles standing in their way. As the writer, you must be true to the story people you've created and let them tell their tale. Otherwise, the reader will sense the puppeteer behind the curtain pulling the strings, and you'll have failed to draw her into your fictional world.

Inseparable from motivation are goals. The first drives your protagonist's need or desire for the second. Your characters will have goals that are both internal and external, and all will be tied into who they are. I discuss goals and how to establish them more deeply in future chapters.

Stop! Wait ... Don't Stop!

A romance novel without *sexual tension* is like a donut without the, well, the donut. It's not even about the icing on top. Sexual tension—that push/pull of the physical "Should I or shouldn't I?" question—is the driving force behind romance. It builds anticipation and both your characters and your readers experience it viscerally. It is expressed in writing through all five senses … with a heavy-lidded glance that causes a heart to race, or a palm on the small of a back that sends a shiver down a spine.

def•i•ni•tion

Sexual tension is a device found in books and movies in which two characters experience physical desire for one another yet are held back from acting upon the physical need. The characters experience that rising awareness of sexual attraction emotionally as well as physically. Sexual tension is the spark that brings the plot to life, that flavors every word spoken, that fuels every response from your hero to your heroine or vice versa.

Sexual tension is more than a woman getting wet and a man getting hard. And it's more than raunchy thoughts and coarse, gritty, nasty words. It's that moment of urgency before a kiss when time stops, when you hold your breath while you wait. It's the way your eyes meet, and you know you are both thinking about sex, even though you haven't said a word.

Sexual tension is the look in Colin Firth's eyes as his Mr. Darcy looks across the room at Jennifer Ehle's Elizabeth Bennet playing the pianoforte in *Pride and Prejudice*. Sexual tension is Daniel Day Lewis's Hawkeye striding through the surgery to find Madeleine Stowe's Cora Munro in *Last of the Mohicans*.

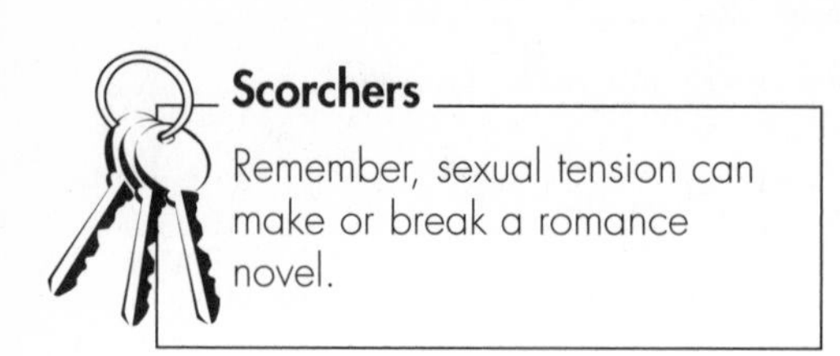

Scorchers
Remember, sexual tension can make or break a romance novel.

Now, everyone familiar with these movies (and what lovers of romance novels aren't?) knows that there is very little sexual content in either of them. Tension is not about the act. It's about the buildup, the sensory awareness. I explore sexual tension fully in its own chapter (Chapter 16). It's that important, that essential.

True Romance Doesn't Happen Every Day

Remember the test? Does your love story carry your book? This may seem obvious, but it's often a complaint by romance readers—that a novel billed as a romance spends too much time away from the love story.

Not only that, readers insist (as they well should!) on seeing the characters fall in love. They want to share and experience the emotional upheaval, the punch of attraction, the nerves and uncertainty of "he loves me, he loves me not." They want to be there for that first kiss, to feel that heart-stopping realization that a character feels when tumbling head over heels for good.

Here's a checklist to be sure you've covered the romance basics:

- ❑ Have I infused my story with sexual tension?
- ❑ Have I shown my characters falling in love through actions, words, and thoughts?
- ❑ Have I explored the sexual component as appropriate, whether on-screen or off-?

I explore this topic more fully in Part 3, but it's worth planting the seed as you begin. You're writing a romance, so don't forget to include the romance!

Scorchers

In his book *Intimate Behavior: A Zoologist's Classic Study of Human Intimacy,* author Desmond Morris describes the 12 steps through which humans progress on their way to intimacy, beginning with eye-to-body contact and ending with sexual intercourse. Exploring this progression is a sure way to keep the love story on track, while skipping a step or two or three can ratchet up the level of your sexual tension.

And They Lived Happily Ever After

Besides a to-die-for hero, the number-one thing that draws readers to the romance genre is the guarantee of a happy ending. Romance offers fantasy escapism, a promise that everything will turn out perfectly in the end no matter the angst along the way.

The stories also offer hope. I can't tell you how many letters I've received from readers thanking me for offering them an uplifting look at romantic relationships. In the end, love conquers all, and what a beautiful way for a couple who has been through so much to triumph.

Slip of the Tongue

Author Shiloh Walker says about the genre's requirement for a happily-ever-after, "I read just about everything, but if I'm wanting a happy ending along with my escape from reality, I pick up a romance. There will be bumps and bruises, but at least I don't have to worry about the main characters—namely the hero and heroine—dying or not ending up as expected, or turning into a thug, or climbing aboard a ship and leaving their beloved behind never to be seen again."

The Least You Need to Know

- Fully developed and realistic characters are the key to compelling fiction.
- A romance novel, like any other fictional work, requires an external plot of rising dramatic tension.
- Conflict must be real, believable, sustainable, and never solved without a lot of work.
- Every action in your story is driven by your characters' goals and motivations.

- Sexual tension provides the electricity that keeps the fire of attraction burning between your characters.
- This is a romance, so let your readers experience your characters falling in love.

Chapter 2

Ready, Set, ... Write!

In This Chapter

- Tips for deciding what you're best suited to write
- The indisputable value of research
- Got your idea ducks in a row? Then start writing!
- Fitting into the market

Now that you've decided to write a romance, the next step is to figure out *what* to write. Obviously, because you've picked up this book, you know that whatever the time period, the universe, the subject matter, or the theme, the sexual content of your novel will be erotic rather than sweet. Believe it or not, that decision is one best made up front, as it colors many of the craft and story elements you will use along the way. That's the good news.

Here's the rest—and it's all still good! Determining your novel's level of sexual heat is only one of the choices you have to make. The next steps involve figuring out what sort of story line will hold your interest for a possible 400 manuscript pages, and whether or not publishers will find your idea marketable in the genre's current climate. Trust me; this isn't as daunting as it sounds, as long as you look before you leap!

What Do You Want to Write?

You want to write a really good book, right? One that gets readers talking? One they can't put down and still think about months after the last page is read? One they shelve with the rest of their keepers and never forget? One they insist their friends must read? One they reread time and again?

Well, that's what I'm here to help you do! The one thing I can't tell you is *what* to write. Deciding on your plot, setting, and subject matter is up to you. But I can offer a few tricks you might find useful if you haven't settled on one idea yet.

The best part? None of the tips I'm about to offer involves anything more painful than taking a look at who you are as an individual and analyzing your interests, passions, and whatever sparks your enthusiasm. In other words, what about you makes your internal author tick?

Writing What You Know

A good friend of mine is a trained first responder. She also served in the U.S. Air Force. One of the first manuscripts of hers I read featured an EMT hero who had worked previously as a medic in the same branch of the armed forces. Her experience gave an authenticity to her work that she might not have managed had she relied on textbook research rather than writing what she knew.

Naughty, Naughty

Whatever you write about, be sure the idea excites you more than a little bit. If you're bored writing it, your reader will pick up on your lack of enthusiasm and be bored reading it. Remember, money isn't everything, and your name will be on that cover forever!

Does this mean you have to be an expert or have experience with your subject matter? Of course not. If such were the case, most of us wouldn't be writing what we do. However, if you're intimately familiar with criminal profiling and have a story idea about a profiler begging to be told, why not? You'll be that much ahead of the game.

Writing What You Love to Read

Probably more than any other motivation, the love of reading drives readers to try their hand at writing a book. If you enjoy reading so much that you're compelled to write a novel of your own, there's a good chance that your favorite topics and themes to read will be the ones that fuel your story ideas waiting to be written.

Writing What You Want to Read

I know what you're thinking. With the number of romances being published each year and the explosive growth of erotic romance in particular, how could anyone have trouble finding anything to read? Well, it happens.

Think of it this way: even with erotica's literary history and the romance genre's domination of the fiction market, someone somewhere had to be the first to say, "Hey, I want my erotica *in* my romance." This is how trends are born—an author comes up with something new and fresh or puts her own unique spin on the tried and true and makes a splash. Got an idea? Go for it! You could be the next big thing!

> **Scorchers**
>
> According to the Romance Writers of America, Inc.'s *2005 Market Research Study on Romance Readers,* in 2004, romance fiction made up 54.9 percent of paperback fiction sales and 39.3 percent of total popular fiction sales. No matter the reason you've chosen to write romance, the genre's popularity allows for enough diversity that you can't go wrong! You have a built-in audience waiting to read what you've written. What are you waiting for?

Writing What Stirs Your Interest

There's a lot to be said for writing about a topic in which you hold a special interest. Not only are you able to write from the standpoint of an expert; you'll naturally infuse your story with an insider's take on the subject.

Maybe you're an aficionado of the American West, having studied the subject for years. Think how much fun you would have writing characters living in a historical era with which you're intimately familiar.

Writing What Stirs Your Emotion

A passion, a cause, an experience—any of these can spark an idea for a story. Believing deeply in an ideal, feeling strongly about an issue, or surviving a life-changing event is often the impetus for wanting to write a book to share that experience. What you need to remember in this case, however, is that you are not telling *your* story, but your characters'. You can draw on your personal experience to give a compelling realism to your work, but you must make the moral of your story subtle as well as have it spring from your story people and their journey—not your own.

Your readers are reading for the romance. They don't want to be lectured or preached to. They will, however, be sucked into any story with a true emotional resonance. Make them feel what you feel, and you'll have a winner!

Researching the Market

No matter what you want to write, one of the most important considerations is whether or not you'll be able to sell your idea in current market conditions. As creators, we may not like the fact that marketing drives so much of the publishing industry, but such is the case. Getting a publisher's marketing department behind you can make or break your book's success, not to mention impact your long-term staying power in the business.

Scorchers

Publishers Marketplace (www.publishersmarketplace.com) is a wonderful online source for seeing what's selling in today's market. The site lists specifics of deals as they're reported by authors and agents and offers an e-mail service that delivers the announcements straight to your inbox. You can also find up-to-the-minute market information at *Publishers Weekly*'s website (www.publishersweekly.com), though much of their site is available only to subscribers of the magazine.

Pixels and Paper: Print vs. Electronic Publishing

Nowhere can the rise in the popularity of electronic publishing be seen better than in erotic romance. Off the top of my head, I can name a dozen publishers with that single specific fiction focus. Even so, print books continue to be the most popular reading format. They are sold online as well as in brick-and-mortar stores, while electronic books are downloaded from sales sites on the Web and read on computer monitors, PDAs, *e-book readers*—even cell phones. Electronic books are available in a number of formats, making them compatible with most operating systems, though specific software such as Adobe Reader or Microsoft Reader may be required. (Both are free.)

def•i•ni•tion

An **e-book reader** is an electronic device made specifically for reading electronically published texts.

Print publishers traditionally pay an average *advance* against *royalties* of 6 to 10 percent of a paperback book's cover price, and those royalties are usually disbursed to the author twice a year. Royalty rates are usually higher for hardcover releases. Some publishers may offer less up-front money initially, and some contracts may specify higher rates for additional sales after a certain number of books are sold. Electronic publishers rarely offer advances but do pay royalties at a much higher percentage (one publisher's website quotes 37.5 percent, another quotes 40 percent) and pay their authors monthly or quarterly.

Print books can—and do—go out of print. Electronic books do not, as long as a publisher continues to list the titles in its catalogue. Print publishers hold back a portion of an author's royalties for a certain time period as they wait for bookstore returns. Print editions of many electronically published books are eventually made available in stores, but electronic publishers often sell print copies from their websites to individuals, negating the entire rationale for holding *reserves against returns.* Most electronic publishers do, however, deduct any individual returns from an author's future earnings.

Consider all these issues when researching the market and deciding which publishing avenue to pursue.

def•i•ni•tion

An **advance** is money paid up front at the time a contract is signed and is deducted from future royalties earned. **Royalties** are a predetermined percentage of the proceeds from the sales of a book paid to the author. **Reserves against returns** are monies held back from an author's earnings in anticipation of bookstores returning unsold copies to the publisher for credit.

The Long and Short of It: Novels vs. Novellas

Romance novels tend to run between 50,000 and 100,000 words. Shorter novels have one main plot, while longer ones allow room for the weaving of a subplot or two. Check the guidelines of the various publishing houses to see what length they look for in their novel submissions.

Novellas are shorter stories, usually between 20,000 and 40,000 words, depending on publishers' requirements, and are most often compiled in collections called anthologies.

Jaci Burton, Ellora's Cave and Bantam Dell author, explains the popularity of erotic romance novellas this way: "I believe the appeal

Slip of the Tongue

Tina Engler, founder of Romantica publisher Ellora's Cave who also writes as Jaid Black, says of the company's stand-alone novellas, "We've found them to be an effective marketing tool for getting readers to try a new author. They are quick, inexpensive reads, designed to show customers what the writer is capable of."

of the erotic romance in novella format stems from busy women searching for a quick, hot, emotionally and physically satisfying love story. They not only can read an entire story in one sitting, but a novella allows them to enjoy several of their favorite erotic romance authors in one book, or to try out new authors without investing a ton of money in buying a more expensive single author title they may not like."

Kensington Brava, a pioneer in marketing erotic romance novellas, publishes a number of three-novella *Bad Boys* anthologies, as well as shorter "six-packs." Romantica publisher Ellora's Cave is one publishing house that offers single-release novellas. Many publishers offer novella contracts only to established authors, while others accept submissions *over the transom*. Look closely at the submission policies for your publisher of choice if you're interested in writing a novella.

> **def•i•ni•tion**
>
> **Over the transom** refers to unsolicited submissions delivered by an agentless author to a publisher.

Size Does Matter: Trade Paperbacks vs. Mass Market

According to a 2005 *Publishers Weekly* article, *trade paperbacks* have become the favorite reading format for many, especially readers of younger generations. This is good news for authors of erotic romance! Kensington's Brava and Aphrodisia imprints are both released initially in trade, as is Harlequin's erotic fiction imprint, Spice. Ellora's Cave publishes their print editions in trade size as well. Also, the new Avon Red and Berkley Heat imprints are publishing their books in the larger size.

Though the price of the larger trade paperbacks is higher than that of the smaller *mass market editions*, the format has proven popular enough to be dubbed the "new hardcover" by many. Another plus is that trade releases are often reissued by their print publisher in mass market 12 to 18 months after their original publication date. This gives readers the option of two reading formats and allows authors to build an audience base with fans of both.

> **def•i•ni•tion**
>
> A **trade paperback** is a book that is smaller than and generally priced less than a hardcover but is larger than the popular **mass market edition** of approximately $4\frac{1}{4} \times 6\frac{3}{4}$ inches.

Researching the Story

Even if you're writing what you know, you won't know everything, right? And if you do? Well, you're writing a romance novel, not a textbook or an instruction manual. Believe it or not, what you leave out is as vital as what you put in. So how *do* you know which details deserve page time and which don't?

It's really pretty simple. What you include must spring logically from the needs of your story and your characters—not from you as the author wanting to share what you've learned. Here's a quick checklist to see if you're on the right track:

- ❑ My research is not only as verifiably accurate as possible but is essential to the story as a whole as well.
- ❑ I haven't bored readers with a massive dumping of information but have woven my research into my story naturally.
- ❑ In each scene, I've only included research details that are absolutely necessary in the moment.

Now, how to research. Lucky you, you're living in the information age with almost everything you could possibly need to know at your fingertips. Deciding where to go first for your instant gratification research needs is probably the hardest part of all! Try these tips on for size:

- **Interviews:** Talking to experts in person or by phone can get you the insider's track to your subject.
- **Internet:** What did we ever do without it? Pull up your favorite search engine, type in your search terms, and a wealth of information awaits.

> **Naughty, Naughty**
>
> When relying on the Internet for research, consider the credibility of the reference, and verify the information with multiple sources.

- **Documentaries:** *National Geographic*, PBS, Time-Life, and the BBC produce amazing factual and informative programs that are often available in VHS and DVD formats.
- **Artwork:** Sculptures and paintings that corroborate other research sources can enhance the finer points of your descriptive scenes.
- **Travel:** There's nothing like hands-on research for accurately depicting sights, sounds, and scents. This is a highly recommended method for getting sensory details just right.
- **Library:** Beyond encyclopedias, check out historical texts, letters, diaries, journals, and archived newspapers for eyewitness accounts and firsthand experiences.

  And don't forget interlibrary loan. Is the Library of Congress the only library to carry the book you absolutely need? No problem! They'll send most books to your local library, where you can read them and make photocopies if necessary.

Slip of the Tongue

Historical romance author Lydia Joyce says of using artwork to supplement her research on underclothes, "Paintings of Queen Victoria playing with her children and other wealthy women in boating parties without crinolines confirms that it was an article of fashion, not decency, and that even upper class women would leave it off when it was impractical. A folktale and its painting finally revealed to me when and why the medieval nobility took their under-linen off to sleep naked and where they put it when they did. But I have to be careful because most painters weren't out to make accurate portrayals of daily life (especially that of the lower classes) but to make Art, which was often idealized and enhanced with props from the artist's studio!"

Note: When using printed materials—magazines, research papers, textbooks, newspapers, theses, and the like—*always, always, always* respect copyright. Also, it's a good idea to use more than one source whatever your methods. Verify your facts to avoid being called on faulty or incomplete research.

Stop Researching Already, and Start Writing!

The time comes when you can't put it off any longer. You have to stop the preparation and the planning and just do it. Write. Get your hands dirty. Dig in up to your elbows. Wallow around in all that juicy information you've discovered and put it to use. Research doesn't do your writing a bit of good if you don't write.

So bite the bullet and put pen to page—or fingers to keyboard—and take the plunge. You won't be the first to flounder or feel as if you've bitten off more than you can chew. It happens to all of us. But there's one universal truth you can't overlook: books get written one word at a time.

Scorchers

Don't feel as if you have to research every detail of your novel before you start to write. Many times, you won't even be aware that you need to know something until you get to the point in your book where it crops up. It's up to you whether you'll stop then and dig for the details you need, or whether—as many authors do—you'll put a placeholder, such as an XXX, in your text and come back to it later. If the detail is only mentioned in passing, the latter trick is invaluable. However, if the research plays a larger part, then take a break and do your homework!

Okay, Now What?

You know what you want to write. Your subject matter stirs you as both an author and a reader. You've studied the market and done enough research that you feel comfortable forging ahead. The only thing left to decide is where within the romance genre's *subgenres* your idea best fits.

def•i•ni•tion

Subgenres are smaller, unique categories within the main romance genre that are divided by time periods, subject matter, or specific elements. The primary subgenres within romance are contemporary, historical, suspense, inspirational, and paranormal, which can also include time-travel and futuristic.

Isn't that obvious, you ask? Not necessarily.

Your medieval-set mystery could be a historical romance—unless the killer is a supernatural being, in which case your emphasis may be on the paranormal. Move the same concept to current times, and you could have a romantic suspense. Make the mystery a secondary storyline, and you might be writing a straight contemporary romance with a suspenseful subplot. See? Things aren't always as clearly defined as you might think.

Obviously, if you've decided to write a Victorian historical because that's what you love to read, or you've decided to write a shapeshifting warlock in outer space because that's what you want to read, or you've decided to put your experience with a surrogate mother into a contemporary romance, then the rest of this section won't apply to you. However, if what you've decided to write is an idea that will work in a number of scenarios, read on.

Let's say you've decided to write about a heroine, Rachel, forced by family obligations to work off a debt owed to the hero, Brandon. Because this will be an erotic romance, such a setup offers a plausible scenario and endless opportunities for interaction between the two. Now, consider the following.

The frequency of the characters' interaction will be determined by word length, as will the development of the plot. You can't do in 50,000 words what you can do in 100,000. This is where it helps to know if you want to write a novella, a short novel, or a longer and multi-layered novel.

The locations of the characters' interaction will be determined by your story world. Rachel and Brandon can go at it in a stable in any time period. Not so going at it under the table in a singles bar or while at zero gravity. Look at your idea, and decide what role your setting will play.

The stakes of the characters' interaction will be determined by the morals and mores of your story world. Yes, people have been engaging in sexual activity since the beginning of time. But the self-perception and societal restraints Rachel faces if she is in Regency England won't necessarily mirror those she will face in intergalactic 2525.

The circumstances of the characters' interaction will be determined by the traditions and cultural expectations of your story world. In a historical novel, Rachel's debt may require marriage to Brandon. In a contemporary novel, Rachel may agree to be Brandon's mistress for a month before they go their separate ways. In a futuristic novel, Brandon may implant a summoning device that forces Rachel to appear whenever he calls.

To determine where your idea best fits, ask yourself these questions:

- ❑ What length of story do I want to write, and will word count requirements limit my publisher options?
- ❑ Is my subject matter or story concept restricted to a particular time period?
- ❑ If not, what fictional scenario will give me the best opportunity for exploring my subject matter or story concept?

Taking the time to consider all your options can't hurt—and might just serve to make your story even stronger!

The Least You Need to Know

- Your enthusiasm for the subject matter of your novel will show in the final product and allow readers to enjoy your work and share your excitement.
- Market research is necessary to be sure your idea is saleable.
- Story research must be integral to your novel's plot and woven seamlessly into your book.
- Taking the time to analyze the best venue in which to tell your story guarantees your novel a strong and solid footing.

Chapter 3

The Romance Genre: It's Like a Box of Chocolates!

In This Chapter

- Writing for a contemporary audience
- Putting history on the page believably
- Keeping the romance in your suspense and the suspense in your romance
- Tapping into the popularity of magic and make-believe
- Maintaining sexual integrity within the context of your story

It's true what they say: romance offers something for everyone. Whether you've chosen to write about current times, past times, pretend times, or frightening times, you won't have far to look for an audience. Every subgenre experiences cyclical ups and downs in popularity, but the wide variety of offerings in the genre as a whole—and in the erotic romance arena in particular—is great news for today's authors. It means there is a huge demand in need of a supply! So get writing!

Contemporary Romance

A contemporary romance is exactly what it says—a story that take place today, no matter when "today" may be. Contemporary offerings include family dramas, romantic comedies, even stories with a *Sex and the City chick-lit* feel. These books are often more accessible to readers who want to see their own world and experiences played out on the page and find it hard to relate to the traditions and expectations or even fictional creations of other eras or worlds.

> **def•i•ni•tion**
>
> **Chick lit** is a genre of popular fiction aimed at young single women, usually in their 20s. The stories feature female characters facing career, relationship, and other challenges that result in life changes and personal growth.

Neither do contemporaries have the same constraints of historical time periods. Contemporary heroines can do and be anything, allowing today's readers to identify with their career options, lifestyle decisions, and sexual choices.

Tried and True Categories

Harlequin Enterprises, Ltd., is currently the only publisher producing *category romances*. Between their Silhouette, Harlequin, Mills & Boon, and Steeple Hill divisions, Harlequin publishes several series lines, and the level of sensuality varies among the divisions. Harlequin Blaze, at 70,000 to 75,000 words, is the only one that publishes erotic romance.

> **def•i•ni•tion**
>
> **Category romances,** or *series romances,* are numbered books published monthly in a specific line that is defined by content guidelines and word length. The books stay on the shelf only until the next month's release replaces them. Each line publishes the same number of books with similar packaging monthly, enabling readers to recognize their favorite series lines on sight. They traditionally have a lower cover price than independently published books.

One of the great things about category romances is that the books have a loyal and dedicated audience, meaning you have a built-in readership. However, this also means you need to read extensively within the line for which you would like to write to know just what those readers are expecting when they pick up your book. Not only do you want to give readers what they're looking for, you'll save yourself editorial revisions by getting the tone and content right the first time out!

Stand-Alone Singles

Single-title releases are books published independently of any line. They may be connected to other books by the same author or be part of a series conceived by an editor and written by several authors who share characters and elements. For the most part, however, single titles stand alone.

The word count for single-title contemporaries is usually no less than 90,000 and rarely more than 100,000. Not only do publishers today traditionally prefer a shorter manuscript than they may have accepted in the past due to paper and printing costs, readers today have more entertainment options and less disposable time to invest in reading a massive tome. Keep it short and sweet while keeping it sexy!

Here and Now

Choosing to write an erotic romance set in contemporary times gives you a wealth of freedom and opportunities to explore your characters' sexual lives. It also assumes you will most likely want to address the responsibility inherent to such freedom. No, you don't have to include a manual on sex education, but you do want to be true to your characters. If they are living and loving in contemporary times, safe sex is an issue they face with every intimate encounter.

Now, you may argue that you're writing escapist fantasy, and readers don't want their entertainment to reflect that much real life. Obviously, this is an individual choice an author must make, because even if there are readers who don't want to read about your hero rolling on a condom, there are many readers who insist on seeing characters behave responsibly and won't accept anything less.

From a craft standpoint, however, such a decision should always be made with your characters in mind. Ask yourself if your heroine, even if she is a risk taker, would forgo a condom or a sexual history discussion with her partner for one night of sensational sex. This isn't about you as the author or about your readers. In the end, you must consider your characters at every turn and be sure their actions ring true.

Scorchers

Weaving quick mentions of precautions taken in the name of safe sex into your text is a breeze: *"He rolled on a condom as she climbed on top."* See how easy that was? It takes nothing away from the scene but adds enough to let your readers know your characters are responsible—not reckless!

Historical Romance

Before erotic romance hit the mainstream, historical authors such as Thea Devine, Virginia Henley, Susan Johnson, Robin Schone, and Bertrice Small were writing erotic historicals. Their steamy stories have become legendary with readers wanting the temperature of their historical romances turned up extra high.

For many, the appeal of these stories lies in the incredible sexual tension between couples who are required to meet strict moral and societal expectations in public—and then come undone when together and alone. If you feel passionate about hot stuff set in the past, following in the footsteps of these tried-and-true authors will take you far!

Ye Olde Mores and Morals

Sex is hardly a twenty-first-century discovery. Men and women have been doing it since the dawn of time. However, just as it's important to be true to your characters and their world's sexual climate when writing a contemporary, you need to do the same when writing about historical times.

Would discovery of your couple's sexual activity result in ostracizing by family or society? Would they be forced into marriage? How do they feel about such ramifications? Is their livelihood or community standing at risk?

I'm certainly not suggesting that any of these strictures would prevent your characters from engaging in sexual relations. But if pregnancy, disowning, banishment, or censure might result, having your characters give consideration to such consequences can only serve to add depth and authenticity to your work.

Naughty, Naughty

If you think readers will be so caught up in the eroticism of your historical romance that they'll overlook historical error, think again! Romance readers are educated, intelligent, and have high expectations when it comes to historical accuracy. Whether you're writing lighter, "wallpaper" historicals or those with a heavier emphasis on the details of the past, prove yourself an author who respects her genre and her readers by getting it right!

How Much History?

If you like to immerse yourself in a story to the point where you feel as if you're living in the time period, then you'll probably enjoy writing books with a similar devotion to historical detail. Many of these novels are so richly textured that the history seems to live and breathe as if it were another character populating your story world. The books of author Lydia Joyce are a wonderful example of how this is done.

If you like your history "lite" with a focus on how your characters interact rather than copious details about the political overtones or societal conventions of the time period, writing books where the history does no more than lightly wallpaper your world will be right up your alley. Once you've set the stage with a touch of historically accurate detail enabling your reader to settle into the scene, you're free to concentrate on the players!

Not All Time Periods Are Created Equal

Westerns are dead. Medievals are dead. Regency rules. How often have we heard similar pronouncements about the demise of a particular historical era as marketable in romance fiction or the praise of another as the next big thing? Yes, certain time periods have fallen out of favor with publishers, while a glut of others can easily cause readers to tire quickly of those periods.

Scorchers

Is historical romance your thing? Keep your ear to the ground. You may have the very idea to bring about a revival of your favorite time period!

Romantic Suspense

Romantic suspense can take place in any time period and in any fictional universe. The only requirement is that your external plot maintains a high level of suspense and that your story's primary hero and heroine are brought together because of it. They cannot be romantically involved independently of your suspense storyline. Let me show you what I mean:

> *Example #1:* Your heroine, Rachel, is a secretary who meets your cop hero, Brandon, at her company's Christmas party. Brandon is attending as his sister's escort

because her husband is deployed overseas. He and Rachel hit it off immediately. When his pager buzzes, he tells her he'll call her later after he's done following up on this newest lead in the murder he's investigating. When Brandon calls Rachel three days later, he asks her to spend New Year's Eve with him, and they ring out the old and in the new together.

Example #2: Your heroine, Rachel, is a secretary who meets your cop hero, Brandon, at her company's Christmas party. Brandon is attending as his sister's escort because her husband is deployed overseas. Except Brandon's sister isn't married. In fact, Rachel's fellow employee isn't even related to Brandon. She's an undercover officer working the same case as Brandon from the inside. The murder weapon found at the scene, an engraved letter opener, came from Rachel's desk. Brandon is just about to take her in for questioning when shots ring out, killing the undercover officer and wounding Rachel.

See the difference between the two examples? Is the first a romantic setup? Yes. Is it a romantic suspense? No. What about the second? Because the suspense plot is the reason your hero and heroine are involved, yes, it is. In the first, your romance and your suspense develop apart from one another. That's fine in any other subgenre. In a romantic suspense, however, the two plot lines must be inexorably linked, as the second example demonstrates.

The Tightrope Act: Balancing Suspense and Romance

Now that you've woven together your suspense and your romance, your next step is to be sure the two plot lines are balanced. You don't want to short-change either one. Readers' top two complaints about romantic suspense are:

- The romance takes a backseat and is never fully or satisfactorily explored because the suspense takes center stage.
- The suspense takes a backseat and is unbelievable and underdeveloped because the romance takes center stage.

Romantic suspense readers come to the subgenre because they want both a fully developed suspense plot and a fully explored romance. This is the only subgenre in romance, in fact, where the external plot holds an equal importance to that of the love story.

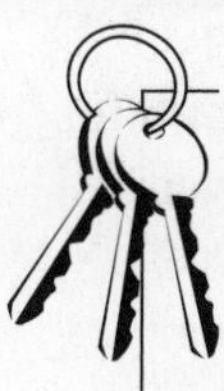

Scorchers

To see if you've managed a good balance of your romance with your suspense, try this trick: on a piece of poster board or even in a spreadsheet program, mark off your chapters and then use colored sticky notes or colored cells and columns to designate your scenes—one color for the romance scenes, one color for the suspense scenes. It will quickly become as clear as a rainbow if you're heavy on one and light on the other!

Crossing the Gross-Out Line: Reader Sensibilities

The "ick" factor. We all have one. Maybe you close your eyes during the opening credits of *CSI: Crime Scene Investigation*. Maybe you shudder at the sight of an autopsied body in the morgue. Maybe you eat it all up along with your bowl of penne pasta and marinara sauce! There's a good chance that whatever your "maybe," you'll find an audience who shares it.

Readers will come to know your work and where you fall on their own ick-factor scale. If you dumb down your gore to make everyone happy, your story will suffer because you haven't been true to your voice. On the other hand, gratuitous slicing and dicing will ring equally false, and again, your story will suffer. While being true to thine own self, don't forget to be true to thine own story as well!

The Danger of Becoming Too Stupid to Live

Picture this: your heroine, Rachel, is standing at the top of the basement stairs, flashlight in hand, after hearing things go bump in the night. Your hero, Brandon, is nowhere to be seen. In fact, Rachel fears the bumps may be Brandon's killer, returned to dispose of his body and pin the murder on her. She heads down the stairs. She must find out what has happened to Brandon at any cost. She loves him. He is her life. She flicks on the basement light switch. The bulb fizzles out. Halfway down the stairs, her flashlight begins to flicker. She bangs her hand against it, dropping her cell phone in the process. The batteries in the flashlight die, leaving her in the dark. Below, she sees the glow of green eyes. Above, the basement door blows shut. What happens next will go a long way toward determining Rachel's credibility with readers.

If she continues her descent into the basement because you as the author want her to just to further your plot, you may be doing Rachel a disservice. Your reader won't buy Rachel's actions as believable and will deem her too stupid to live if her reasons for continuing on aren't motivated by her character. Maybe she knows the green eyes are from a glow-in-the-dark Halloween mask. Maybe she knows there's a hunting knife and a butane campfire lighter hanging on a pegboard two steps down. Whatever Rachel knows, be sure your reader fully understands the motivation for her actions, or they might be first in line to lock the basement door and keep her down there!

Romancing the Action-Adventure

A subset of the romantic suspense subgenre is action-adventure. In these books, the reader is usually in on more of the behind-the-scenes maneuverings while along for the ride. The movie *Romancing the Stone* with Michael Douglas and Kathleen Turner is the perfect example of an action-adventure romance. Add an erotic component, and you've just given your audience an even more exciting read!

Terror Sex

The elements of danger inherent to romantic suspense, the hazards your characters will face, the risks they will often be forced to undertake—all these things present opportunities for heightened emotions, sensations, needs, and desires. As long as there's no imminent threat pounding on the door, having your characters seek shelter and safety in one another's arms is a believable human response.

Take a look at the physiological responses of the human body to arousal, and notice how they mirror the responses to fright:

- Dilated pupils
- Flushed skin
- Sweating
- Labored breathing
- Rapid pulse
- Tingling sensations

It's not hard to understand fear and desire going hand-in-hand after making the comparison between the two. Just be sure your characters' actions are believable and that they're not putting themselves into even more physical danger by making love!

Paranormal Romance

Paranormal romance has grown so popular over the last few years that late in 2005 even *Newsweek* ran an article on the phenomenon. Within erotic romance, the paranormal subgenre has exploded.

Slip of the Tongue

"There's nothing like escaping to a world filled with magic and mythical beings, especially when the stories take place within our world today. I love magic and mystique. There's something so exciting to me about imagining that these beings—faeries, witches, shapeshifters, and more—live amongst us unseen, that we can reach out and touch them, kiss them, know them, and have adventures beyond even our wildest dreams," says author Cheyenne McCray.

Whether it's delving into the thrill of the unknown and unexplainable, the fairy tale/ fantasy factor, or the challenge of taming the beast within, paranormal romance offers something for every reader—and for every author. The only limit is your own imagination!

Vampires

If only Bram Stoker could see what he started with his *Dracula*! From J. R. Ward's *Black Dagger Brotherhood*, to L. A. Banks' *Vampire Huntress Legend* series, to Laurell K. Hamilton's *Anita Blake Vampire Hunter* books, to Lynn Viehl's *Darkyn* series, vamps are hot, hot, hot. As with anything, trends come and go, but lovers of vampire stories can't seem to get enough. And the neck-nibbling eroticism inherent to the mythology makes vampires the perfect protagonists for erotic romance.

Shapeshifters

Werewolves, selkies, mermen, dragons, etc. It's no wonder shapeshifters have found a welcome audience in erotic romance; the myths and legends have existed since the days of ancient Greece and permeate our culture. From Tom Hanks and Darryl Hannah in *Splash* to Michelle Pfeiffer and Rutger Hauer in *Ladyhawke* to the earliest incarnations of the Frog Prince tale, shapeshifter stories explore the legends of these fantastical transformations.

Naughty, Naughty

When writing erotic scenes between human and shapeshifting characters, make certain in your narrative that it's clear your shapeshifter is in human form. Taming the beast is a proven romance fantasy. Sleeping with him is borderline bestiality—and no romance publisher is going to want you to go there!

Futuristic/Science Fiction

So you think Han Solo deserved better than Princess Leia? Are you one of the many romance readers who have begged Ann Maxwell (Elizabeth Lowell) to continue her fabulous *Fire Dancer* series with Rheba and Kirtn? Or like me, were you hooked on the subgenre the first time you read Amanda Glass's (Jayne Ann Krentz) *Shield's Lady?* If futuristic or science-fiction romances ring your bell, you're in good company.

Slip of the Tongue

Author Sylvia Day has this take on the popularity of and demand for erotic romance's science fiction and futuristic stories: "A large part of erotic romance's appeal is the inherent fantastical aspect. Exploring science fiction and futuristic settings is a natural extension of this. One of Ellora's Cave's top selling genres is futuristic, and I think the reason for this is twofold. One, New York print publishers are not accepting futuristic romances in large numbers, which leaves a void in the market. And two, characters who are adventurous in the bedroom may also be adventurous out of it."

Fantasy/Fable/Fairy Tales

The most well-known fairy tale erotica may be Anne Rice's (writing as A. N. Roquelaure) take on the Sleeping Beauty legend in her *Beauty* trilogy, but others have taken similar childhood stories and added their own grown-up twist. Check out Cheyenne McCray's *Erotic Elves and Wonderland Kings* stories from Ellora's Cave.

Out-of-This-World Characters

There are any number of otherworldly characters who you might cast in an erotic romance. Witches and warlocks are a perfect example. Whether they are your protagonists or antagonists, characters who circulate in a world where the supernatural exists offer authors a chance to explore the truly frightening risks—and the magic—involved in falling in love.

Characters with the ability to read minds or communicate with the spirit world are also a popular choice with readers. The movie *Ghost* is a perfect example of a love story that, though lacking the romance genre's happily-ever-after ending, touched viewers' hearts. Even the great romantic classic *The Ghost and Mrs. Muir* is a wonderful example of emotions refusing to be limited by earthly boundaries. Imagine a hero wondering if the heroine is truly in tune to his needs or is simply reading his mind. Imagine a heroine unable to let go of a lost love. There are two story ideas. Take them and run!

Time-Travel

Not without my morning coffee! Oh, wait. This isn't about me! Imagine your heroine Rachel traveling back in time to find herself married to a Viking warrior. Or imagine your hero Brandon traveling into the future where men are used solely as breeders to impregnate the female population of a matriarchal society. Time-travel romance provides instant conflict—a wonderful bonus, as conflict is what drives romance!

Sexually, Anything Goes!

This is your world, your creation. Not only will you build your physical world, you'll also be the big guy in charge of what sexuality means to your world's inhabitants. Taboos, customs, traditions, the cultural norm—you get to decide.

You might want to put your own twist on the mythology of *droit du seigneur*—the right of a feudal lord to have intimate relations with a vassal's bride on her wedding night. It might be an acceptable practice for new brides to spend their wedding night with their groom *and* his best man—or to share her maid of honor. Sex in your dying world might be solely about procreation, or in your hedonistic world, solely about recreation. Perhaps sexual intercourse is only practiced by an underground society while oral sex and mutual self-gratification are considered as far as proper couples should go.

Look at your characters and your universe to discover what sexual practices best suit your world and your story's needs. And then let your imagination run free!

The Least You Need to Know

- To hook your reader, you must create admirable and sexually responsible characters—no matter when or where the world they inhabit exists.
- The history in a historical romance can serve to wallpaper your setting or can play the role of a character with which your protagonists interact.

- Lovers of romantic suspense want a clear balance between the romance and the external suspense plot, even while demanding the two be intertwined.
- The opportunities for exploring romance in the paranormal subgenre are limited only by your imagination.

Chapter 4

Planning Erotic Romance: Giving Sex Its Due

In This Chapter

- The keys to believable sexual encounters
- How to decide what sexual content fits your story
- Exploring your characters' sexual personalities
- Successful methods for pushing the envelope

The sex in an erotic romance is integral to both your novel and your characters' individual journeys. As such, it deserves high priority—yet not at the expense of good storytelling or good craft. By adding sex scenes to an existing manuscript in an attempt to turn it into an erotic romance, you risk the possibility of your scenes coming across as gratuitous padding or seeming disconnected from the rest of the book. By including sex scenes for no other reason than pushing the envelope, you do the same.

Readers want erotic romance with a meaningful physical relationship, not a lot of casual sex with no meaning at all. The best way to accomplish this is to plan what you can of your book's sexual content the same way you work out in advance your characters' goals, motivations, and personality traits. In fact, when developing those traits, explore the sexual natures of your story people as well.

Planning Sexual Encounters

Wait a minute, you say. Shouldn't my characters be the ones driving the sexual content of my book? Isn't it *author intrusion* if I'm the one making things happen? Yes, it is. But sometimes you will want to plan. Sometimes you won't. It all depends on what shift in story dynamics each sexual encounter brings about. Remember, in erotic romance, sex is never just about sex. In erotica, yes, it can be. In pornography, for the most part, it is. But this is romance where sex always ends in love and emotional commitment—or at least the promise of one to come. That genre tenet necessitates that your characters' sexual encounters play a larger role than your hero and heroine just gettin' some satisfaction!

def•i•ni•tion

Author intrusion is anything the author does to remind the reader that she is reading, jarring her out of her immersion in the story. It is the author imposing her will on the characters and inserting herself into the plot and the characters' lives so the reader sees her pulling the strings.

No, no, no, you argue. What about spontaneity? Doesn't preplanning take all the fun out of things? First of all, I'm not encouraging *your characters* to do any preplanning. They can be as spontaneous as their personalities dictate! You are their creator, and you are the one who knows them best. And you're the one I'm talking to!

def•i•ni•tion

The term **pantsers** refers to authors who write by the seat of their pants, avoiding any major plotting or outlining.

Second, many of you may be *pantsers* rather than detailed plotters. You don't know where your story is going until you get there. That doesn't mean you can't be thinking about the changes your characters will go through after they become sexually involved. Neither does it mean plans won't change, even for those of you who've outlined every scene. Mice and men know full well that they do!

Writing is organic; plot lines and character arcs ever-evolving. Knowing all that doesn't discount the value in planning—even if your story flips your planning on its head. The work you've done in advance won't be wasted. Instead, it will give you a heads-up that the changes are coming, and you'll be that much more ready to revise if you need to.

In Chapter 12, I take a closer look at reasons why your characters engage in sexual intimacy besides expressing their love through such acts. Considering those reasons during your novel's developmental stages—no matter how much or how little planning you do—will help you put your plot back into gear the morning after and allow you to ramp up the emotional conflict with no more than a flip of the planning switch!

Location, Location, Location

Why would you need to plan where your characters do the deed? The answer is simple when you remember from earlier that the sex in an erotic romance is never solely about sex.

Scorchers

Not every location where your characters indulge will need to have meaning, but don't forget to explore the ones that do!

Say Brandon's goal is to impress Rachel with his rags-to-riches success. Making love with her on his penthouse balcony shows her how far he has come from those days when she knew him as a penniless boy. On the other hand, sleeping with her in the single room of the hovel where he spent his formative years proves to her that his wealth has not changed the person he's always been.

Maybe Rachel wants to spend her first night with Brandon—a night of sex that's long on physical relief and short on emotional involvement—on the sofa in her office. Why? Because that's where her ex brutally dumped her, and she's desperate to obliterate the connection between the place and the man. Look to your own characters and see if you can use location to increase their conflict or add a new layer to their depth.

Cards on the Table

Will sleeping with Brandon pose a risk to Rachel's upcoming promotion should their dalliance be discovered? If so, how will that impact your novel's plot? Will making love with Rachel destroy Brandon's credibility as a prosecutor when he learns after the fact that she is a star witness for the defense? Will having sex with Brandon ruin Rachel's family's respect for her? Will Brandon lose a friendship he's nurtured for years if his buddy finds out that he's doing the wild thing with the same woman who left said buddy at the altar?

In a plot-driven novel, the stakes your characters find themselves facing will be largely external and tied directly into the action in which they're involved. In a character-driven novel, the stakes will be linked more closely to internal goals and motivations, as well as to your characters' self-perceptions and their standing in the eyes of others. I talk more in Chapter 6 about the differences between the two types of novels. For now, just remember to consider the stakes of your characters' every sexual encounter.

Planning Sexual Content

Once you've established that your story's sexual content is relevant to both your plot and your characters, the next thing you may want to consider is what exactly you want them to do once they're in bed. Or in the shower. Or beneath the table in a restaurant. Or up against a wall. Because the acts will spring from your characters, their preferences, etc., the primary reason for planning them in advance is to be sure you get things right—otherwise known as doing research!

Is such research really necessary? It can be, especially if you plan to include sexual activity with which you have no personal experience, or with which your personal experience has been less than satisfying. I once heard an author say she would never include anal sex in her erotic romances because it was so painful. Obviously, such is not the case for everyone. Were this author to decide to write an anal sex scene, she would need more than personal experience to draw on for her readers to buy into the fantasy. For many, this sort of research is best done before attempting to write a compelling and believable scene.

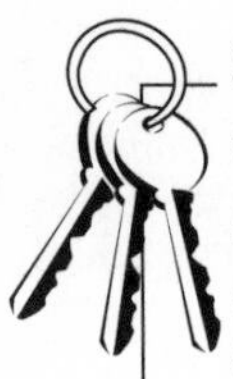

Scorchers

Writing honestly with an open mind is the only way to go. Anything less, and readers will spot your discomfort!

Scorchers

As with anything else you write, you need to know what you're talking about—even when it comes to sex! So don't scrimp on the sexual research!

A reader involved in a submissive lifestyle will be able to spot a false representation of the same. A reader who enjoys bringing toys to bed will sense your hesitation if playthings don't do it for you. A reader who wants to be forcibly bound might not relate to a more politically correct version of bondage. You have to decide what audience you're writing for as well as how far you can comfortably go.

For many readers and authors of romance, "having sex" simply means penile-vaginal intercourse. In erotic romance, it can mean that, but it can also mean more. Anal sex, oral sex, masturbation—both solo and mutual—among other acts, are commonplace within the subgenre. Not every book includes all these acts, but many books will explore each of them as well as others. Whatever "having sex" means to your characters, be sure you know how to line up their tabs and slots correctly!

Getting Kinky

Kinky behavior works best when tied into your characterization as an intrinsic part of your story people and their psyches. Take a look at the following examples:

- A powerful and controlling CEO heroine may get off to being bound by her lover to the point where her powerlessness causes her to lose control.
- A stock broker hero may be a high-stakes gambler, one who drives fast, parties hard, loves extreme sports, and gets a charge out of taking exhibitionist risks.

- A sports-loving heroine might lie to get out of dinner with her parents so she can attend a game knowing that her boyfriend will spank her later as punishment.
- A stressed-out and uptight corporate exec might release the day's tension by masturbating and describing the act in explicit detail to a stranger in a chat room.

Now, it's your turn.

Doing What *Doesn't* Come Naturally

If it's not obvious by now, let me state again that I'm a firm believer in a story's every action springing from its characters, not from author manipulation. If you want your characters to explore sexual acts or a sexual underworld or even a sexual kink about which they are hesitant, you'll need to establish the basis for that desire when you create your characters and their personalities.

There's no place you can't take your reader if she believes your characters are acting true. Let's look at a few reasons a character might want to explore the unfamiliar:

- A character bored with her routine challenges herself to try something new.
- A character dares another to take her where she's never been to see if he's all talk and no action.
- A character starting over believes she needs to break out of her shell.
- A character determines to prove she's gutsier than her lover believes her to be.

As long as you keep your characters in character, there's no such thing as a scenario that's too far-fetched.

Planning Character Change

Sex changes people. We get naked; we get intimate; we can't expect things to stay the same. Maybe the only change is that we never want to see the other person again. But hey, that's a change, isn't it?

In all fiction, but especially erotic romance fiction, the changes are vital to the characters because the sex is vital to the story. And in erotic romance fiction, even though the characters may not be *in* love when *making* love, the readers know the truth of the matter and expect the changes to be profound.

Slip of the Tongue

New York Times best-selling author Tess Gerritsen says of writing love scenes, "Ask yourself, as a writer, what your love scene is supposed to accomplish. If it's just to show that your hero is a normal guy having sex, that's about as interesting as watching him eat bologna sandwiches. No, the best sex scenes are those that accomplish something far more profound. They offer us a deeper understanding of character, or show us emotional awakening or healing. When I write I'm also thinking of hearts and minds as well—and how this love scene will forever change these people."

Aftershocks and the Ripple Effect

The morning after doesn't stop at noon. In fact, it should be called the "life after," because after your characters have hit the sack, they can never go back! Consider a heroine sitting at her desk at 10 A.M. the morning before. Now consider her sitting at the same place at the same time the morning after. It doesn't matter if she loved how she spent the night or if she regretted every minute of it, she *will* be thinking about it. Her giddiness may spill over during a big presentation she's scheduled to make. Or she may be sullen during her weekly gripe-and-gab session with her girlfriends. Whatever her reaction, use it, don't lose it!

A night of passion will also cause a ripple effect your characters must face. Think about a stone dropped in a pond and the circles that spread outward, displacing anything floating in their path. Now drop your character's sexual encounter into the big fat circle of life, and there you go! While aftershocks are more the waves our characters will feel individually, the ripple effect is felt by everyone around them. Our heroine who is sitting at her desk at 10 A.M. the morning after? The one who giggled through her presentation or moped through lunch with the girls? Watch the reactions of her co-workers and friends and then figure out how to use *them* to increase *her* conflict.

The Big Reveal

One of the most important things to think about in your planning stages is what your characters will discover about themselves after they've slept together. This can be something as minor as your heroine figuring out that she really doesn't like to have her toes kissed, or as major as her realizing she's betrayed a promise she made to herself not to drink and date, or as eye-opening as coming to grips with her ex's claim that she never gave anything of herself to their relationship beyond sex. Don't forget to explore all these revelations!

Planning Character Sexuality

Over the course of your writing career, you'll no doubt create enough characters to populate a small village. No two characters will be the same. They will each come complete with their own views on sexuality, their own sexual histories, even their own sexual weaknesses and appetites. The role their sexual activity will play in their development and that of your story's plot is all-important in an erotic romance. Because of that, the more you know about your characters' sexual natures, the better off you'll be.

Your Characters' *Whys*

Not every character you write will feel the same about sex. You may write a heroine who will only sleep with a man she loves, while her best friend may sleep with anything in blue jeans as long as the man involved can make her forget the one who got away. You may write a hero who is tired of sexual encounters lacking any hope of romantic involvement, or a hero who doesn't believe in romance at all but does believe in sexual monogamy.

What you have to do now is figure how *why*. What in the character's past was the catalyst for these views? After you nail it down, you've got a lot of good baggage to carry your story!

Your Characters' Experiences and Preferences

With life comes experience of all sorts—including sexual. Knowing your characters' sexual history is important. Equally important is how they feel about their past sexual encounters. Is there anything your hero regrets? Anything your heroine is ashamed of? Why did they make the decisions they did? How many relationships were about love? How many were about convenience? How many were about nothing but orgasms? If your heroine has been promiscuous, does she hide that fact from the man she is falling in love with? So much to consider!

Slip of the Tongue

Never fear planning your book's sexual content, because no matter how much you do, you'll be in good company. Best-selling author Angela Knight says, "I definitely plot sex scenes as a means of character advancement or plot development. They shouldn't be inserted just because it's time for nookie." Author Lydia Joyce agrees: "I always plan them as a part of the character arc, though sometimes my characters surprise me."

Along with preferences for chocolate over caramel, theater over movies, flats over stilettos, or uptown over downtown, your multitude of individual story people will have sexual likes, dislikes, and favorite things. If you know these in advance, you can set up the perfect situation to use them down the road to further their growth.

Planning to Push the Envelope

One of the descriptive tags often given to erotic romance is "edgy," but what exactly does that mean? Readers of erotic romance want stories with sexual content that's daring and provocative, that goes farther and is more explicit than what is traditionally found in even sensual romances. It's also a vital component of your erotic romance plot. Such content not only fills a need in your reader, it challenges your characters to examine who they are and what they believe about their own sexuality.

> **Naughty, Naughty**
>
> If you push for the sake of pushing and not for the sake of story, you may end up writing a threesome in one book, a foursome in your next, then a fivesome, a sixsome, etc., because you'll always be working to top what you've done before. Push only for the sake of the story.

But most of all, it demands that you as the author be aware of what you're doing. The decisions you reach must be made on behalf of your characters and because of their story. In other words, it isn't about you. It's all them!

> **Slip of the Tongue**
>
> Author Jo Leigh offers this insight into pushing the envelope: "Pushing the envelope is another way of saying you want to take your characters outside (sometimes way outside) their comfort zones. You want to force them to see the truth about themselves, and that happens only when they are the most vulnerable. Remember: character is revealed through conflict. We learn the most about people when they're most desperate."

Why?

In Chapter 7, I cover motivation. But it's important to ask yourself during your planning stages *why* you want to push the sexual envelope. Following are a few reasons I've come up with that might work within a story's context. What others come to mind?

- To confront a character's self-perception; she doesn't think herself capable of taking a risk.

- To test a character's willingness to trust; she equates trust with being stabbed in the back.
- To ease a character into overcoming a bad experience; she gave a man similar liberties before and ended up hurt.
- To press a character into facing her feelings; she's been told all her life she has nothing to offer anyone.
- To give a character an incentive to surrender control; she believes submission equals weakness.

How Far?

One of the dangers of pushing the envelope is that eventually there's no place left to go. What is edgy and brilliant becomes old hat. No one lifts an eyebrow anymore. The envelope is nothing but the same ol' same ol'. Lather, rinse, repeat.

You want your readers to come back to your books looking for even more of what you've given them before. And how do you guarantee that will happen? By making sure you push only as far as each individual story allows and demands. Keep your focus on the book at hand, and take those characters—and only those characters—to the limit.

Naughty, Naughty

Don't forget when pushing your characters to keep your happily-ever-after in sight at all times!

To Where?

The forward motion of your story propels your characters to their final destination: romantic involvement. Along the way, however, your characters will make personal, internal-demon-facing pit stops. Whether you start with mini-monsters and build gradually toward a showdown, or whether you hit them with the biggest brute right out of the gate depends on their story.

In What Ways?

Is the push you're planning going to be purely sexual? Or are you considering forcing your characters into situations that will drive them into making an uncomfortable self-examination? About where their lives are headed? About dangerous risks they're taking to get their sexual kicks?

The first, the sex part, is fun. The second, the self-analysis, is not. At least not for your characters—which is why it's one of the best things you can do as an author. Make 'em laugh. Make 'em cry. Make 'em sweat their backsides off while you put 'em through their envelope-pushing paces!

Whose Envelope Is It?

Whose envelope is it that you're pushing? Is it yours, or is it your characters'? There's nothing wrong with wanting to challenge yourself as an author. We all want to hone our craft, take our storytelling abilities to the next level, etc. In fact, most of us are doing so consciously all the time.

That's not what I'm talking about. I'm talking about is pushing for the sake of pushing. Writing a sexual scenario that no one has written before (is there such a thing?) just to say you got it into print. Being the first at your publishing house to describe a role-playing, cyber, BDSM, voyeuristic ménage. (Is there such a thing?)

Pushing the envelope is not about what you can pull off or get away with. It's about taking your characters to another level of conflict, about challenging their self-awareness, about forcing them into taking a stand or making a choice or defending their decisions. It's about showing them a pleasure that changes their lives forever. That's the real test of boundaries, the real show of edginess. Keeping it all about your characters is how you keep it real.

The Least You Need to Know

- Planning your story's sexual content in advance will not prevent your characters from being spontaneous.
- Sexual activity should always bring about change, whether within your characters or your story's dramatic tension.
- When creating your characters, don't forget to develop their sexual natures—including their histories, preferences, and beliefs.
- Pushing the envelope is a vital part of challenging your characters' limits.

Chapter 5

Writing 101: World-Building

In This Chapter

- Walking the research tightrope
- Description that pulls its weight
- Fitting your characters into your story
- Stacking your world's building blocks
- Sex as a plot device

No matter the subgenre you choose, whether your setting is real or make-believe, and no matter the time period, whether past, present, or future, you must create a viable world for your story people to inhabit. Even if you're writing characters living in your home city and state, you want to get your details right to suck your reader into the daily lives of your novel's hero and heroine, as well as into those of their family, friends—and hey, maybe even their enemies!

Let's take a look at several ways to accomplish just that.

Have You Done Your Research?

Whether you're dealing with the specifics of Navy SEALs' BUD/S training, the NYC Transit subway schedule, or the management of a sugar plantation in Barbados during the 1800s, peppering your prose with tidbits of detailed research gives your readers an accurate depiction of the world in which your characters live and allows your audience to experience the sights, smells, and sounds right along with your story people.

Readers, however, should never see your research in action. It should be as organic to your story as every other element. All those details about medieval times should appear to stem straight from your characters, not from your research books. There's no need to impress the reader with every morsel you've uncovered. You may have dug up an incredibly yummy crumb about your subject, but if the story doesn't require the information, don't create a need for it. You don't want to risk bogging down your pacing or losing your narrative thread as you go off on an unnecessary tangent—no matter how tempting!

Do Enough to Be an Expert

As the author of your story, you are the expert behind your plot, your characters, and every facet of your novel. Fully knowing your subject matter enables you to write with an expert's skill. The better your insight, the more complete your understanding, and the easier it will be for you to weave in details naturally as needed. There's no such thing as knowing too much. But there is such a thing as showing off! Remember, *if your story doesn't require you use all you've learned, don't create a need for those extraneous facts.* Your reader will thank you for giving her only what she needs!

Scorchers

For an excellent look at world-building, check out author Holly Lisle's online workshop, "How Much of My World Do I Build? at www.hollylisle.com/fm/Workshops/how-much-do-i-build-workshop.html.

However, while you're busy making sure not to use what you don't need, do be certain to include what you do! You don't want your readers questioning the decisions reached by your story people or being confused by the actions they take.

Effective world-building—like most writing—is not an easy task. You have to decide on just the right moment to reveal just the perfect detail. Give too much, and you bore your reader. Give too little, and you leave her shaking her head.

Take a look at the books you read, the ones where you feel you know exactly what you need to know, and study the author's technique for weaving in her research. If you find yourself caught up in the story and having to really look for those details, that is weaving done well!

Infodumps vs. Exposition

An infodump is not the same as *exposition*. An infodump is simply what it says: dumping a lot of information on your reader all at once to get it out of the way. This is often seen as a long section of backstory in chapter 1 or a full-out explanation of a character's conflict when a gradual exposure through her thoughts and actions is much more effective.

Exposition gives readers what they need when they need it to better understand what's going on. Basically, exposition is good. Infodumping is bad.

def•i•ni•tion

Exposition is explanatory prose that conveys information your reader needs to understand what's happening in your story. It can be told by your story's narrator rather than shown actively in a scene because it has no impact on the forward motion of the plot. A clever author can almost hide her exposition so her reader absorbs the information without even being aware of it.

Slip of the Tongue

Author Sarah Monette says, "Infodumps are authorial intrusion, because they mark a point where the author has decided there's something readers Need To Be Told. They can be camouflaged well, and they can certainly serve their narrative valiantly if done correctly (which may or may not involve camouflage). But world-building by minimalism is what I strive for because it allows the story and the sheer brilliant joy of the world-building to co-exist."

Description Doesn't Require a Thousand Words

A picture may be worth 1,000 words, but painting one for your story doesn't require you use that many. Doing so successfully, however, does require thoughtful use of the right words! The ones you choose for your descriptions do double-duty. Not only do they allow you to paint a visual representation of your setting and your characters so you can ground the reader in the scene; they evoke an emotional, visceral response as well. They also reveal bits and pieces of your characters' personalities.

You should remember, too, that not every word is created equal. Tossing the first one that comes to mind into your manuscript might possibly shortchange the power of your description and fail to create the full picture you want your readers to see. *Red* is not the same as *vermillion* or *cherry*. *Wood* is not the same as *pine* or *maple*. Make your words work for you, and don't settle until you find the ones that do!

Don't Write a Laundry List

Which of the following descriptions is more evocative?

> *Example #1:* Rachel stepped into Brandon's well-appointed bedroom. To the right of the door, a shaker-style chair sat in the corner and held several books stacked on the seat. His bed, covered with a handmade quilt, had been pushed up beneath the room's single window covered by mini-blinds rather than drapes. There was a desk on the opposite wall, and an entertainment center housed his collection of movies and music.

> *Example #2:* Rachel stepped into Brandon's bedroom, catching sight of the chair full of books next to the door. He'd told her he'd gathered the stack to drop at the library on his way to pick her up but then had forgotten. He'd been too distracted, he'd admitted with the cutest apology, to do more than toss the quilt his grandmother had made him for his birthday over his sheets before leaving. He hadn't even cleaned his desk after last night's bill-paying session or returned the music that had helped him get through the money-spending nightmare to his entertainment center. He'd been all about getting to her.

The first example isn't bad until you look closer and see that it's nothing but a list of the room's furniture. The second mentions the same items as the first but personalizes the description, making it important to the scene. Not only that, but in example #2, the description is threaded into the scene along with Rachel's internal thoughts, rather than being unloaded all at once.

The purpose of description is to give readers a sensory grounding in a scene. One of the best explanations I've read on how to do this comes from author Elizabeth Bear. She says, "Grounding the reader lies at the heart of good fiction writing. It's the writer's attention to the kinesthetics of the viewpoint character, the way his body moves in space, the way he holds his head, the way the cold in the room soaks through the soles of his socks and the sweater doesn't keep that thin line between his hair and the top of his turtleneck warm. It's the exact color of a blown-glass sphere, not mauve, or purple, or lavender, but the color of a dusky sky along the rim of the horizon. It's evocative and it's a kind of super reality, the way the golden light lies slanted over the Vermont hills at four o'clock on an autumn afternoon and likewise the different way the brutal ultraviolet of an uncompromising sun hammers perpendicular on the metal roofs of packed cars on a Las Vegas freeway."

Through a Character's Eyes

Stories are told primarily from the viewpoints of your story's main protagonists, usually your hero and heroine, although often you'll use secondary characters' viewpoints as well. What you show the reader should only be what the viewpoint character sees. And what the viewpoint character sees depends on how he or she fits into the scene. When Rachel walks into Brandon's bedroom for the first time, she sees everything because she's never been there before.

Scorchers

By delving into your character's viewpoint, you can make your descriptive details reveal characterization as well as set the scene's stage.

Brandon, on the other hand, will only be concerned with the things that are out of order, or with wondering how Rachel will react to his lack of decorating skills. It would not be in character for him to notice that his bed is pushed up beneath the room's only window or that he has mini-blinds instead of drapes—unless he bought drapes to impress Rachel and hasn't had time yet to hang them.

What *Does* a Reader Need to See?

Do your readers need to know the style of the chair sitting inside Brandon's bedroom door to the right? Well, that depends. Does it mean something to Brandon? Does the style have a purpose in the scene? Is the mention of the style nothing more than you as the author wanting to set a Martha Stewart–type stage?

If Brandon had previously told Rachel about the shaker-style chair his grandfather had made as a wedding gift for his grandmother, bringing it to the reader's attention makes perfect sense. If this is Rachel's first visit, she would most likely notice it and recall the conversation. But if the chair means nothing to the characters living in your story world, it makes sense that your reader has no reason to see it. Think twice before including it in the scene!

Old Blue Jeans or New Shoes: Your Characters' Fit

Your characters' comfort and familiarity with their surroundings is a large part of your world-building. In fiction, the reader sees your story world through your characters' eyes. If your heroine is fearful of her surroundings, she will fit differently than if she knows the streets of the city like the back of her hand. If your hero is a rancher

Scorchers

Consider how your characters fit within their world, and keep their actions consistent with their situation.

who spends his days on horseback, he'll no doubt be pacing his banker's office rather than sitting still while working through a financial plan.

So what happens, you ask, when you have one character who is a fish out of water and another who loves swimming with his home sharks? What you'll be doing is introducing your reader to your story world through multiple viewpoints, showing her the good, the bad, and the ugly. That depth allows her to feel as if she's a part of the same world to which your characters belong and to draw her own conclusions about it—and that's the whole point of world-building!

Home Sweet Home

A character at home in his surroundings may find a wonderful comfort in having close all he holds dear. On the other hand, he may feel trapped and consider his circumstances stifling. Still another character may have accepted his lot in life as inevitable and be in the grips of an apathy he's given up trying to shake—or happily be making the most of his life.

Whether home is indeed sweet or whether familiarity breeds contempt, writing about characters living in a world they know well offers endless possibilities for exploring their feelings about their surroundings—from the gossip that comes with having the same neighbors for so many years, to watching childhood friends experience traumatizing events, to managing a sex life under such a microscope. What home means to your protagonist depends on the character you've created and the story niche into which you've fit him.

Stranger in a Strange Land

A heroine who has sailed across the ocean to the new world. A hero who has slipped through a wormhole from one dimension to another. A teacher who has moved from a one-horse Wyoming town to Manhattan—or vice versa. An exchange student. A renowned surgeon from Houston treating earthquake victims in a remote village in Afghanistan.

In any of these scenarios, your character has to deal with not only making new friends, but with learning everything from what is expected socially of a person in that position, to where to shop for groceries, to managing currency (cash, credit, barter), to the accepted customs of courtship and seeking a mate.

Against Their Will

Not all prisons are constructed of steel bars. Obligations, promises, debts—any of these can keep characters in a place they long to leave. How they deal with their situation defines the way your reader sees their world.

One character may ooze resentment while another does his best to accept what cannot be changed. Take a look at how your character's attitude influences those around him and whether he's made a friend or an enemy of society.

Naughty, Naughty

Your reader's perception of your story world depends on your viewpoint character. You can use point of view as a tool to manipulate your reader into a calm when she's actually stepping into a storm. If you do that, however, be sure the pay-off is worth the deception if you expect your reader to pick up your next book!

Revisiting Old Haunts

Maybe you've written a character who once had a fling as a counselor at a summer camp. Years later, he makes a sudden detour while driving by the old place, wondering if any of that magic remains. What will he see now that he overlooked then? What difference will 10 years make in the lay of the land—or in the heart of the man?

Back to the Beginning

I'll admit it. I have a favorite "back to the beginning" book: Karen Robards' *One Summer*. Her hero, Johnny Harris, has spent several years in prison, and upon his release, he returns to his small Kentucky hometown and his former English teacher. In this case, the hero and heroine have a history, and the hero a checkered past.

Not all stories in which characters return to their roots will follow that same format. A heroine might be hoping to start over in the town where she was born after a bitter breakup. Or a hero who has spent the world globe-trotting may want nothing more than to spend the rest of his life comfortably at home. The fun comes when what they're expecting is not necessarily what they get!

Scorchers

When building or choosing your story world, don't forget to consider how it will impact your characters' conflicts and their sex lives. Take advantage of every opportunity to trip them up with roadblocks thrown their way!

A Brave New—or Old—World

Tell me something about your story world. Are you setting your novel in the present day? In our world's recent history? What about in an alternative version of that same history? Or are you starting from the ground up with a fictional universe?

No matter where your story is set, your world will be governed by laws, rules, even principles of religion and tenets of society. All will play a part in the construction of your story world, and many in the development of your plot.

Gods of Old

If you are creating an entirely fictional world, does it require a mythology? Does it need a history of biblical proportions? Does it demand its own folklore and legends that have been handed down through generations and to which its inhabitants look for guidance? A wonderful example of an intricately plotted mythos is J. R. Ward's *Black Dagger Brotherhood* series. Check it out!

Religious Rights and Lefts

Politics and religion. Two things best not discussed. Or are they? Think about the issue of morality in how your story plays out. I covered this a bit when looking at sexuality in a historical context in Chapter 3, but it's worth revisiting here. How might characters react were the morality of their world to be legislated? Or flip it and explore an amoral world and the story people who call it home. Food for thought, yes?

The Bride Wore White After Labor Day

Every world, whether real or fictional, has traditions and customs, holidays, rules of courtship—the list goes on. Think about the roles these will play in your story. What is the purpose of your world's traditions? Are they outdated, useful, or harmful? Does your society think of its customs as hard-and-fast rules or fun and games?

Is your heroine perhaps caught up in a family tradition of selecting a mate from a pool of men chosen by her sisters and doing everything she can to extricate herself? Hmm. That gives me an idea ….

Scorchers

Consider how your characters fit into society. Are you writing about the misfits or the cool kids? Are your characters pleasers or rebels? Do they care what society thinks about them? What *does* society think?

Big Brother Is Watching

Every world is governed by rules of law and order. Turn on any television channel any night of the week, and you'll see our fascination with the same. The government of your story world may serve as a background element, or your characters can be fully involved in fighting corruption and working for change. Perhaps they flaunt regulations they believe violate whatever rights they are guaranteed. Lots to think about!

Blinded by Science

Any laws of science and nature you create for your fictional world must make as much sense in your universe as do our own. You can look at science in much the same way we looked at history earlier and go either the full-immersion or wallpaper route.

For those of you writing s/f or futuristic stories, don't go breaking your own rules from one page to the next! And if you're writing a story set in our own existing universe, be sure you get it right!

Head of the Class

What role does education play in your story world? Will only men be allowed in academic circles, and what power will such circles wield? Will women be considered lesser beings if they're not educated? Will a character's financial situation determine whether or not higher learning is made available to him? Is school voluntary or mandatory?

If you're creating a fictional world rather than using one with an established educational system, give a hard twist to the accepted standards, and see where you end up!

Logic and Consistency

Logic is probably the most important consideration when world-building. If a reader scratches her head and says, "That doesn't make any sense," then you've fallen short in the logic game and need to take a second look at your explanations.

And if logic is the number-one most important thing to keep in mind when world-building, then consistency has to be number two. Contradicting your world's rules from chapter to chapter or breaking them without reason will not win you many fans.

Scorchers

To come up with an idea that is unusual and unique instead of just a variation on something that has been done to death, never settle for the first thing that comes to mind. In fact, never settle for the first five. Stretch your imagination. Make a list of 10 possibilities, and only then pick the one that most excites you!

The Five P's of Your Sexual Universe

You're writing erotic romance, so sex will play an important role in your story world, no matter whether or not that world even exists in our solar system! In Chapter 12, we take a closer look at characters engaging in sex for reasons other than love and romance. For now, I'll list for you five scenarios that could easily work within a fictional world—or even possibly within our own in the hands of a clever author!

- Procreation
- Pleasure
- Payment
- Prize
- Punishment

I've come up with five. Now you take a stab at it and see where your imagination takes you!

When considering the part sex will play in your story, don't forget to take a good look at your characters: their motives, goals, and most important, their conflicts. If you can use your world and the role of sex to deepen your characterization, go for it. Never let such an opportunity pass you by!

The Least You Need to Know

- Exposition should never be unloaded on a reader in one massive information dump.
- The most effective description is the one that reveals only what is important to your viewpoint character.
- How your characters fit into your world will be determined by the roles you've created for them to fill.
- All worlds, whether fictional, alternative, or true to life, are bound by rules and laws.
- The role of sex in your fictional world does not have to be solely about love and romance.

Part 2

Lust at First Sight: The External Journey

Although the love story is a romance novel's main appeal, there must also be an external plot. This series of events drives the dramatic tension and is the reason the hero and heroine find themselves together. Yes, the sexual component is paramount in an erotic romance, but there has to be more than sex going on. Whether the couple is brought together freely or against their will, the plot gives them a reason to be in the same place at the same time and a reason for sparks to fly.

In an erotic romance novel, the sex may be great, but it also introduces complications and trouble into a character's world. That trouble is the heart of the external journey. In Part 2, I show you not only how to assemble your novel's plot elements to play up that trouble, but also how to set up the external conflict, motivation, and goals that drive your story forward.

Chapter 6

What *Is* Going On?

In This Chapter

- Outlining from start to finish
- Ways to wing a plot
- Clearing up erotic romance misconceptions
- The driving force behind your story

At its most basic, plot is what's happening to your characters, what's going on around them, or what they're doing as they fall in love—and all the reasons why. In a romance, plot consists of the love story and the external events that propel it forward. Your job as the author is to sequence these events logically as demanded by your characters' journeys.

Additionally, you have to be sure your plot includes rising dramatic tension with sustainable conflict that keeps readers on the edge of their seats, wanting to find out what happens next!

Let's take a look at plot—including how to map out a story with erotic potential.

Plotting from Beginning to End

As soon as I tell you that you must plot your story from beginning to end before you write it, dozens of authors will contradict me and say it just isn't so. They'll point out all the books they've written without knowing where the plot was going when they sat down to put pencil to paper. They'll talk about letting their characters surprise them. They'll discuss growing tired of the book and feeling as if they've already written it if they know in advance where it's headed. They'll explain that they trust their story to unfold organically.

You know what? They're right. There are too many successful, list-making authors who don't outline for me to insist it's a must for anyone. So I won't!

What I will say is that it won't take you much time at all to discover if you need a solid blueprint to work from or if you can wing it. I do plot, and I made the decision to do so when it became clear that without a guideline to follow—one complete with a clear beginning, middle, and end—I floundered aimlessly, going off on tangents unrelated to the flow of my story's narrative intent. I'm not a natural-born storyteller. I need structure. I also know that not everyone else does. Do I plot out every single scene? No, but some authors do, and their outlines are so detailed that they can reach up to 50 or more pages. With such detailed outlines, these authors can concentrate on the scene at hand rather than deciding what needs to happen in the scenes that follow.

The Dreaded Synopsis

One of the first things I sit down to write is my synopsis. I've yet to meet an author who didn't cringe at the word *synopsis* the first few times spent writing one.

def•i•ni•tion

A story **synopsis** is a short narrative outline telling the events of a story in the order they occur and describing the driving motivational elements of the characters' journeys.

We do, however, eventually come to realize the value of a synopsis. Some publishers use them to pitch to overseas markets. Others use them as guidelines for cover copy and cover art. Our agents use them to pitch our ideas to editors. Then there's the simple fact that once established, an author is often able to make a sale based on nothing but a synopsis.

As hard as it is to admit, a synopsis truly is your friend. Learn to love them … and then realize what you end up writing will more than likely bear only a passing resemblance to your original outline! That said, unless you proposed a contemporary romance and turn in a historical, don't worry. Editors understand the nature of a story's development and expect these changes to occur.

Scorchers

Publishers often want two lengths of a synopsis: one a short, back-cover-blurb-type recap, and one a longer, fuller outline of the story, complete with any subplots you've included. It's a good idea to learn to write both; you never know when you'll need one or the other. Additionally, because some established authors are able to sell based on nothing but their synopses, learning to write one before you write a book gives you a head start on getting contracted and having that all-important advance money in hand.

A Story in Three (or Five) Acts

Telling a story in three acts harkens back to Aristotle. When broken down, each of the three acts does a distinct job in showing a story's setup, confrontation, and resolution—or, more simply, beginning, middle, and end. Romance authors might break this structure down into boy-meets-girl, boy-loses-girl, and boy-gets-girl.

Scorchers

If you feel your idea would fit into a three-act parameter, check out Syd Field's books on screenwriting for a more in-depth look at this plotting method.

The five-act structure is most commonly and often associated with Shakespeare's plays. This method consists of an initial act of exposition to let the reader in on the backstory followed by acts of rising or complicating action, a climax, falling action, and then the catastrophe or denouement. Authors today often use a *prologue* to convey any necessary exposition before moving into the first scene that launches the plot's dramatic tension.

A Multitude of Methods

There are so many plotting methods that work for so many authors, I'll only be able to touch on a few here. In the end, you are the one who'll have to decide what resonates with your writing personality—whether you go with one of the concepts I mention here, or combine several ideas into a workable solution. Maybe you can't work alone at all but need to bounce ideas off a brainstorming partner. I know of several authors who meet with plotting groups across the country a couple times a year and hash out story details with the input of trusted and intuitive friends.

Scorchers

For those who enjoy a little electronic stimulation, a variety of plotting programs are available to walk you through developing a plot based on the criteria you input in response to the software's prodding. Many companies offer downloadable demos that enable you to give their programs a trial run. *Power Structure* is one of many popular programs available at www.write-brain.com. *Dramatica* is another, found at www.dramatica.com.

My own way of plotting has its foundation in Christopher Vogler's *The Writer's Journey* based on Joseph Campbell's *The Hero with a Thousand Faces.* The diagrams and story analyses in his book appeal to me because I'm a character-driven author, meaning I start with ordinary story people and put them into extraordinary situations. I look at plot through my characters' eyes and their roles as heroes, villains, mentors, tricksters, etc. I then combine Vogler's circle of instruction with a basic three-act structure, throw in tips and tricks I've picked up over the years at various workshops and seminars, and voilà! After 15 years of writing, I've honed a method that works for me!

Scorchers

If one technique doesn't work for you, don't worry. We all go through trial-and-error phases as we discover what suits our individual writing personalities. In the end, we can only employ what meets our unique needs as an author. Don't ever let yourself feel like a failure because the most touted guide for writing help … doesn't!

Now it's time to come up with a process that works for you! Here are just a few of many other plotting methods you might want to research. Just plug them into an Internet search engine or check with your local library. You'll find numerous articles and suggested references to explore.

- The "W" Plot
- The Four-Act Structure
- The Mountain Plot
- The Nine-Act Structure
- The Episodic Plot

Plotting by the Seat of Your Pants

If you start writing with just a vague idea of what you want to happen in your book, then you're the pantser I described in Chapter 4—an author who writes by the seat of her pants. Maybe you have a dynamite opening scene and you create a story from there. Maybe you've decided on a theme you want to explore and can visualize a dramatic confrontation between your main protagonists and have to get it down on the page before you can figure out where to go next. Perhaps you've come up with a couple whose story you want to tell and need to get to know them by writing scenes in both of their viewpoints. Whatever your launching point into your story, know you're in good company by working this way!

Flying Into the Mist

Flying into the mist is not for everyone, but there's no denying it's a method that works well for many authors. You may not be able to see where you're headed, but the unknown factor of what lies ahead is part of the fun. It's a very instinctive way to work through a plot, discovering your story through the process of actually writing it.

I equate it to taking a leap of faith. Doing so means you trust your intuition to show you where to go and your writing skills to get you there. You also trust that the characters you've developed will tell you what direction to take them next!

Writing to Road Signs

Writing to road signs is a method of partial plotting that was described in a workshop I attended years ago. The author talked about how he outlined from one major point in his story to the next. He didn't plot from beginning to end; he wrote one scene or one section and then worked out the details of the next based on what had gone before. If flying completely blind terrifies you, this might be the next best thing.

Working Out of Order

Many authors can't see the forest for the trees. They don't know the whole of their story, but they're able to see bits and pieces of their characters or plot in action. They write these scenes as they come to them, not knowing how they'll fit in the book, and then assemble them after the fact, much like they would put together a puzzle.

Scorchers

If you write scenes out of order, don't forget when putting them together to thread through plotlines and character development that may have occurred in one section while you were writing elsewhere. You wouldn't want the character growth you added to chapter 3 to be missing in chapter 6 and then to appear again in chapter 9! Neither would you want a subplot to vanish for pages and pages, only to emerge just in time to be conveniently wrapped up at "The End."

If you use this method, don't be afraid of throwing away scenes you can't use. The worse thing you can do is force an unnecessary sequence of events into a book. No writing is ever wasted. A scene may not be right for a story, but you've still flexed your writing muscles, possibly improving one skill or even learning another!

The Revision Factor

Many authors who plot by the seat of their pants or write out of order wind up at the conclusion of their book needing to do extensive editing and revising to be certain they have a seamless and logical story narrative.

Don't let this put you off from discovering if this method works for you. Although it might seem contradictory, just as many plotters have to do the same thing when they reach the end of their outline. Such is the temperament of stories that morph and evolve as we write.

Reversals of Fortune

No matter your method of plotting, one of the elements that makes a plot zing is a *reversal.* A plot reversal occurs when a character's decisions result in an outcome opposite of what was desired. This throws a new obstacle in the way of his reaching his goal.

It can happen as well by his learning something he didn't expect to learn that makes him rethink his goal. A reversal results in a climactic moment, changing a character's good fortune to bad.

def•i•ni•tion

A **reversal** is a point in the plot at which things shift in a new direction, often unexpectedly, because of a character's choices or actions.

Plotting with Erotic Potential

You're here because you want to write erotic romance, so then, looking at the erotic potential in your ideas makes sense, doesn't it? Whether you start with a basic story idea or begin with characters, you want to be sure you're working with a concept that courts eroticism.

The first thing you want to do is be sure you've developed story people whose sexual natures lend themselves to a close examination. They will be under a microscope, their every move examined closely. Not only will readers be given a voyeuristic look into their sexual lives, they'll be privy to the decisions your characters make regarding sex, i.e., who to have it with and why. Your hero and heroine must stand up to that intense scrutiny.

Once you understand your characters' feelings about sexuality and know their sexual personalities, you'll want to place them in situations that challenge those beliefs. Push them to the edge. Take them to the limit. Yes, they'll get pleasure out of sex, but they'll also be forced into the sort of self-examination that's critical for growth.

In Chapter 1, I listed several scenarios with built-in opportunities for characters to become close and find themselves in situations conducive to sex due to forced proximity. Using such a plot device is not required, however. What is required is a situation or theme where sex is woven intrinsically into your story's fabric. An erotic romance where the sex has to be wedged into the plot … well, it isn't an erotic romance! A story with one sex scene after another is a story with a lot of sex, yes. To be an erotic romance, it needs more. The sex must be tied so tightly into your story that if you cut it loose, your story would no longer make sense. Tell that to the naysayers who claim that erotic romance is easy to write!

Scorchers

Your readers must understand and respect your characters' choices, even if they may not agree with them.

Naughty, Naughty

Don't settle on what's been done a dozen times before. Think up unique situations in which to drop your characters. Readers tire easily when fed a diet of the same ol' same ol'. Give them something new to gobble up!

Plotting Misconceptions

Let's face it: not everyone is going to be comfortable with or approve of sex being written about so openly or explicitly. This group of people is not your audience. There is, however, a segment of the reading public that doesn't know what erotic romance is because they've never been exposed to the extent or the quality of what the genre offers.

Eroticism, like beauty, is in the eye of the beholder. Where one reader may experience a sexual twinge when reading about a kiss, another needs a graphically detailed consummation scene to feel the excitement. Luckily, the genre offers both. But that's not all it offers ….

Misconception #1: Erotic Romances Have No Plot

Tell *that* to the authors who slave over their novels, making sure their stories tell the compelling tales of fully developed characters on believably motivated quests.

Scorchers

Why anyone would think eroticism equates to lack of plot is a mystery to me! No discerning reader looking for a fulfilling romance is going to want to read a book with nothing but sex on the page. And no discerning editor is going to buy a romance without a story.

Of course erotic romances have plot! They are novels, after all. And yes, because they are erotic romances, the sex plays a large part in the stories. In fact, in the best erotic romances, the sex fuels the plot—just as a murder fuels the plot in a mystery. Genre fiction is genre fiction because of its specific requirements. The main story element required by erotic romance is eroticism.

So yes. Erotic romances do have plot. But then you already knew that, didn't you?

Misconception #2: Erotic Romances Are All About Sex

As discussed in the previous paragraphs, erotic romances by nature have a high sexual content and a focused emphasis on eroticism—the same way a romantic suspense has a high suspense quotient, the same way an inspirational romance has a focused emphasis on spirituality. Each is still a romance. What sets one apart from the others are the expectations of that subgenre's readers.

Romance novels are the stories of two people finding each other against all odds and falling in love. While the couple in a romantic suspense is caught up in external events and the couple in an inspirational story has a spiritual calling, the couple in an erotic romance experiences much of their personal growth through their sexual encounters. It really is that simple.

Who's Behind the Wheel?

Here's where I talk about who or what provides the driving force of your story. If you're writing a family drama, obviously the interactions between the characters are going to be one of the most important aspects of your novel. The same will be true for an erotic romance that's focused on two characters battling internal rather than external challenges before finding true love.

If you're writing a suspense novel or one with a lot of action and adventure, outside events will propel the dramatic tension forward. The same holds true for any story where external forces bring your hero and heroine together. In these situations, the story is carried forward by the momentum of the plot.

The Characters

Earlier I mentioned that I plot out my books based on my characters. I do that by developing my story people and putting them into situations that will test them and challenge them and throw roadblocks into their path. In Chapters 9 and 11, I talk more in depth about how to bring your story people to life. If you find that your plots stem from the choices your characters make rather than from situations with which they find themselves dealing, you are more than likely writing books driven by your characters rather than external events.

The Plot

A book that is plot-driven is often one in which the plot happens to the characters. They are active participants, never passive, but they are caught up in series of events. Whether the incidents are of their own making or are ones over which they have little if any control, the things that are going on around them are responsible for the forward motion and rising action of the story.

The Sex

As discussed earlier, erotic romances, because of their nature, have a higher potential—and need—for a sex-driven plot than books in other genres. Again, this does not mean a series of sex scenes strung together equals an erotic romance. Gratuitous scenes take away from the developing romance and damage a story's credibility.

The sex that drives an erotic romance must be intrinsic to the novel's development. It must do one or more of several things:

- Force a character into examining his belief system
- Increase the conflict, whether internal or external
- Provide twists and turns to the plot
- Up the stakes for all characters involved

Slip of the Tongue

Author Pamela Clare says, "I have a general idea when I'm writing a book when the sex scenes will happen, but I also try to be spontaneous. Also, I do try to think out scale, i.e., which will be the most tender scene, the hottest scene, etc. In writing my first novel, *Sweet Release,* it dawned on me that sex in a book needs to have the same range as, say, a piano keyboard. The high notes can only be truly appreciated if contrasted with the low notes. If you want to make something seem *hotter,* in other words, start out cold and build slowly."

The Least You Need to Know

- Plotting a story from beginning to end gives you a solid outline from which to write.
- Diving into a story without preplanning allows you to discover your characters' journeys as you write.
- By tying a couple's sexual activity intrinsically into the plot, you can dispel many misconceptions about erotic romance.
- A plot can be driven by the characters or by the story's external events.
- For the sex scenes in an erotic romance not to be gratuitous, they must play a larger role than providing physical pleasure.

Chapter 7

Plot: Establishing Motives, Goals, and Conflict

In This Chapter

- Digging for motives
- Establishing where goals come from
- Finding the perfect conflict
- Working the sex angle

A character's outward desire (goal) and the exterior force behind it (motive) create the momentum of the external plot. Both the desire and the force behind it must be clearly defined, as together they will push the character into making choices and taking action. Throwing obstacles (conflict) between a character and his goal makes for compelling fiction, as it gives readers a hero to root for.

We'll look at internal goals, conflicts, and motivations in Chapter 9. For now, let's examine what a character wants from the world around him, what's keeping him from getting it, and why it's so important to begin with.

Motives: Wanting What You Get

Characters don't just wake up one morning and decide they want something. Well, other than maybe coffee or sex. They want what they want for a reason. A motive. One that fuels every step they take on their quest. Their goal could have been a long time coming, having built up over the years, or it could be a sudden decision. Whatever it is, there will be a reason behind it. (I guess coffee and sex would work! More than a few characters, when opening their eyes, have been motivated to seek out coffee because of the need to wake up and to seek out sex because of their early morning arousal!)

If your hero's goal is a job promotion, his motive could be as simple as big money or a big corner office. If what he wants is a sports car, his motive could be a love of speed. There's more to it than that, of course, and I'll explain further in a bit. But so far, so good, right? Then let's go on.

Scorchers

I've found it of great help to figure out the goals and motives for all my characters—including villains—before I start my books. In fact, it's one of the first things I do, even before outlining my plot. The direction of every scene you write will be determined by what a character wants, what he'll do to get it, and why. It's a good idea to keep this information forefront in your mind!

Goals: Getting What You Want

Goals and motives are so inexorably linked that it's nearly impossible to talk about them as separate elements. Whatever your character wants, he's been driven to seek it out for a specific purpose. His quest is the reason your story exists.

It's also difficult to look at the external goals and motives without bringing the internal into play, although I'm going to give it a shot. No story, however, is complete without the entire package—a package with elements that your planning has helped you link together. How so, you ask? Well, here's an example:

External goal: Brandon wants to buy a condo in Aspen.

External motive: He's loved skiing all his life.

Internal goal: Brandon wants to regain the joy of his childhood that's missing in his adult life.

Internal motive: He's never been happier than when he was skiing as a boy with his father, who died last year.

See how that works? Every element is connected, intertwined, and dependent on the rest. If Brandon's father hadn't died, for example, he might not be thinking back on the fun they'd had together skiing when he was a child, and the condo in Aspen wouldn't be a priority.

But back to goals. An external goal can be a tangible item, such as the sports car I mentioned earlier, or a piece of beachfront property. It can also be something intangible, like the job promotion or even a ski trip to Aspen.

If a relaxing ski trip is your hero's goal, the story might be a lighthearted romantic comedy taking place on the slopes, while if the beachfront property he's after once belonged to his grandfather, you might be writing a family drama. Then again, you could flip the ideas and make the ski trip an unplanned journey home and the quest for the beachfront property a romp.

Scorchers

Once you've established your character's external goal and motive, you can then have fun deciding how to tell his or her story.

Conflict: It's Brewing

Conflict is what makes a book impossible to put down and keeps readers coming back for more. Reading about characters who never have to struggle and have everything go their way means we have no one to root for, nothing to look forward to in terms of character growth. No one with whom to share the fight to beat the odds.

Think about your favorite books and all the obstacles thrown in the characters' ways. If they hadn't been forced to face their enemies or interfering family members, if they hadn't had to keep one step ahead of a ticking clock or a consuming fire, if they hadn't needed to deal with an ongoing fear of failure or the stigma of being the family's black sheep, then their triumph in the end wouldn't have been as satisfying.

In my own book *Indiscreet*, for example, my heroine, Annabel Lee, refused to get emotionally involved with my hero, Patrick Coffey, because the career for which she'd worked her entire life was finally within reach, yet would more than likely take her out of state and away from Patrick. Patrick, on the other hand, brought dangerous external baggage to his relationship with Annabel, and having already lost one woman to the story's villain, he was not about to risk losing another.

Neither character was able to move forward with the relationship until their external conflict had either been conquered or a compromise made. That didn't keep them from having an incredible sex life, but even the sex had a poignancy to it, as they weren't sure if what they'd found was going to last.

Slip of the Tongue

Author Lynn Viehl takes this approach to creating her characters and throwing conflict into their path: "...every character I imagine takes form by answering three basic questions: *Who are you? What do you want? What's the worst thing that I can do to you?* When I have those three answers, I've got my protagonist, and the foundation for his or her novel."

Interpersonal Conflict: Man vs. Man

Having one character in conflict with another gives you the opportunity to explore a human relationship outside your story's romance. This conflict can be between your protagonist and someone close to him, a lifelong enemy, a person he just met, or someone he doesn't even know. Interpersonal conflict pits two strong individuals, with equally well-motivated and opposing goals, against one another. Readers get to know both parties as real people and often have their loyalties torn, knowing only one will triumph in the end.

Scorchers

Giving your hero a truly worthy antagonist, no matter who it turns out to be, is the best way to prove his mettle!

The person who causes conflict in your protagonist's life is as important to your story as is your protagonist. Whatever his role in your plot, he exists to turn the world as your main character knows it upside down. This can be intentional or accidental, malicious or just for fun. His exploits are the catalyst that spur your character into taking action. How your character reacts sets not only the tone of your story but defines the sort of person he is.

The Bad and the Ugly Guys

Villains don't have to be overtly evil or wicked, even if Alan Rickman's Sheriff of Nottingham in *Robin Hood: Prince of Thieves* was to die for! This type works well in movies made from comic books or in cartoons, but many of the villains who intrigue us most are those who are so compelling that we don't know for sure if they're good or if they're bad.

Also, consider the tension of a protagonist not realizing he's dealing with a villainous type until it's too late to sidestep the inevitable conflict. Believable, credible bad guys give your story punch. Make them as interesting as your good guys, and your reader won't be able to stop herself from getting caught up in your book!

Scorchers

When you develop the goals and motivations for your hero and heroine (and any secondary characters who may have subplots of their own), don't forget to do the same for your villain(s). No one likes reading about flat, cardboard characters. The best bad guys are the ones who are as fleshed out as the good guys, because they show your readers what your hero is made of when he takes them on!

Close-Knit ... or Not!

Is there anyone who can send us into an emotional upheaval quicker than a family member? There's sibling rivalry. There's well-intentioned meddling, overprotective coddling, or what seems like constant criticism wrapped up in the guise of love. There's also true animosity, jealousy, bitterness, etc.

Dealing with these issues and exploring their basis can try your hero or heroine for all they're worth—and that's what the best conflict does! Such trials allow for the very character growth and change you want to portray in your novel, so delving into them as deeply as you can is a good thing!

Stiff Competition

Bidding on the same job. Hunting for the same mysterious artifact. Even going after the same girl—or guy. A serious competitor can create huge conflict for your protagonist. Every time your character gets one step closer to his goal, he's thwarted by the competition who's as on the ball and determined as he is.

A good competitor, though a source of conflict, can be as much of a good guy as your hero—or heroine. In fact, watch out, or he'll be demanding a story of his own!

Naughty, Naughty

Don't give your character a competitor he could steamroll or one who isn't up to the challenge. What fun would that be for your protagonist or for your reader?

Gone but Not Forgotten

The, ah, *unpleasant* ex-wife, fiancée, girlfriend, or lover is a romance novel staple—and a romance novel cliché! There's absolutely nothing wrong with using a former spouse or significant other for your story's antagonist, but give the ex more than an ax to grind because of being dumped. Remember, you want your villain to ring as true as your protagonist. Otherwise, there's no reason for your reader to care.

> **Scorchers**
>
> In addition to looking to your hero and heroine for your antagonist, look to your story's premise and theme, as defined in Chapter 8. Linking all these elements closely helps maintain the focus of your story.

An ex forced into your character's life against his or her will, for example, or even one who will always be around because of a shared business venture or joint custody of a child provides conflict that's not easily—if ever—resolved. This is the sort of conflict that will make your story stand out.

Mystery Men

When crafting the antagonists who will create conflict for your story's main characters, take a big cue from your hero and heroine. Who is going to keep them from reaching their goal better than anyone? Who can toss the biggest, baddest roadblocks in their way? Who will best test their strengths and weaknesses? And something to consider in erotic romance: who will add grief of a sexual nature to the mix?

No element in your story stands alone, and the more tightly together you can weave each one, the more powerful and effective your story will be.

Internal Conflict: Man vs. Self

A character is often his or her own worst enemy. Decisions and choices he makes can get him into hot water that only he can get himself out of—no matter how much others try or want to help. Pride could be keeping him from accepting or from reaching out, or he could be determined to find his own way through the muddle. And even though the conflict is internal, its existence will cause him problems beyond what he suffers privately.

> **Scorchers**
>
> A character's unique personal problems often present the perfect kindling for keeping the conflict flame burning high.

In erotic romance, we are given opportunities to use a character's sexuality not only internally, but also as an external conflict. Perhaps your hero's extracurricular activities don't sit well with conservative neighbors who are none too pleased with his hot tub parties or other sexual conduct that fills his exhibitionist needs. Perhaps a co-worker who learns of a heroine's preference for bondage makes advances that force her to file a sexual harassment complaint.

Don't think internal issues or a character's personality traits can only present internal conflict. These things present problems externally as well.

Much Obliged

A character's obligations, how he feels about them, and what he does to live up to them tells your reader a lot about the type of person he is. Said obligations also provide for great conflict. Being the only family member available to an ailing relative might require he give up a dream of accepting a job in another city. A promise to help a co-worker work up a bid for a construction project, feeling bound to represent an ex-lover in a court case, or the need to follow through on vacation plans made with a friend—scenarios such as these present an internal sense of obligation that can cause external conflict in a character's life. It's up to you to provide it!

I Just Don't Know ...

Doubt can take many forms. A character can wonder whether or not she is doing the right thing when she agrees to go home with a man she just met. Another might be concerned that she doesn't have the skills necessary to finish a job or the experience necessary to please a new lover—even though she's more than happy to try. Doubt can eat away at a character's self-confidence—and give you as the author a great opportunity to add complexity to your characterization.

Can't Get Enough

Battling an addiction to food, alcohol, gambling, drugs, sex ... any of these can provide a character with a serious internal conflict that shows itself in the light of day. Waging a war on such a large personal scale means not a day—or even an hour—goes by that your character isn't beset with conflict. Dealing with it will either make him or break him, proving him to be a character worth reading about.

Naughty, Naughty

If the main source of conflict in your book is an internal issue that manifests externally for your characters, be sure not to let your story dissolve into nothing but pages of introspection. You still need active scenes to move your story forward and to keep the dramatic tension high.

These are only a few examples of innumerable conflicts stemming from within a character while coloring his dealings with the world around him. I'm sure you can come up with dozens more that will help you tell a compelling story!

External Conflict: Man vs. Outside Forces

Characters have little or no control over outside forces. Where they might be able to manipulate a human antagonist, no can do with a storm or other natural disaster. Where therapy or a lot of beers with the girls or boys might help them through personal conflicts that keep them from reaching their goals, neither of those will stop an impending deadline.

Putting a character on a collision course with an external disaster gives readers a chance to see him in action. How does he cope? Can he think on his feet? Does he back away, needing time to plot and plan, or does he barge forward, full steam ahead and consequences be damned?

Any of these scenarios can have any number of outcomes. The theme of your story and the premise you want to prove will determine the direction your character takes. And the direction your character takes will fuel your plot as well as his personal growth.

Tick Tock

I absolutely love using a ticking clock for my external conflict, because it offers so many opportunities to keep the tension high. Characters can't escape it. They can't change it. They have to deal with it, or they're the ones who lose. What do they lose? Anything from a chance to see their favorite sitcom because they've arrived home too late … to their life. It's a great plot device because it provides a believable source of conflict—or it does as long as it fits believably with the rest of your story!

Scorchers

A ticking clock conflict can exist outside action-adventure or suspense plots. These subgenres quite often use the device, but it can also be used on a smaller scale. A deadline set by a family member's will, for example, forces characters into action. The date a character is scheduled to leave home for college or to move across the country may require he face issues he's put off for too long before leaving.

Stormy Weather

Natural disasters create an obvious source of external conflict between a protagonist and his goal. (If you don't believe me, think of the movies that have been made about them: *Twister, Volcano, Earthquake*, etc.) In fact, if the disaster is the basis for your plot, it will most likely be the motivating factor behind said goal.

An emergency worker's goal would be obvious in such a situation—working to save lives—while another character's goal might be simply to get out of the path of destruction. Characters might also find themselves caught unexpectedly in the path of a fire or a storm and be forced to rethink their goals. The opportunities for tension and suspense in these situations are endless. Use them!

Filthy Lucre

Another conflict in many characters' lives is their need for financial security. They put in long hours at work and more long hours pursuing their education. Having their time eaten up by this intense drive for success can provide conflict in a number of ways—the most obvious of which is their inability to be available to friends and family, even to their significant other. Look to the reasons why your character has this love affair with money, and use it to give depth to what might seem to be a shallow, materialistic conflict.

Fitting Sex into the Mix

As if I haven't said it enough already, I'll say it again: the erotic romances that work best are those where the sex is inseparable from the story as a whole. In fact, I'd go so far as to call this a tenet that makes the genre work.

The plots are advanced through the characters' sexual encounters. Their individual story arcs evolve and their self-perceptions are challenged through their sexual encounters. Thinking of the sexual content of an erotic novel separately from the other story elements is courting trouble.

Slip of the Tongue

In talking about fitting sex into a plot with a high level of external conflict, author Shannon McKenna says: "The great thing about the emotional byproducts of a suspense plot—danger, fear, rage, etc.—is that they blast the hero and heroine wide open and get right to the raw, scary stuff inside. This creates instant intimacy and increases the range of emotions you've got to work with. If a horrific villain is trying to wipe you out, you skip the small talk, and dark, problematic sex becomes more believable, as well as more, well … forgivable. Like, you're-in-on-the-plot-to-kill-me-but-I'm-too-turned-on-to-care sex."

That doesn't mean developing a story with a theme and premise that supports a high level of sexuality is easy. Far from it. But the end result will please editors and readers alike and, most important of all, you'll be pleased to see the fruits of your labors so well accepted.

The Least You Need to Know

- Making your goals, motives, and conflicts inseparable adds to the compelling nature of your story.
- A character's goals must be fueled by believable motivations.
- The best way to test a character is through conflict that has substance.
- Using a character's sexuality as a source of conflict adds depth to an erotic romance.

Chapter 8

Writing 101: Putting It All Together

In This Chapter

- Maintaining a story's forward motion
- Looking through the right set of eyes
- Keeping your reader involved
- Finding and using words that work best

One of the most important parts of novel writing, whether you outline from beginning to end or plot by the seat of your pants, is structuring your book, i.e., putting it together in a cohesive package. This holds true for an erotic romance novel just as it does for a novel in any other genre.

Assembled correctly, your book will have your readers whipping through the pages. On the other hand, throwing together a jumbled mess will leave her confused, unable to follow along, and moving on to the next book on her shelf. To keep that from happening, you as the author must consider several things. Let's take a look at those now.

Theme and Premise

The theme of your story is a recurrent idea presented throughout via the action, the characters … basically, all the story's components. A premise then puts forward a specific belief based on your theme. Yes, I know. It's confusing! Let me see if I can make it clearer.

If your theme is the power of love, then your premise would be something along the lines of love conquering all, and the actions of your characters will prove that very thing. Establishing your theme and premise before you get started and then keeping both on the front burner while you write helps guarantee you'll end up with a strong, focused book.

Lights, Camera, Action!

I first ran into the concept of structuring scenes in Dwight Swain's wonderful book *Techniques of the Selling Writer*. Next to Christopher Vogler's *The Writer's Journey*, Swain's book has had the most impact on my writing. Not only has it helped me shape my chapters, it also has enabled me to fix most of the pacing problems that cropped up in my work when I began to write. As I did with Vogler's book, I took from Swain's what resonated with my way of writing and tweaked it until we were a perfect fit!

Let's take a closer look at what it means to write in scenes and how doing so can improve the framework of a novel.

What Is a Scene?

A scene is a vehicle for delivering the action of a story. Each character in a scene needs to have a goal—one he or she wants to accomplish in that short span of time as opposed to an overall story goal that won't be met until the end of your book. (If the goals of your scene's characters are in opposition, all the better!) Your characters are then thwarted from reaching said goals by some sort of obstacle. (Are you seeing a pattern here? Just as a plot needs characters with goals, motivations, and conflicts, so does a scene.) This conflict results in a scene reversal or other upheaval that makes things worse for your story people while hooking your reader's interest. Whatever the trouble, it keeps her turning the pages, raising questions for her *and* for your character about what happens next. It's a sure way to build a successful scene!

What Follows a Scene?

Once you've written a scene, you'll want to write your characters' response to it. This is where a character, usually through an introspective passage, processes what has happened and makes a choice as to what to do next. (If you're reading Swain's book, check out his section on scene and sequel.) Basically, this creates breathing room for your reader. Along with your character, she is given time to digest all that's gone before as well as a chance to observe your character's reasoning process as he considers his options.

> **Scorchers**
>
> Each scene you write needs to act as a puzzle piece and fit into your story's overall arc. Think of a scene as a building block containing its own mini-arc that helps support the larger framework. If you're interested in a more in-depth instruction about the structure of a scene and each of its components, I recommend reading Robert McKee's *Story.*

I recently read an article that argued that this method of structuring a story was outdated because readers reading in today's fast-paced society don't have time to spend slogging their way through the long introspective pages. Who said anything about long introspective pages? You can convey a character's thoughts in a matter of sentences! Want to see how?

> Brandon waited until Rachel stepped onto the subway before scrubbing his hands down his face with regret. He should have waited until tonight to tell her about his trip to Tokyo. Over dinner would've been better, giving them time alone and all. In fact, screw their usual Monday night burgers. She deserved wine and candlelight and her favorite shrimp scampi. They could finish up the conversation then. He bounded up the stairs, pulling his cell phone from his waist to call for reservations.

See how quick that was? You have the response (regret), the predicament solved (finishing conversation over dinner), then the step (making reservations) that propels Brandon into the next scene. Following up an intense action scene or one that is highly emotional with this sort of short break allows your reader a bit of downtime and also creates a way to move easily from one scene to the next.

The Eyes Have It

The viewpoint character in a scene is the one through whose eyes we are seeing the action, whose thoughts we are privy to, and whose feelings we experience. Novels can be written in any number of viewpoints. The most common in genre fiction are the following:

- **Omniscient.** An all-seeing narrator who knows the thoughts and feelings of all characters and can insert editorial comments and observations at will.
- **First person.** A single character narration (I, my, me) where the character telling the story is relating a personal experience—or one she has witnessed—and only relates her own thoughts and feelings.
- **Third person.** A character or multiple characters relating their individual perspectives and often sharing the narration as required by the story's forward motion.

Which point of view you use and how you use it will depend on what you want to accomplish with your story. I've read books in which the author has successfully mixed first- and third-person viewpoints in alternating chapters, and others in which the author has kept to one narrator in third person the entire time. In romance, most authors choose to switch between the viewpoints of their hero and their heroine, as each character plays an equally important role in the story, and readers enjoy seeing the romance develop through the eyes of both.

def•i•ni•tion

Head-hopping refers to jerky, tennis-match-style (think of a spectator following the ball back and forth) point of view switches in a scene that leave the reader unable to keep up with whose head she is in.

Though every author will have her own preference for sticking with one point of view in a scene or switching between the viewpoints of the scene's characters (I could write an entire book on this particular subject!), all authors agree that the one thing you want to avoid is any reading confusion caused by awkward *head-hopping*. Transitions between viewpoints need to be smooth and clear. When a reader can't keep up with or figure out who is doing the thinking in a scene, then there's a big problem with the way point of view is being employed!

Naughty, Naughty

The biggest problem inherent to head-hopping is the distance you create between your characters and your reader. Moving her into the head of one character when she's just settled in comfortably with another can pull her out of the story, and that's something no author wants to do. When switching viewpoints, be sure you do so smoothly, as well as for a desired effect, not just because you're in the mood for a change!

Setting the Pace

Have you ever been reading a conversation between two characters where one stops to think about something, and by the time the author returns to the dialogue, you've forgotten what the conversation was about? This is a pacing problem easily solved by writing in a format similar to the one I described earlier. The conversation should be completed and *then* the characters involved can stop to consider its implications and how it made them feel. You want your reader with you at every step. The downtime is a necessary part of a story's flow, but the middle of a scene's action is not where you want it to occur.

Many authors are born with a pacing gene. I was not and had to develop this structure to write my way out of horrible pacing problems. Give this method a try and see if it won't work for you, too!

Rising Tension

Every scene should contain conflict that prevents characters from reaching their goals, so every scene should cause a story's overall tension to rise, as if in increments. Think of each scene as a rung on a ladder that reaches into the unknown. The beginning is solidly grounded, the middle might waver a bit, and the top seems forever out of reach. The higher you climb, the greater the danger of falling, and the greater the fear of what awaits at the top. All this adds to your story's dramatic tension and keeps your reader on the edge of her seat.

Scorchers

A notebook, pen, set of highlighters, and DVD-player remote control are great tools to use to analyze how the weaving of a story's threads help build its rising tension. Choose a movie to analyze, watch it to figure out the main subplots, and make a list of the movie's scenes—in order. Assign each subplot a different color and then highlight your list and see which story lines were given most screen time and how they converged at the end. You can do the same with a book.

Careening to the End

Once you approach your story's finale, your pacing should have reached a breakneck speed. All your plot threads are converging, and your reader can't read fast enough to find out what's going to happen. Think of how well this is done in action movies where the villain and the hero prepare to collide in a final showdown. Use the same technique in your book, and see if you don't wind up with a powerful ending.

Weaving Threads

I like to think of weaving a story's threads (or subplots—both the internal and the external) together as I would braiding hair. I did a lot of that for my daughters when both were younger, so the analogy of starting with multiple sections, plaiting them in and out and around each other, and binding them together at the end works for me.

It demonstrates exactly how a whole is produced from its parts. It also gives each thread equal significance; no one is more important than the others. The braid analogy proves how each thread is dependant on the others. If you remove one, you don't have a finished product, only sections. And finally, it shows the value of a tight knit, because loosely woven hair—and plots—fall apart easily.

Suspension of Disbelief

If you want your readers to stick around for your novel's full ride, they have to believe everything that's going on—even if what's going on is a paranormal fantasy set in a futuristic dimension!

Believability does not require a world be based in our own reality, but it does require the solid world-building I described in Chapter 5. It also requires consistent characterization. If a reader buys into your story people and story idea, you can convince her of anything—including that the moon really *is* made of green cheese!

Show, Don't Tell

We hear this advice as soon as we begin to write, and many authors take it to mean that they should never tell anything in a book—which just isn't true. I'll explain more on that in a moment. For now, take a look at the following two examples:

> *Example #1:* It was almost noon. Rachel was going to be late for her appointment. The traffic had tied her up. She pushed the button for the elevator. She stepped in when the car arrived, and chose her floor, pushing that button, too. The elevator door closed. The car began to rise. When the door opened again, she stepped out and headed down the hallway. She found the right office, reached for the door handle, and turned it.

Example #2: The clock ticked its way to noon. Rachel cringed. Her stomach knotted at the thought of walking into her meeting late. Damn traffic. And damn slow elevator, she grumbled to herself, jabbing her finger at the call button repeatedly. When the car finally arrived, she shoved her way inside, smacking the button for her floor and holding her breath. She hated elevators, the way her stomach dropped to her feet. This ride up was no different, and by the time she reached her floor, she was so dizzy she wasn't sure she'd be able to find the right office. That's what a horrible case of nerves did to a girl.

The first example tells us what is happening with Rachel. This sort of writing creates a distance between your character and your reader and keeps your reader from feeling immersed in the action. The second example shows the reader the same thing happening, but does so through evocative details that let her experience what the character is feeling—both physically and emotionally.

Scorchers

There is a time for both telling and showing. Knowing when to use which is the key!

We often gloss over unimportant details to get to what matters, and that's fine. Telling a reader that a heroine got up, made her bed, drank her coffee, brushed her teeth, and headed out the door to work is all we need to do if her morning routine has no bearing on the overall story. If we show her in active detail taking care of each of those things, we will bore the reader to death and waste manuscript pages better devoted to the meat of our plot.

Passive vs. Active Writing

Active writing gives your reader exactly what it implies—a sense of something happening, i.e., action. You do this by choosing words to convey that the character is the one in motion, the one acting and reacting, and is not a passive bump on a log while things are done to him or around him.

Look at the following:

Example #1: The chair was picked up by Rachel.

Example #2: Rachel picked up the chair.

Example #3: Rachel hoisted the chair overhead and hurled it to the floor.

See how in the first example the subject, Rachel, is a passive participant? In the second example, she is actively lifting, and the third example takes it one step further by giving more life to her movements with evocative words. And notice that I didn't settle for *picked* when *hoisted* made a better fit for the emotion of the scene. Look at your prose, and be sure your chairs aren't in charge!

Let's look at a few more examples to demonstrate the power behind the right action verbs:

> *Example #1:* Which choice works best if Brandon is in a hurry to get to Rachel and settle an argument?
>
> Brandon *walked* up the stairs from the subway to the street.
> Or:
> Brandon *bounded* up the stairs from the subway to the street.
>
> *Example #2:* Which choice works best if Rachel is hurrying to clean her apartment before Brandon arrives?
>
> Rachel *loaded* the dishwasher and *closed* the door.
> Or:
> Rachel *shoved* the dishes into the dishwasher and *slammed* the door.
>
> *Example #3:* Which choice works best if Brandon wants to take his time making love to Rachel?
>
> Brandon *unbuttoned* Rachel's blouse and *removed* it.
> Or:
> Brandon *eased* open the buttons of Rachel's blouse and *slid* it down her arms.

Get the most action you can out of your verbs.

Cause and Effect

This is one of my personal bugaboos—maybe not so much with the big picture, but definitely with smaller ones that need the same attention—and I find similar gaffes in books I read. I tend to get too caught up in the rhythm or construction of a sentence and end up reversing my cause and effect. For example:

> *Example #1:* Brandon walked through the door and slammed it. Hearing the latch catch, Rachel turned.
>
> *Example #2:* Hearing the latch catch as the door slammed shut, Rachel turned to see Brandon walk through.

Obviously, the latch catching on the slamming door is what causes Rachel to turn. The first example shows the correct sequence of events. The second doesn't, as it has the door slamming before Brandon has even walked through! Be sure you don't put reactions before the actions that cause them!

Verisimilitude

I was introduced to the word *verisimilitude* at the first writing workshop I ever attended. It was given by author LaVyrle Spencer. I had read everything of hers I could get my hands on, and hearing her speak was a dream. Since then, I've seen the term most often associated with the work of Stephen King.

> **def•i•ni•tion**
>
> **Verisimilitude** is something that seems to be real or has the sense or appearance of being true. As an author, you lend verisimilitude to a scene by using specific words and descriptors, such as saying a character drove "a 1965 cherry-red hot rod" instead of saying he drove "a car."

Broken down into its etymological roots, *verisimilitude* means "very similar." By refusing to settle for any descriptive word and reaching for the one that is perfect, just right, the exact fit, you can give your work the verisimilitude that helps draw your readers into your story. You do the same when relating various incidents by looking for universal situations everyone reading can relate to.

Effective Repetition and the Rule of Three

There's a difference between using repetition for a reason and carelessly repeating the same words or phrases throughout a manuscript. With all the words we have to choose from, I can't think of any reason to repeat a word unless it's done for a specific purpose such as narrative rhythm or emphasis.

When you do a final read-through of your manuscript before submission, look for overused words throughout, as well as the same words popping up time and again on a page. We all seem to have one or two words we reach for too often.

Repetition isn't all bad, though. One very effective and meaningful use of repetition is grouping things into threes. This tool can also add to your rising tension—which is a good reason to give the third item in the list the most power and punch, as it's the one readers will remember. Here are a couple examples of writing in threes:

> **Naughty, Naughty**
>
> A reader notices repetition, and if she's noticing anything in your book, she's holding onto it, looking for it to mean something down the road. If it doesn't, she feels cheated. Be sure anything she's retaining pays off for her in the end.

Brandon grabbed his wallet, his keys, and his watch and headed for the door.

Brandon wanted nothing from the Tokyo partners, nothing from his co-workers here, and right now, he wanted absolutely nothing from Rachel.

Brandon hated feeling angry, powerless, and more than that, used.

Basically, it comes down to this: if you want something to be noticed, mention it three times. For example, say you have a physical item you need your reader to notice because it will come into major play later in your book. You mention it three times before you use it, and in doing so, you have planted the seed in your reader's mind.

Between the Style Sheets

Yes, grammar does matter, as does punctuation, spelling, and all the other elements of style. In the past, editors had time to mentor authors, to overlook these sorts of errors to get to the story. Perhaps there are still some editors who do, but for the most part, an editor's workload means an author who has done her English 101 homework is going to be the first to catch her eye.

Look at it this way: if you were faced with 200 manuscripts to go through, wouldn't you skip the ones requiring extra work on your part and concentrate on the gems? And yes, of course, we all send in manuscripts with errors sprinkled throughout. But there's a difference between a soft sprinkling and a downpour!

The Least You Need to Know

- A smoothly structured novel with clear point of view switches and consistent pacing is more enjoyable for a reader than one with a jerky feel.
- The smaller goals and conflicts contained in individual scenes push your plot forward and provide impetus for character growth.
- You can draw your reader into your scenes by selectively choosing the words that portray your characters as active participants in your story.
- Turning in a polished manuscript is the sign of a professional.

Part 3

Who Do You Love? The Emotional Journey

Romance readers read for the love story and the characters' emotional journey along that road. They want to experience the novel's hero and heroine falling in love. To make this happen, the author needs to create characters as real as the reader's next-door neighbors. Stagnant characters are boring characters.

Readers want to witness the growth and upheavals in the lives of the people populating a novel, and Part 3 focuses on how you can create believable characters your readers will love. It also takes a look at what your characters are looking for when it comes to love, sex, and romance—and how to give it to them!

Chapter 9

The Building Blocks of Story People

In This Chapter

- Digging into a character's past
- Discovering the influence of friends, family, mentors, and loves
- Looking at what lifestyle reveals
- Understanding deep-seated motivations

Bring your characters to life by exploring the whole of who they are, from past to present. No one exists in a vacuum, even fictional characters. Their backgrounds and life experiences will play a part in their sexual natures and the romantic relationships they nurture.

What has made them who they are? What determines compatibility? Why is one character repressed and another a sexually open book? All these questions can be answered through detailed character development. Let's take a look at how to create characters from the ground up.

Where Did They Come From?

Brandon was born in the year 1975 on the wrong side of the tracks.

Okay, maybe we don't need to go back quite that far, but if you want to, more power to you! Such detail can only add to the depth of your characterization. If Brandon was born on the wrong side of the tracks, lived in poverty and shame, and was bullied as a child, he'll bring that to the table as he grows. His outlook on life could be defensive; he had to fight back for so many years that he automatically prepares to do so now. Or his outlook on life could be such that he expects to get kicked when he's already down and has given up trying to make things go his way. Whether you give him a background to fit your story's theme, premise, and plot, or whether you develop those around the character you've created, just be sure you know him as well as you know yourself!

Naughty, Naughty

Don't take the easy approach to characterization. Don't assume, for example, that a hero raised in poverty is going to be obsessed with money. That's the cliché everyone expects. To keep your writing and stories fresh, add twists where you can. Instead of an obsession with money, a hero raised in poverty could realize he turned out just fine and eschew material wealth, preferring to give to others and live a monastic existence!

The Wonder Years

From preschool to grade school and beyond, our formative years play a huge role in our development from children to adults. It's no different with our story people. One character might have been bullied as a child, while another did the bullying. One might have participated in extracurricular sports, enrolled in dance or gymnastics, or studied piano or a foreign language; another might have spent most of his time at home alone reading; while a third interacted socially with others through computer role-playing games.

Also, consider how sex was viewed in your character's home. Was it an open subject? One that was very hush-hush? Did your character grow up believing sex to be a bad thing or consider it an intimacy to be enjoyed and celebrated? How these things helped or hindered a character's growth is up to you as the author to discover—and then to use in brush strokes to paint your characters onto the page.

Trial and Error

Have your characters been involved in romantic relationships before your story opens? Are they divorced? Have they broken off an engagement for any reason? Have their affairs been strictly sexual? Whatever their situation, the reasons behind their relationship history—and any regrets or fall-out suffered following a break-up—will have an influence on how they interact with potential mates now and in the future.

We don't want to read about a character in an erotic romance who is hung up on an ex to the point of being unable to move forward—that would defeat the purpose of the book being a romance! But knowing what your characters have gone through, from first love to last, will give you the insight you need to understand how they'll approach a relationship this time around. One character might be cautious while another throws caution to the wind. A reader will believe any reaction that's believably motivated!

> **Scorchers**
>
> Even if all of what you discover while developing a character doesn't make it onto the page, it's there for you to draw on as you write. You won't have problems with consistency or continuity as you show them acting on and reacting to their own needs or the demands of outside forces.

A Helping Hand

Coaches, professors, troop leaders, Sunday school teachers, and, yes, even parents. Mentors play a huge part in a young person's development. Look back at your characters as children and see who had the biggest positive influence in their lives. Did one particular teacher turn your heroine onto a subject of study that she eventually made her career? Did a coach offer a willing ear when a parent was too busy and is still one of your hero's best friends?

Don't forget to look to your characters' mentors, too, to see if anyone gave them sexual advice or shaped their views on sexual relationships. Where a parent may have encouraged a child to finish school and get a degree before thinking about a serious relationship, a psychology teacher may have explained about a human being's emotional growth, giving a character the tools to make such decisions on his or her own.

Funeral for a Friend

Consider the traumatizing events that have shaped your story people. Death, divorce, moving from school to school, natural disasters, learning there is no Santa Claus, being bullied at school, losing their virginity, abuse … the list is endless. How they handled these incidents at the time—taking the blame, withdrawing, fighting back, working to fit in—might depend on the support system they had around them. Or it might depend more on who they saw themselves to be.

> **Naughty, Naughty**
>
> Don't assume a character will look at a traumatizing event in a negative light. Having experienced heartbreak at an early age might just be the catalyst that has made him strong as an adult. Dig deep to make your characters worth reading about rather than settling for clichés or stereotypes.

While one character may have embraced the nomadic concept of picking up and moving on a whim as an adventure, another may have grown hostile toward his parents, and yet another may have decided he was old enough to live on his own and run away. If you have a character who as a child lost his entire home—including his collection of toys, books, baseball cards, etc.—to a natural disaster, what impact is that going to have on him as an adult? Look at the disasters that may have occurred during your characters' early years and see what you can do to bring them forward into the present. Doing so makes for great character development!

Another thing to think about is where a character's sexual experimentation fit into the bad times. If a heroine was in a first crush relationship, a disaster might have her turning to her boyfriend for comfort and going all the way for the first time—or have her backing away and wanting to be alone. She might react similarly today to bad news. It's always interesting to consider these responses from every angle!

Mom Liked You Best!

A character's position within his own family plays a big part in his emotional growth. An oldest child might turn out to be a leader, having been forced into that role by parents who expected him to help with younger siblings, or even by those siblings who looked to him for guidance. On the other hand, he might have decided enough with the responsibility already and gone on to choose a career that never requires he hold a supervisory position.

Then there's middle-child syndrome. Never given the same responsibility as the oldest and never receiving the same coddling as the baby of the family, a middle child character might be an independent soul who felt she had to make her own way. Or she might be a rebel who bucks against her second-class status and finds herself in trouble. She might feel unloved, different, misunderstood … while the baby of the family basks in the family glow and never has to vie for attention because it's freely given.

What about a sibling's boyfriends or girlfriends, or your character's own? Did the inclusion of one or the other into the family push your character even further away? Or did your heroine, for example, find herself becoming best friends with her brother's girl … or lusting over and flirting with her sister's boy? If she was a boyfriend-stealer as a teen, does she do the same now as an adult?

Scorchers

None of this background information on your characters *has* to go into a story, but adding some of it could give your story even more sexual punch!

School Days

I don't know anyone who doesn't look back on his or her days in high school or college from time to time. Some might wish they had paid more attention, studied harder, and earned better grades. Others may just miss the camaraderie, the school spirit, and the innocence and freedom from the stress of adult life.

While some characters might still need the adoration they received from classmates and continually look for ways to find it, others might have continued to be students because they love to learn. If your character is pursuing an advanced degree, why is he or she doing so? Knowing the reasons will allow you to be sure your reader understands who your character is. And the answer could be almost anything:

- Love of learning
- Opportunity for career advancement
- Comfort in academic surroundings
- Occasion to discuss issues with like-minded peers

There's also the very high chance that your character's first sexual experiences occurred during high school and college. A heroine might have wished she waited longer, or have chosen a different boy to give her virginity to. On the other hand, she might have always wondered what happened to said boy … and my muse says it's time for her to look him up!

Where Are They Now?

Now that you know where your characters have come from, what building blocks make up the foundation of their belief system, their personality, their outlook on life, etc., it's time to understand more about who they are during the period of their lives when your story occurs. A grad student working as a bartender won't be in the same place in his life as a corporate CEO, for example. Let's look more closely now at your characters and their current situations.

It's Not Just a Job

Your characters' career choices can be tied to almost any number of things in their pasts. I've heard authors say they started writing stories with crayons and knew early in their lives what they wanted to do. A character could have had a youthful fascination with cable television medical shows and become a doctor. Another may have sat at her mother's feet while she sewed and longed to be a fashion designer. Others may have inherited a family business and had the choice taken away … and how do they feel about that? Perhaps the daughter who sat at her mother's feet only wanted attention and became a preschool teacher to give other children the same.

Scorchers

As with anything else, giving twists to the reasons behind a character's career decision can add a unique bent to your story.

Then again, your characters' career choices could be rooted in other things, such as financial opportunities, endless possibilities for travel, the chance to work independently, an occasion to use unique skills, or a desire to help others or give back. Look at your characters and think the way they think to discover what drove them to pursue their own careers.

Circle of Friends

The people with whom your characters surround themselves are often closer to them than family members. They might see them more often—daily if they're co-workers or roommates—and consider them a second family.

On the other hand, friends might just be casual buddies your characters know from a yoga class or a bowling league or a book club. If the latter is the case, why? Does your character have one best friend who's been with him through years of thick and thin and is his number-one drinking buddy whether things are up or down? Understanding how your characters choose their friends and interact with them will help you understand even more about them.

Scorchers

Not all stories you write will star large casts of secondary characters, but I've had great fun writing ones that do. I've had two series from two different publishers featuring co-workers who were also the best of friends. In the male-dominated series, my heroes knew their buddies had their back at every turn; things were the same in my female-dominated series. Both sets of characters offered me a chance to explore the changing nature of friendships.

All in the Family

What sort of relationships do your main protagonists have with their family members—parents, grandparents, siblings, extended family, etc? Has your heroine remained living in the same small town where she grew up so she could stay close to her folks? Did she leave that one-horse town as soon as she could, and if so, how did her family take it? Does she have a sister who is also her best friend and whom she calls every day? Has she cut all ties with her relatives after a perceived slight—or one that was malicious and real? A heroine's interaction with her family might possibly be the catalyst for a hero's deepening interest if he is a strong believer in home and hearth—or if he is an independent sort, he might break things off with her rather than see her tied down.

Scorchers

Families can be the bane of a character's existence or the most important support system she has. Don't forget to develop your characters' familial relationships if they're important to your story—whether the relationships are close or not!

And in My Spare Time ...

If your characters take time to relax (and if they don't, you'd better know why), what do they do? What is your heroine's favorite form of entertainment? Does she knit or sew? If she reads, does she belong to a book club to discuss the literary merits of a chosen work, or curl up on her sofa with a juicy paperback?

What about your hero? Does he spend his downtime at the local art house taking in foreign films? Does he volunteer at a food pantry? Do either of them participate in organized sports or play street hockey with the neighborhood kids? Giving your characters hobbies and interests are just one more way to add to their characterization.

No Place Like Home

Take a look at the humble abodes your story people inhabit. Do their living arrangements fit with who you've created them to be? Would a heroine who grew up as an only child, rambling around in a house big enough for six siblings, live alone in a similarly spacious loft? Or would she live alone in a tiny efficiency? Or maybe even cram three roommates into a two-bedroom apartment?

> **Naughty, Naughty**
>
> Try not to give your characters special interests just so they'll have something to do on the page that works as filler for your manuscript. Sure, hobbies can be solely about entertainment, but they can give a boost to the story if they come into play in the plot!

The feelings imbued by her childhood living conditions—whether freedom, abandonment, loneliness, or fairy-princess entitlement—will play a big part in the home she chooses to make for herself now. And if you give her a hero who wants the peace and quiet of country life when she thrives on the chaos of the city, then you've just upped the conflict ante!

The Color of Money

I once wrote a character who surrounded himself with material possessions, ones he had worked for and provided for himself. He had grown up on the streets and was later taken in by a well-to-do family who taught him the value of self-sufficiency. What might have seemed like greed or an obsession with *things* was instead the way he proved to himself that he didn't need to rely on anyone for anything.

How do your characters feel about money, and why? Do they struggle to live comfortably yet not mind a bit doing so? Or do they work so many hours that they don't even have time to enjoy or appreciate their wealth? Look to their pasts for any events or experiences that have had an impact in determining their outlook on financial security.

Internal Needs and Desires

In Chapter 7, I went over a character's external goals and the external motivations driving him to accomplish them. I also showed you briefly how to tie the internal to the external to give a solid and cohesive strength to the entire novel package. Now let's examine the inside of things.

The problems your characters face internally are the essence of who they are. All character growth stems from the challenges they face. So let's look more closely at what drives your characters from within and how these elements can serve as the basis for your story's theme and premise—as well as being a big part of your character's story arc.

Scorchers

As part of forcing your characters to face challenges, try putting their internal goals and external goals at odds. Also, be aware that a character may never recognize the root of his desire. You as the author, however, must know it and convey it to your readers.

In the following chart, I've listed some sample goals and motivations, both external and internal, showing you how to tie them together. See how this works?

External Goal	External Motivation	Internal Goal	Internal Motivation
visit old hometown	look up old friend	seek friend's forgiveness	lost valuable friendship
give up gambling	financial security	regain father's respect	failed his expectations
take on new identity and go undercover	expose corporate corruption	clear lover as suspect	prove self worthy as mate
enter bull-riding competition	win money	keep bank from foreclosing on ranch	protect inheritance

This is obviously a very simplistic chart, one that doesn't ask for detailed characterization or plot points. It's only a rough draft of the basics. It does, however, show you how to link your goals and your motivations from the inside out.

What Do They Want?

Just as your characters have external goals they want to accomplish, they have internal goals as well. In most cases, in fact, the external goal is a direct offshoot of the internal or a surface manifestation of a deep-seated desire. Whatever it is your character wants, it is that inward, emotional desire that serves as the basis for character growth.

Why Do They Want It?

Characters are often driven to seek out their goals by events in their lives. These events can be life-changing or simply ones that have caused them to think—or rethink—how they feel and then take action to change. Any number of emotional triggers can provide the impetus for a character's internal motivation. Here are a few:

- An emotion
- An experience
- A moral value
- A belief

Any of these can be the drive behind a character's internal goal. Look at the story people you've created, and match them up with the triggers that will work best in their situations.

Scorchers

One of the best tips I ever received for writing believable and compelling internal motivation was to ask a character "Why?" He has to give his answer in a "Because …" response, and I then follow that up with another "Why?" We keep doing this until he can't give me anything but a simple "Because. Just because."—no more than that. Doing this causes the character (and me) to dig to the root of what drives him, and his story is all the better for having a deep-seated motivation rather than going with the first—and often shallow—reason he's willing to admit to!

The Least You Need to Know

- Digging into a character's past will give you all manner of events from his childhood to use to bring him to life.
- The quality of a character's lifestyle, including hobbies, interests, spending habits, and material possessions, reveals a lot about his priorities.
- A character's interpersonal relationships with friends, family, co-workers, and strangers are a good indication of his personality type.
- Internal motivations are often so deeply seated, a character may not even be aware of what is driving him toward his internal goal.

Chapter 10

What's Love Got to Do with It?

In This Chapter

- Looking for love
- Finding love without looking
- Love that won't go away
- Realizing true love has been there all along
- Old flames, ex-lovers, and high school crushes

The end game of an erotic romance novel is a happy ending, just as it is with a traditional romance. Your characters may not realize they are making the journey to commitment until they're wrapped too tightly in love's web to break free. A big part of their development comes from exploring whether they will accept the inevitable as what is meant to be or fight the attraction tooth and nail. Much of this will depend on each individual's situation—whether she (or he) is actively looking for love, or whether she (or he) is blindsided when love comes around.

The sexual component of your story that is tied tightly to your plot will also play a huge part in how your characters react to an impending romance.

Single and Seeking

Obviously, a character looking for love will be in a different place in his or her life than a character whose eyes are closed because he doesn't want to see the freight train of love bearing down. Characters who are single and seeking can be doing so for any number of reasons.

Biological clocks could be ticking—yes, even in erotic romance, characters can be ready to settle down and raise a family. Others might be tired of coming home to an empty apartment, tired of ordering Chinese take-out for one, tired of watching reality TV alone, tired of not having a sexually compatible companion.

Characters who know what they want make for great erotic romance protagonists—and they don't even have to be contemporary characters who order Chinese! A character looking for love can happen in any time and any place. It's how they go about it that makes their story unique.

A futuristic heroine may be able to dial a mate and try a few potential heroes on for size before settling on one who rings her bells. A heroine in a paranormal may be able to conjure up a hero with just the right equipment to keep her happy instead of club hopping the way mere mortals do!

Erotic romance is the perfect place for a character to get out and go for it. Our characters have unlimited freedom to pursue their desires. And as long as we as authors create intelligent, savvy, and well-motivated story people, there's very little readers won't buy!

Naughty, Naughty

Don't think single and seeking is limited to 20-somethings! Love and romance have no age barriers, and neither does eroticism!

Scorchers

Our sexually adventurous heroine loves romance. She loves being courted and flirted with and wooed. But she also doesn't mind a hero who makes no bones about wanting to take her straight to bed. In fact, she might very well be the one who makes the first move and takes him. In erotic romance, traditional courtship is often skipped completely and our heroes and heroines discover their compatibility through making love. So if hearts and flowers don't fit your story plan, no worries!

On the Make

For some reason, the idea of a character on the make always makes me think of Samantha from HBO's *Sex and the City*. She was always dressed to kill, was rarely caught off-guard, and was eager and ready for anything. A similar character with a mix of aggressiveness and determination would make a great erotic romance character—especially when you consider whether it's better to give her thick or thin skin!

Look, too, at how the character on the receiving end of her boldness reacts. Does he welcome her without a second thought, or does he run screaming into the night? Maybe he has issues about making the first move and walks away, or maybe he enjoys a woman who goes after what she wants.

What happens when you get two equally confident characters together? Do sparks fly from the attraction … or from the butting heads? Consider every possible scenario to come up with the perfect one to fit your characters.

Blind Dates

The concept of blind dating is rife with opportunities for self-doubt, self-deprecation, and a whole lot of panic. What happens if your heroine doesn't like the man she meets? Or what if she does, but he doesn't return the favor? Then there's the slut factor to consider. If they share a mutual attraction and hit the sack first thing, does it change how she feels about herself?

In many situations, secondary characters and their feelings come into play, as a friend or co-worker probably arranged for the setup. Will it ruin a heroine's relationship with her best girlfriend if she dumps on the blind date guy? Is she willing to take that chance?

Scorchers

Think outside of the blind-date box. Instead of making the date the beginning of a relationship, make it a source of conflict in your heroine's life.

Matchmaker, Matchmaker

A matchmaking setup would be very similar to a blind date except, perhaps, for the identity of the matchmaker. A mother making a match for her son with the daughter of her oldest friend might ignore the truth that a first date could end up with the couple in bed for a one-night stand, preferring to think long term!

Also, family obligations might play into a matchmaking scenario, depending on the character's culture. The 2001 movie *Monsoon Wedding* is a perfect example, with a wonderful twist at the end!

Caught Unawares

Characters who aren't looking for love and end up falling anyway—and falling hard—are some of my personal favorites to write. The heroes in my *SG-5* series for Kensington Brava have almost all been loners and were knocked off their feet by the women who came into their lives. I especially love creating characters who have sworn off love completely and then end up stumbling over themselves when they meet the person of their dreams.

Scorchers

Characters who are caught off-guard by the possibility of love and romance may come to the relationship first for a purely physical reason or an emotional reason having nothing to do with love!

Some characters will fight it. They have a degree to complete, a career to advance, too many bad memories of relationships gone bad haunting them, or just not enough time to devote to anyone but themselves. Other characters will dip a toe into the waters, testing things out before taking the plunge. Even more will embrace the unanticipated surprise and take it for a spin. There's no end to the stories this one idea can spawn. I've written at least a dozen!

Fighting Tooth and Nail

Even if under constant familial pressure to find a mate, or repeatedly witnessing friends who fall hard and fast, some characters just don't want anything to do with a relationship. They have plans for their life, and bringing another person into the mix will disrupt everything. They've seen too many of their friends who've fallen have to pick themselves back up in pieces … and who needs to go through that pain? Nope, they're perfectly happy on their own. Lonely? Never. Horny? When it happens, they know how to take care of it. Now, bring in a character who refuses to take no for an answer. Talk about tension and conflict!

Sweep Her Off Her Feet

It's the fault of all those fairy tales. We loved seeing both the princesses and the commoners swept off their feet by true love. Yes, it's a fantasy, but it's one universally understood. At times, we've all wanted to be rescued by a knight in shining armor, no matter how independent we are as women and how proud we are of that fact.

Being able to lean on someone else once in a while doesn't make us weak. It makes us human. So being swept off our feet by a hero who's caught us unawares? It's the perfect erotic romance fantasy.

Blindside Him

Readers love seeing a hunky alpha male brought to his knees by his female counterpart. There's nothing like a man capable of taking on the world yet who is unable to resist a woman to remind us how quickly the power dynamics in a relationship can switch. Will your man fight the attraction? Will he give in? Don't make it too easy on him, okay?

Friends to Lovers

There's just something about pairing up a hero and a heroine who know things about each other that no one else would ever have reason to know. There is also the fabulous shortcut this plot line provides. Let me explain …

Do you ever have trouble writing or, when reading, getting through long "get to know you" conversations two characters have? Matching a hero with a heroine he already knows lets you bypass the do-we-have-anything-in-common or this-is-who-I-am-who-are-you discussions and get right to the nitty-gritty of the conflict they're going to have to work through!

Scorchers

The idea of long-time friends who realize they've fallen in love and stepped over an established boundary is a reader favorite.

Cubicle Mate

Ah, the office romance, often forbidden and complete with a whole host of secrets and lies. In the early days of genre romance, boss and secretary stories were released regularly. Today they're not as abundant, which may be in part to sexual harassment charges making such scenarios politically incorrect.

But that doesn't mean consensual hanky-panky in the office wouldn't work as an erotic romance. After hours? That comfy leather sofa? That conference room table that's big enough for two … or three? Keep your characters smart, make them admirable, and readers won't miss a beat.

Roommate

In my 2005 Harlequin Blaze, *Kiss & Makeup*, I wrote about platonic roommates who really were platonic. My heroine got her guy elsewhere, while her male roomie got his girl, too. But wouldn't platonic roommates who just can't stay that way make for a great erotic romance?

Scorchers

Because much of erotic romance is pure fantasy, many readers simply want to be carried away by a hot and sexy romance—and will have little concern for politically correct scenarios. They understand that what they're reading is fiction, not an account of real-life events!

First of all, they see each other when it's time to get up and when it's time to go to bed. They shower and change clothes in the same close quarters. The towel rack in their shared bathroom may end up being used as a clothesline for drying delicates. Maybe one borrows the other's razor …

They're familiar with each other's habits, favorites, likes and dislikes—even with each other's scent, whether perfume, soap, shampoo, or skin. And if they're really good friends, they may know even more. Who wouldn't want to write their story?

The Boy Next Door

If your hero and heroine grew up together from the time they were toddling around in diapers, think of how many things they'll know about one another without even realizing it—not only personality traits, favorite this-and-thats, but secrets, too. Maybe even lies. One could have used the other as an alibi when sneaking out after curfew.

Bringing this knowledge—and your characters' feelings about it—into the sexually charged present will make for all sorts of fun and games, don't you think? The characters could wonder why it took them so long to connect, or even wonder if they want to connect, using the past as a reason not to!

Rekindling a Flame

Reunion romances are another reader favorite. Like friends-to-lovers romances, they allow you to bypass a lot of back story and introductory conversations. They also offer the opportunity to explore character relationships that may have been interrupted before having a chance to develop, or ones that may not have ended well, resulting in baggage the characters need to unload.

Reunions are also hotbeds for sexual tension. All those years of buried memories come flooding back, all those years of wondering, all those years of harboring grudges and regrets, maybe even guilt over betraying a best friend with her boy, or cheating on a steady guy with someone close to him.

I have a reunion romance in the works for Harlequin Blaze (*Infatuated*, November 2006) and my 1999 Harlequin Temptation, *Four Men & a Lady*, was a reunion romance that was so popular, I wrote spin-off stories for each of the main male characters. Some of my favorite parts of that book were the flashbacks from each of the 4 years the characters spent together in high school as friends. Seeing the main couple interacting during that time gave an added depth to their relationship when they found each other again as adults.

Scorchers

Many authors prefer not to use flashbacks in stories, but I have received terrific reader response when I've done so—and each time, the story has been a reunion romance!

Reunited

Characters who may have been young lovers come to the table with baggage other old friends will not have. Not only do they have the memory of the shared intimacy between them, they will likely have a closeness that neither may want or acknowledge. Even if the breakup was mutual and amicable, unanswered questions could still remain—especially questions that, at the time, they were too young to answer. Talk about a source of conflict and of sexual tension! Use it all!

Scorchers

In my May 2002 Harlequin Blaze, *Bound to Happen,* I wrote a flashback scene exploring my couple's first sexual experience when they were teenagers. While their scenes as adults were sizzling, the scene from earlier in their lives was emotionally sweet with far less sexual detail. This offered a glimpse into the characters' past, enabling readers to see the changes they'd been through during their years apart.

Unrequited

While some reunion romances may feature old flames, others explore high school crushes or other one-sided attractions. The best part of these scenarios is that the characters are most likely on a more even footing at this later stage of their lives.

A science club geek who crushed on a cheerleader may now be the chief technical officer for a Fortune 500 software firm. When she happens to run into him, does he tell her to stuff that in her pom-poms and shake it? Or does he see exactly how far he can take her, as he's the one in the driver's seat now … or is he? What if beneath his designer Italian suit, he's still that geek at heart and walks away rather than face rejection? What will your cheerleader do now?

First Love, True Love

What if the person with whom your character is reunited was her first true love? What if their relationship was the best thing either had ever experienced? What if they expected to spend the rest of their lives together but were interrupted by … a cross-country move? A lie told by a jealous friend? A parent who felt they were too young for such an intense relationship? A misunderstanding they *were* too young to comprehend? Besides a physical longing, what emotions does the reunion set off? Anger? Happiness? Pain? Guilt? Shame? Sorrow?

> **Scorchers**
>
> Characters who fell in love at a young age and were then forced apart will more than likely have many unresolved issues for you as an author to discover!

Even if they broke up without outside interference, they may not have ever settled or worked through what happened between them. Writing their story will give you many opportunities for exploring what went wrong, what has happened during the years since, and then the ultimate joy of seeing them live happily-ever-after.

Commitmentphobes

Why buy the cow when you can get the milk for free? Ever written a character who uses that excuse to explain balking at commitment? While men may seem to put up the biggest resistance to committing to an exclusive arrangement, many women are equally hesitant—no matter how good the sex!

Why do characters resist commitment and exclusivity? As in real life, there are innumerable reasons. Your characters are the best ones to reveal for you their whys and wherefores, but let's look at a few universally held ideas that can present as conflict between your hero and heroine:

- Loss of freedom
- Loss of independence
- Loss of self
- A mate is an anchor rather than a buoy
- Life stops being fun and turns into a "honey-do" list

- No more Friday nights out with the boys or girls
- A white picket fence takes all the fun out of sex
- Being part of a couple means giving up alone time

Eventually, of course, your characters will realize that a good partnership can only make their lives better, but getting them to that point is half the fun of reading and writing their stories!

A Ring on Her Finger

Does the genre's requirement of a happily-ever-after mean an erotic romance has to end in a marriage ceremony or at least a marriage proposal? No, it doesn't! I've written several couples involved in a plot with a very short story timeline.

Eli and Stella, for example, the protagonists in my 2005 Brava novella *The McKenzie Artifact*, spent only a matter of days together. They came to the end of those intense hours knowing little about one another. They were not yet at a place in their lives to make a long-term commitment—or even to see each other exclusively (although the reader always knows the truth)! They did, however, agree to see where things would go, and Eli invited Stella to join him in New York to do just that.

Even though romance readers want that commitment at the end of a story, they're not going to believe in one that has no basis or in a relationship that hasn't had sufficient time to develop. They want to be along for the ride as your characters fall in love, but they don't want to be *told* that a couple has reached that point. They want to be *shown* the relationship developing into something more than lust, and they especially want to understand why these two story people are meant to be together. Be sure they do!

Naughty, Naughty

Avoid taking your characters on a sexual journey without developing their emotional relationship sufficiently. If readers are unable to point out specific incidents that have brought your characters close, they won't buy into a commitment of any sort—whether marriage or a simpler agreement to see where things might go. Don't wait until the last 10 pages to *tell* your readers that your characters have feelings for one another. *Show* their feelings growing from the first moment they meet!

The Least You Need to Know

- Erotic romances can feature characters looking for love as well as those never expecting to find it.
- Don't forget to consider secondary characters and their relationship to your protagonists to add even more conflict to your story.
- Writing about friends who fall in love takes away the necessity of introducing characters to one another and enables you to explore the nuances of an already-existing relationship.
- Giving characters believable reasons to avoid committing to an exclusive arrangement will add to the story's conflict.
- A happily-ever-after ending does not require that an erotic romance end in a marriage ceremony or even an engagement.

Chapter 11

Writing 101: Characterization

In This Chapter

- Finding value in character charts
- Revealing character need-to-knows
- Conducting character interviews
- Tapping into a character's self-perception
- The all-important sexual history lesson

Nothing in a novel is more important than the characters. It's their story you're writing. They are the ones whose actions drive the plot forward. In fact, many authors agree that plot *is* character.

In Chapter 9, we looked at building your people from the ground up. Now we'll look at getting to know the people they are now so well that writing their actions and reactions are second nature to you. After all, if you don't know your story people as intimately as possible, how can you do them justice or be true to who they are?

What Do Character Charts Really Reveal?

The purpose of a character chart is to help you create a protagonist worth writing about, one you know so well you never have to stop and think what he would do or say in any given situation because you know. You know immediately and precisely. You know him as well as you know yourself.

The questions that help you get to that point are the ones you want to pay the most attention to, and only you can determine which ones those are! Let's look at a few of the questions character charts often ask:

- Full name and nickname
- Age and date of birth
- Eye color and hair color
- Height and weight

Physical characteristics are important for your descriptions. If you need to write them down to remember them, do so. If you prefer, you can work with a picture in front of you. Whatever you require to keep the details straight, do it. The last thing you want is for a copy editor to miss the eye color change you made between page 100 and page 200—and a reader find it!

Many authors are so involved with their main protagonists that they might only need to do this for secondary characters to avoid bungling descriptions. I'm definitely one who's had to look back at what I've written to be sure I'm being consistent with my cast of extras!

Scorchers

Do the answers to the questions asked on many detailed character charts really matter? That depends. If they play a part in your book, then they definitely do. The ones that don't? They can come in handy, too, if only for sparking your creativity. If you find filling out a character chart in great detail jump-starts your story and character development, go for it! Any tool that gets you thinking about goals, motivation, conflict, and plot twists and turns is a tool you don't want to give up. However, if you don't use the answers to many of the questions, concentrate on the ones you do.

How Much Do Favorites Matter?

Confession time. I have never once, in more than 30 published works, found a need to know in advance a character's favorite color—at least none that I can remember! I might have mentioned it in passing when a character was describing why she'd painted her bedroom red, for example, but I don't remember doing that either. A character's favorite color has never played enough of a role in a book I've written for me to need to settle on it before I started writing.

And that's the answer, isn't it? A favorite color *could* have so much meaning for a character that she buys a black car, wears nothing but black, decorates her home in a monochrome color scheme of black and white. Now, that would cause a few brows to raise and mean you need a ready answer! So when a character chart asks such things as the following, you have to decide if the answers play into your plot somehow, or if these are items you can afford to discover about your characters as you write:

- Favorite food
- Favorite movie
- Favorite book
- Favorite music
- Clothing style
- Type of car
- Pet(s)

Am I implying that these things don't matter? No, that's not what I'm saying at all! You might not know what your heroine drives until she heads out to her driveway. Or if you've developed her to be someone focused on the environment, you might put her behind the wheel of a hybrid while fleshing out your chart.

Scorchers

Only you know how important lifestyle details are to your story—and whether or not you need to figure them out in advance!

The same thing with clothing and food. Food might matter more to a chef than to a bike messenger. Then again, if your bike messenger only takes time for one meal a day, what he wants might be of great significance. And if he eats the same thing day in and day out, there's probably a good reason behind it—even if it's only about saving money on groceries so he can pay for a new bike. It all depends on who he is, and only he can give you the answer.

What about charts that ask for a character's occupation? Again, how important is it to your plot? If you're writing a romantic suspense and your hero is the lead detective, then I'm pretty sure you won't have to write that down on a chart! But if you're writing a romance between two characters who meet while on a ski trip to Aspen, you might need to jot down a note of job details for continuity's sake!

Who Are You Really?

Ah, now we're getting to the good stuff. If you're single and seeking and you meet a man with the most gorgeous eyes and perfect washboard abs, yet he finds fault in everyone around him and is unable to say a kind word to anyone ever, well, off he goes to the curb! Who has time to waste on an inconsiderate jerk, no matter that he makes for tasty eye candy!

Here are a few personality traits worth considering, as they say a lot about who your character is and how he or she will interact with the rest of your story people:

- Introvert or extrovert
- Optimist or pessimist
- Uptight or laidback
- Go-getter or slacker
- Conceited or self-effacing
- Sensitive or thick-skinned
- Judicious or foolhardy
- Impervious or paranoid

Scorchers

Personality traits matter because they get to the heart of who a character is. Not only that, they're a big part of one person being attracted to another instead of to his neighbor down the hall.

Additionally, certain mannerisms or peculiarities might make a character annoying or endearing to his story mates. Not everyone can deal with someone who constantly flips back her hair or checks her reflection in every mirror she passes. Your other characters will have to decide how much they'll put up with. They might even have to decide how much they'll put up with in bed!

Scouting for Talent

Do your characters possess any special talents or unique skills that will come into play in your story? Or even any that will work as a hindrance while they pursue their goal? Using a unique talent as a source of conflict truly keeps it close to the bone.

A character who is not a convincing liar would make a poor undercover officer, while one who does amateur theater would have no trouble slipping into the role. An accountant hero who is good with numbers would be the perfect guy to help your heroine organize her sorority's charity fund-raiser. Don't let good talent go to waste!

A Hard Habit to Break

Smoking, drinking, swearing, spending money like it grows on trees. What other habits might your characters have that could influence how they feel about themselves and how others see them? Do they want to change, try to change, think they need to change? If the answer is no, what if they're asked to do so by the person with whom they fall in love? Do they walk away, compromise, or tell their lover to take it or leave it? So many things to think about!

Not all habits, of course, are bad ones. A character with the habit of keeping every receipt she receives will come in handy when another character asks her to prove—in court—where she was at a particular time!

Outlook Express

What sort of outlook on life do your characters have? What philosophy colors their dealings with other people? This should be an easy one to figure out based on the background you've given them.

While one character might go through his days believing "life's a bowl of cherries until you choke on a pit and die," another will go through hers believing "when life gives you lemons, make lemonade." Now, put those two together and see who comes out on top … so to speak!

Scorchers

Opposing life philosophies make for a great source of conflict, as they color every action a character takes as well as all his decisions. Pit an optimist against a pessimist, and you'll never lose your story's tension.

Don't Look Back

If given the chance, is there anything your characters would want to do over? What do they fear? Do they harbor any regrets? How do they deal with knowing they can't change what has gone before—or do they deal with it at all? Perhaps they look over their shoulder constantly, waiting for their past to catch up with them and bite them solidly and where it counts.

The fear of repeating past mistakes or of being haunted by them forever can also impact a character's sex life. If a break-up didn't go so well, a character might be less willing to put her heart on the line, no matter how good the physical loving. If a hero let himself be used in the past, he may be bitter and on a payback mission. Dig deep for your characterization, and use everything you can!

Under Pressure

Are your story people ones who roll with the flow or freak at every roadblock life throws in their way? Pressure from one's career or family or even friends isn't something that can be pushed to the side for long. It just keeps coming back. Problems, too. If not taken care of, they keep rearing up with their ugly ol' heads.

Changes, if made willingly, can still cause a character to go through an emotional upheaval. If she accepts a promotion that takes her to a new state, for example, she has to leave behind good friends. Changes she's forced to make might cause her to break down or cause her to buck up, depending on who she is. And then, as with everything in an erotic romance, there's the issue of sex.

Scorchers

When considering all these character traits, look to how you can use them to initiate the character growth and change for your protagonist's personal character arc. If a character is less than satisfied with how she reacts under pressure, that's a big signal that she's ready to switch things around.

A heroine might have sworn off love forever and have to deal with pressure from friends and family about cruelly leading on the perfect guy. She might even have trouble with the guy himself; he might turn her rejection around and remove all emotion from their sex life. Whether or not she cracks will be part of her character arc. See how the sex is a fundamental part of the story?

Religion, Politics, and Class Warfare

Politics and religion won't necessarily come up in conversation during your story or as story elements needing attention. But knowing if your characters are spiritually minded or have strong political views will give you an edge in writing scenes in which their beliefs may be challenged or even tested privately.

Another thing to consider about your characters is their social standing. Beyond being upper, middle, or lower class income-wise, are they perhaps movers and shakers in society? Community leaders? Well respected in their fields? Entrepreneurs? Business owners?

Maybe you're writing about a starving-artist bohemian type of character who defies any sort of convention and disregards all edicts handed down by her building's tenant association. Mix things up. Cause conflict. Match a free spirit with a stick-in-the-mud—much as I did with Leo Redding and Macy Webb in my 2002 Harlequin Blaze, *All Tied Up.*

The Life of the Party

Do your characters fit in easily with new people? Do they have trouble making friends? Do they know—or care—what others think about them? Do they put on a front in public, playing the extrovert, and collapse later in private like the introverts they truly are?

Are they social butterflies when it comes to sex and dating? Is it easy for them to hook up? Do they ever suffer morning-after regrets, or do they just get on with the day at hand? In erotic romance, we write about sexually adventurous characters, so seeing how they fit socially with others who may not share their dating philosophy is great fun and makes for excellent tension and conflict!

The Character Interview

A character interview often produces some of the most revealing details you need to know about your protagonists. A character chart is primarily a list of items that gets you started; an interview can dig deeper into that list by making a character explain decisions and choices he's made in his life in his own words.

You might think you know what he's going to tell you, but don't be surprised at the details he reveals. If he responds in a *stream of consciousness* monologue, let him. Take notes. Pay attention. He might mention tidbits of information that he hasn't let onto in the past. Not only will you know the "what," you'll know the "why"—and the "why" is the all important motivation that drives everything your characters do.

def•i•ni•tion

A **stream of consciousness** is an unedited and continuous flow of thoughts and feelings running through the mind.

Taking one of the subjects I mentioned in Chapter 9, such as how a character came to his career, and asking him about it in depth can help you understand the road he took, whether he knew from childhood what he wanted to do, or whether one particular event, conversation, or even a newspaper article he read for an English project set him on the path that brought him here.

To give you an idea of how this works, let's ask Brandon about his trip to Tokyo and what it's going to mean to his relationship with Rachel:

- What prompted you to become an attorney?
- How important is your career?
- If you had to make a choice between making partner and losing Rachel, what would you do?
- Are you going to remain faithful to her while you're away for the next 6 weeks?
- Do you believe in compromise in a relationship?
- After you're married, will you continue to travel if it puts a strain on your marriage?

These and similar questions can help you better understand your character. He, in turn, will then better understand himself.

Scorchers

The first character I ever interviewed was Ben Tannen, the hero of my 1999 Harlequin Temptation, *Four Men & a Lady*. I was still working my day job, commuting, and that day I was on a city bus headed from downtown to the park-'n'-ride lot 40 minutes away. I usually spent my commute time writing, but my story wasn't going anywhere, so I used the time to get to know Ben better. It was an indispensable lesson in how valuable a character interview can be.

Who Am I Really?

A protagonist's self-perception is one of the most important aspects of her character development, as it will have a huge impact on her *character arc*, as well as on how the plot brings about growth and change. A character who is happy with where she is in life won't feel she needs a major personality overhaul the way one who is looking to find herself might—but that doesn't mean winds of change won't be blowing her way!

def•i•ni•tion

The growth, change, or emotional transformation a character makes during the course of the story, one fueled by the story's events, is his **character arc.**

You might even want to know what your character likes best about herself physically and how it influences her interactions with others. Does she want to change something so much—the size of her nose, her inherited overbite, her height—that she avoids certain people or situations?

Ask your characters what, if anything, they would want to change about themselves, whether physically or emotionally, and why. The answers may surprise you enough that they cause you to rethink the direction of your story!

A few telling things you might find worth knowing about your story people (and why they feel as they do about each) are the following:

- A great strength
- An unforgivable flaw
- A big secret
- An unequaled accomplishment
- A regrettable failure

How a character sees herself will be based in who she is and where she's come from, her experiences, her expectations—basically, everything you've discovered during the creation process.

Sexy Beast

You're writing erotic romance, so it's vital that you know your characters' sexual histories, sexual personalities, sexual preferences … all of it. You as the author need to know everything—even the things your story people may never tell another living soul. Sex is a driving factor in both plot and characterization, and because of that, you can't scrimp on this element. It would be like scrimping on the development of the suspense in a suspense novel!

Look back to Chapter 9 for a quick refresher on questions to ask your characters as you develop their sexual histories. The discussion there should launch you into making even deeper discoveries on your own. And if you love erotic romance (which you obviously do or you wouldn't be here), this is truly one of the most fun parts of writing in the genre.

Scorchers

As much as I've stressed the importance of developing your characters, there's nothing wrong with figuring out who they are as you write their stories. Some authors will be more comfortable conducting character interviews and filling out charts before starting, while others will get to know their story people as they go, only stopping to dig deeper when they get stuck. At that point, asking a character questions pertinent to his situation should get the writing ball rolling again. Whether you do the work as part of your preplanning or wait until hitting the spot where your story demands it be done may depend on your writing style, whether you're a detailed plotter or a seat-of-the-pants writer.

The Least You Need to Know

- The value in a character chart is twofold, first revealing details that will play a part in your story, and secondly helping you get to know your story people intimately.
- Interviewing a character about his life or about a particular plot point can give you more insight into writing it from his point of view.
- When you know your characters well, you never have to stop and think about how they will react in any given situation.

- Understanding a character's self-perception will help you bring him to life on the page.
- It's important to understand a character's sexual past, sexual nature, and sexual beliefs when writing an erotic romance.

Part 4

Tangled Sheets: The Physical Journey

In an erotic romance, the physical relationship between the hero and heroine is as important as the emotional—if not more so. Eroticism is about arousal and anticipation. You don't want to ever shortchange an erotic story's erotic content.

Take your characters to the limit. Push them to the edge of what they think they know about their own sexuality, because the sex in which they engage, while satisfying in the moment, must raise even more issues with which they'll be forced to deal.

The main topic of Part 4 is sexuality—how to keep sexual tension running high before and after intimacy, characters who work best in an erotic romance, and sex that has nothing to do with love! I cover each of those subjects in depth in this part and show you how to make them work.

Chapter 12

Sex Isn't Always About Love

In This Chapter

- Connecting physical and emotional pleasure
- Using sex as a plot device in erotic romance
- Discovering the most intense and intimate reassurance of life
- Curing a character's ills

You are writing a romance novel. That one single caveat—that this is a genre novel meeting genre expectations—guarantees the sex that occurs between your hero and heroine will be integral to the story and make a lasting impact on the characters involved as they journey to falling in love. At the outset, it may seem that the sex has nothing to do with the romance, but stay tuned; the truth is out there!

You're writing an erotic romance novel, so the sexual activity between your starring couple (or even secondary players) does not have to be solely about commitment. (Note this is not a license to write purely gratuitous sex!) In fact, many authors of erotic romance turn tradition on its head by having love spring from a sexual relationship rather than the reverse, which has been the genre's mainstay for years.

Your reader trusts that you will be providing her with a happily-ever-after. She doesn't expect every sexual encounter to be replete with hearts and flowers and whispered sweet nothings. You are the author, the expert, and as long as you stay true to who your characters are; make them smart, honest, and interesting; and fulfill the requirements of their plot, the sky's the limit on how far you can push the sexual boundaries within an erotic romance.

With that in mind, let's explore reasons other than love that send characters into each other's arms—and into bed.

The Pleasure Principle

This one is simple. Sex is a pleasurable physical activity. It feels good. We like to do it. Our characters do, too. If not, they wouldn't be human. (Although many characters are not, we'll stick with the humans for now!) Just "doing it" means a whole lot of chandelier-swinging, headboard-creaking, down-and-dirty fun.

It also means a whole lot of complications—from your characters questioning their own beliefs about intimacy to making small talk with a stranger over coffee after a night of unbelievable sex. In an erotic romance, there must always be a price paid for the pleasure gained—and I'm not talking about cash!

I'm talking about emotional challenges, shattered expectations, unwelcome changes, unexpected tension, a shift in relationship perceptions, and the recognition that the person your character has made love with is about to turn his or her world upside down. Then again, isn't that exactly what's supposed to happen?

Wondering what sort of scenarios would allow you to turn what seems to be nothing but a physical relationship into something more? Let's take a look at a few examples.

Scorchers

When you add the word *romance* to the erotic mix, you're promising your readers more than pleasure for pleasure's sake. If your characters want to take their libidos for a ride, let them. Just remember, your characters must make a lot of stops on their journey to falling in love. Look closely at these sort of scenes and setups. You don't want to waste even the smallest opportunity for furthering characterization and your story's emotional depth.

One-Night Stand

Your heroine is traveling alone for business, attending a conference far from home. Following an intense day of meetings, she decides to unwind in the bar of the hotel where she's staying. There she meets your hero. He's sexy. He's attentive. He's interested. Suddenly, relaxing with a drink isn't half as appealing as multiple orgasms. After an amazing night together, your hero and heroine go their separate ways in the morning with no plans to ever see one another again.

Because this is a romance, your reader knows your couple's one-night stand is only the beginning. So why not surprise her? Rather than relying on the cliché of the hero being the heroine's new neighbor, new co-worker, or even her new boss, put your imagination to use. Have their next meeting be equally as unexpected as the first. Kick off their romance in a way neither saw coming with creative twists and turns unique to your story. Your readers will appreciate the effort you put into keeping things fresh and new.

Bed Buddy

There are times when we humans—and your characters—need a physical connection. Not stimulating conversation. Not a night out on the town. Simply a convenient, warm, and willing body.

So what happens when your hero decides he wants more? That he'll remain celibate while your heroine makes up her mind, but that he's tired of being her boy toy? If she doesn't want what he wants, can she find herself someone new to warm her bed? What happens when that ultimatum causes her to realize she does want more, but she wants it on her terms and she turns his challenge into a game? Oh, the endless possibilities!

Casual Affair

Unlike a relationship with a bed buddy, a casual affair often involves more than sex. Say your heroine is an attorney who puts in 80+-hour weeks. Romantic involvement? Who has the time? Nurture a relationship? Who has the energy? That doesn't mean she won't have the occasional professional function to attend requiring an escort. Or that she wants to eat Chinese take-out seven nights a week. Or that sleeping alone won't get old and buying batteries even older. What fun to watch a character go into what she believes is a casual affair only to find herself falling in love with the man she is sleeping with.

Naughty, Naughty

In Chapter 17, I talk about your comfort zone as an author. But if the idea of sex for reasons other than love puts you off, erotic romance may not be your fictional niche. The good news is that romance is such a broad genre, it offers a niche for everyone. Don't force yourself in where you don't have a comfortable fit!

Ups and Downs

We've all been there. A bad day, a good day. A need to unwind and forget. A need to celebrate and share. Sex in these cases is rarely planned but is, instead, a spontaneous emotional response. Got that? *An emotional response.* But notice also that nowhere did I mention the word *love.*

Slip of the Tongue

Author Sasha White feels strongly about the emotional component of a sexual encounter. She says, "Love is not the only emotion out there. What about awe, pleasure, shame, joy, happiness, contentment? Are these not emotions? Just because the characters aren't in love does not mean there is no emotion."

The sex in erotic romance can occur for many emotional reasons. All you have to do is be sure it works in the context of your story. More important, you need to be sure it works for the story people you've created. Don't have them act out of character if engaging in sex is not how they would react to an emotional need.

If it would be more in keeping with your story to have your heroine go out for a night of margaritas and dancing with her girlfriends to share the joy of her good news, that's the way to go. If it would be more in character to have your hero hit the track to work out his anger over the course of a few miles, write that.

Always, always be true to your characters. Their actions and responses must come from who they are, not from you as the author intruding and manipulating them to further your plot. Readers can spot your fingers in the pie, so keep them to yourself!

Flying High

Your heroine comes home, bursts through the front door, shouts to her roommate that the promotion she's been chasing down for months has come through. Not only that, the money is more fabulous than she realized, the corner office she's secretly coveted is hers, and her first client appointment is in Paris. The only problem is that your heroine's roommate isn't home. Instead, her brother—who's visiting from Anchorage and who's made it clear he's interested in making more than eye contact with your heroine—walks into the room.

He lifts your heroine off her feet and swings her around until her laughter bubbles over like festive champagne. Then he sets her down and backs her into the nearest wall. He threads his hands into her hair and brings his mouth down on hers.

Her heart is racing, her skin tingling, her adrenaline running high. She kisses him back, her excitement and joy overwhelming. The next thing she knows, she's ruined a brand-new pair of pantyhose, she's missing her panties, and she's smoking without ever having lighted a cigarette.

That scenario is not so hard to imagine now, is it? It's what follows, what the two characters do with their unexpected sexual involvement, that moves the story from one that's simply erotic into being an erotic romance. Their intimacy may have started out as a blissful celebration, but now it's time to notch it up to the next level.

Scorchers

As with any sexual situation you create, the turn your story takes afterward will depend on whether your character has celebrated or grieved or simply worked off frustration with someone she knows or with a stranger. Knowing the story's outcome beyond the obvious happily-ever-after, as well as the emotional journey you have planned for your characters to take, will help you decide on the best sexual partner for each.

Sinking Low

Your hero has just discovered that his business partner has walked off with their most prized client, noncompete agreement be damned. He's furious, livid. Almost too much so to answer the bell at the delivery door. When he does, he finds it's the cute female driver for the service providing his firm's computer and video parts. They've flirted for months. They've shared career war stories. She sees he's in a bad mood and tries to get him to talk.

He doesn't want to talk. He closes the door and grabs her by the waist, setting her on a crate and stepping between her legs. She wraps her arms around his neck and pulls him down for a kiss, her hands soothing, her whispers calming. He doesn't use words to ask. He tugs at her clothes. She tugs at his. He knows what they're doing is crazy, but long hot minutes later, he's reeling from the most incredible sex he's ever imagined.

Again, what happens next makes this scene work. You're writing living, breathing characters. They have flaws. They're not perfect. Dealing with what they've done is paramount. In an erotic romance, neither will simply walk away from the experience. Neither will be unchanged. They'll face the challenges thrown their way by this emotionally charged sexual encounter. And that's the very seed of an erotic romance.

Emotions: Resonance and Honesty

Try to come up with your own scenarios for other emotional experiences that could result in a sexual encounter. Here are some examples to get you thinking:

- A heroine *longing* to renew an old flame looks up her ex-boyfriend during a trip home.
- A hero *stressed* over a business proposal finds a sexy female co-worker in the file room after hours.
- A heroine *panicked* over finding a new roommate before the rent is due turns to a male neighbor.
- A hero *angry* over the vandalism to his sailboat makes a pass at his insurance adjuster.
- A heroine *awed* by the response to her sculptures ends up in the arms of the gallery owner.
- A hero *bored* with his programming project hits on the coffee shop barista when he takes a break.

> **Scorchers**
>
> Stuck for an emotion to move your story? Try on loneliness for size. That's a big one—a character needing to know she's not alone in the world, that she can reach out and connect with another human being. Such an identifiable emotion will resonate with readers!

Now it's your turn. Remember, any situation ringing with true emotion will work to drive your characters into one another's arms as long as they are honest and responsible in their actions.

The Means to an End

Historical romances especially have long included situations in which sex—or at least the promise of sex through an arranged marriage—is used for material gain. Land, gold, jewels, and livestock have all been traded for sex. Additionally, fathers and guardians in these stories have promised daughters and wards to their enemies, to their friends, even to withered old men. Why? To protect their borders, to increase the size of their kingdoms, or to make an alliance or pledge allegiance.

With the surge in popularity of erotic romance, the same scheming machinations used in historical romances are now taking place in boardrooms, executive jets, villas in the south of France—even over hands of Texas Hold 'Em. Only now the deals are less likely to be made by fathers or guardians. Instead, they're worked out by the men and women who will be enjoying the sexual benefits of the deals—and who will eventually be falling in love.

What a cheap and tawdry tactic, you say, using sex as a means to an end. Not if you've developed and motivated your characters properly. Don't forget—in an erotic romance, your characters by necessity are strong, self-assured, and, most important, in charge of their own sexuality. If your hero and heroine agree to a sexual contract, both must be well aware that the outcome might not be as simple as one resulting from a handshake.

Bargaining Chips

The women in erotic romances understand their sexual power over men. The men in erotic romances understand they have what it takes to drive women wild. Characters of both genders know they can use the promise of sex and the lure of that incredible physical pleasure to get what they want, even when it's only business. A leverage in negotiations. A concession. An incentive.

Once they've given into lust, however, the tables are turned. What had seemed to both characters to be nothing but an intimate closing to a business transaction or the sexual sealing of a merger is now a piece of baggage they're both going to have to deal with if they expect their lives to return to normal. We, of course, know that nothing will ever resemble "normal" for them again.

Naughty, Naughty

By definition, an erotic romance offers more freedom and leeway in sexual situations. As the author, however, you are often buying yourself extra work to build characters who would believably engage in sexual activity that would be questionable in nonerotic stories. Keep that in your mind as you create your story people. If such deep characterization doesn't come easily, erotic romance might not be your cup of tea.

Power Plays

The world we live in is run by sex, money, and power—who's getting it, who has it, and who wants it. To gain the second two, people throughout history have been known to do outrageously stupid things when it comes to the first. Sex has been used countless times to destroy a career, to tarnish a reputation, even as ammunition for blackmail.

Sexual attraction is notorious for guiding men and women down paths they would not otherwise choose to take. For centuries, women have accused men of using what's in their pants rather then what's on their shoulders to make their decisions. Men, however, are not alone in doing so. Women who are normally sensible, rational, and sane are equally liable to give in to the powerful pull of pheromones.

The fun begins when one character believes he or she holds all the cards in a power play, only to be sideswiped by lust and wrapped around his or her opponent's little finger. Watching the sparks fly, the sheets heat up, and the attraction grow from lust into love is a perfect example of an erotic romance in the making—one that begins with sex being used as the means to an end.

The Last Remaining Virgin

Although it's not impossible to create a contemporary character who has reached adulthood with her virginity intact, it does present a challenge. Readers will be much more inclined to buy her decision to remain chaste if the reasons spring from her self-perception, her views on sexuality, and her moral beliefs—not that she simply hasn't found a man to turn her on.

Using those internal, character-based motivations allows you to give depth to her lifestyle choice. And because you have created this fully developed character, when she finally does give herself to a man, the experience will be that much more rewarding for both her and your reader!

Sex Education

A character who has lost her virginity yet is not in a serious relationship may feel she is missing out and simply want a more comprehensive sexual education. Or perhaps she is experienced but wants to better understand a certain sexual lifestyle.

Slip of the Tongue

Author Jaid Black shares this "sex education" scenario: "A book I wrote called *The Possession* features a highly educated (Ph.D.), geeky heroine who has always wanted to know what it feels like to be a submissive sex kitten. She makes the decision to work for one week at an exclusive gentlemen's club in order to live out her desires and ends up falling for the hero, one of the club's patrons."

Contemporary characters are inundated daily with sexually explicit advertising, magazine articles, and the like. Knowing the mechanics of the acts, the sensations to expect, and the ramifications of an intimate encounter is not the same as living the experience. As long as you create a character with whom your readers can relate, they'll support her in any decision she makes.

Affirming Life

Is there anything other than sex that makes us feel more alive? (Sorry, chocolate doesn't count!) The primal connection with another human being. The possibility of creating a new life. And is there a genre other than erotic romance better suited to sexually exploring the full potential of what it means to be living and breathing creatures? Think about these scenarios:

- The world as your character knows it has ceased to exist (think time-travel romance).
- The possibility exists that your character might not make it out of a situation alive (think romantic suspense).
- There's no way tomorrow could possibly in a million years be a better day, and your character might as well quit (think, uh, anything?).

Any of these situations can give rise to a character's need to prove he or she is a vital and viable human being. And how better to prove just that than with a romp in the sheets!

Getting Out Alive

You're a CIA operative on the run. You have nowhere to turn. What lies ahead is unknown, a real danger. Behind is an even bigger threat, one from which you've escaped. You're in a safe house. You turn to your partner, looking for his assurance that you will both get out of here alive. He gives it to you. Boy, does he give it to you. He gives and gives and gives.

And then you wake up …

Naughty, Naughty

Don't let characters using sex to affirm life be stupid as they're doing the deed. If a bomb is ticking outside their door or if armed gunman are minutes away, they had better be getting out of Dodge—not into each other's pants.

In the midst of danger and disaster, sex offers hope, a human connection. Like the bonobos (members of the great ape family) who engage in sexual activity when faced with aggression, characters facing their own mortality are strongly motivated to reach for life, to defy death by making love. Sex offers what may very well be that most basic affirmation of being alive.

Let's Procreate!

Sometimes a character engages in sexual activity for no other reason than wishing to become pregnant. Nothing will ever be that simple, of course, because you're writing a romance. One character may not be ready for parenthood. A promotion may be at risk because of maternity or paternity leave. Families and friends may be unsupportive. Whatever the conflict, procreation is still one of the most natural motivations for intercourse.

That's a Relief!

Sex. Those few (or many!) minutes of nothing but sexual pleasure can offer some amazing relief found nowhere else.

Satisfying the Urge

Let's face it. Our characters are just as likely to feel sexual urges as we are. Many will take matters into their own hands. Many will prefer a little assistance from a member of the opposite sex. Many who choose the latter will think a one-night stand is the solution. Others prefer a week of indulging!

Wait. What kind of behavior is that for a romance novel character? How about human behavior? Aren't our characters human?

Looking for sexual relief from a willing body makes perfect sense in the context of an erotic romance. As with any other sexual activity, the suspension of disbelief is tied up in your characters. Have you given the reader reason to believe your heroine (or your hero) would engage in a one-night stand? If so, go for it. If not, head back to the drawing board.

Killer Stress

It's a fact: stress can damage a character's sex life. Over time, financial pressures, familial demands, even paper-training the new puppy can all put the damper on a character's libido. On the other hand, engaging in sex relieves stress. The endorphins released during orgasm are naturally calming, producing a long-lasting state of relaxation.

If you're writing characters facing highly stressful situations, having them turn to sex for relief is a proven physiological solution for what ails them. Have them turn to an ex-lover, a platonic friend, or a co-worker to whom they're attracted. Stress could very well be the start of a beautiful relationship!

Slip of the Tongue

Author Cheyenne McCray gives this example of how she used sex as a major nonromantic plot point: "In *Wonderland: King of Hearts,* my bestselling romance at Ellora's Cave, there is a 'bonding' scene toward the end where Alice is required to bond with the King of Hearts and his three brothers (Kings of Spades, Diamonds & Clubs). Because Jarronn is the High King, and Alice will be the High Queen, she must be bonded with all four brothers as protection against an evil force and any other threats that may challenge the kingdom. The scene is a fivesome and is a very important scene in the book. The bonding scene is definitely one where sex is used for other than love and romance."

The Least You Need to Know

- Physical pleasure is one of the most basic reasons characters choose to engage in sex.
- Sex in an erotic romance can be about many emotions in addition to being about love.
- Using sexuality as the means to an end is a practice as old as time, one with numerous historical examples.
- Affirming life through sexual contact is a primal human response to facing one's own mortality.
- Sexual activity provides relief from stressful situations as well as assuages arousal.

Chapter 13

Sex: Make It Count!

In This Chapter

- Understanding why sex matters
- Keeping it fresh
- Unexpected revelations
- Using sex as a basis for character change
- A new look at what a character wants

Sex for sex's sake? Not in an erotic romance! As discussed in Chapter 12, sex doesn't have to be about love. Not initially. But neither can it be thrown into the story's mix solely to increase the heat. The sex act itself must have a purpose. The time your characters spend in bed (or wherever) must not be only about pleasure—even if that's all they think is going on!

If you can remove the sex and nothing in the story changes, it doesn't need to be there. Following every sexual encounter, the story's status quo will change. The characters cannot wake up the morning after and be the same people they were the night before. The sex must propel the plot forward and sweep the characters into another level of involvement. Now to see how this is done …

Starting from Scratch

The sex in an erotic romance is what defines the book as belonging to the genre and, therefore, is vital to the book's success. Not only does the sexual activity in an erotic romance need to impact the plot, it also needs to affect character growth and change.

Because of its inherent importance to the novel as a whole, a story's sexual content needs to be as much a part of the development process as any other element. Making the sexual content count as more than sex accomplishes several things:

- It keeps the sex from being gratuitous.
- It keeps sex scenes from seeming like padding or filler.
- It guarantees the book will be about more than sex.
- It keeps the sex from becoming monotonous and repetitive.
- It makes it impossible to remove the sex and still have a viable novel.

One of the easiest ways to be sure the sex in your stories stays fresh is to *start* fresh each and every time you begin a story. What does that mean? Basically, you should think twice or three times before adding sexual content to an existing book. And if you do? It should never be for the sole purpose of "sexing it up." Turning a traditional romance into an erotic romance can be done, but it's hard to do well and to do seamlessly.

For one thing, the book in question needs to have the right tone, with an existing physical relationship between the characters that allows for the added eroticism. There's also a good chance you'll have to revise extensively to reveal plot twists and character growth in the new sexually charged scenes instead of in the scenes where the same information was originally made known.

Scorchers

To find out if your story works as an erotic romance, ask someone to read your novel but skip the love scenes. If she still understands everything going on—including how your characters fall in love, when and how they change, and every plot twist and turn—then the sex scenes don't need to be there because they don't provide anything essential to your story. If, however, she feels she's missed vital information, then your story works! Congratulations!

Sex scenes added after the fact often come across as nothing more than an attempt at increasing a manuscript's page count or upping its level of steam separate from the dramatic tension and characterization. Rarely is the sex in such a situation intrinsic to the plot of the story, nor does it act as an impetus for character growth and change.

These are the scenes a reader skips because they really don't belong. The only purpose they serve is filler, or they exist solely for marketing reasons. Trust me. Readers can tell the difference between authors who have passion for their work and those hoping to hitch a ride on the erotic romance bandwagon! Be sure your passion shows!

Change Is in the Air

It's doubtful any character in an erotic romance enters a physical relationship thinking, *I wonder exactly how this encounter is going to change me.* But these encounters do just that. They *need* to do just that. The fact that change happens through and because of sex is what drives erotic romance.

Looking more closely at a few of the specific reasons characters engage in sexual relations as outlined in Chapter 12 will give you an idea of how change comes about based on the motivation for the sexual encounter:

> **Scorchers**
>
> So many story elements are their strongest when inextricably linked, so planning in advance how a sex scene will act as impetus for character change is not a bad thing—especially if it's not second nature to the way you write!

Flying high: A character who finds herself unexpectedly celebrating a job promotion with her roommate's visiting brother will no doubt discover that her relationship with her roommate has changed—not to mention her own feelings for the brother and possibly her self-perception. If she's never done anything like this in the past, she may be surprised to find she had it in her to be so bold, and when she takes her next step out into the world, she does so as a completely different person.

Sex education: A character looking to expand her experience and sexual knowledge will have undergone obvious physical changes while using her body as she hasn't before. However, digging for deeper changes will make her a character readers can truly care about. If things didn't go well, perhaps she wonders what's wrong with her rather than questioning her partner's lovemaking skills and loses her hard-won self-esteem as a result. If things did go well, perhaps she wants to go even further with someone new and begins to wonder who she really is that she's suddenly thinking about sex as a sport.

Let's procreate: A character engaging in sexual intercourse for the sake of getting pregnant will, of course, wake up wondering if it's happened. She may start choosing baby names, thinking of colors for her nursery, decide to start a college fund—none of which she would have paid as much attention to when there was no chance she could be pregnant. Doing the deed has, for her, resulted in a change to her way of thinking—even perhaps in how she looks at herself, because she could very well be on her way to motherhood.

Scorchers

Another way to ensure that a character changes as the result of the action in a scene—a sex scene or any other—is to look for a specific and significant shift in emotions or values that happens between the beginning and the end—e.g., sad to happy, panicked to soothed, intense to mellow—and explore the deepest possible motivation for the switch.

Getting out alive: A character wanting nothing more than to feel alive in the face of impending death may have to face the fact that she wasn't in as much danger as she thought, as she's obviously still alive. She now has to consider how her actions will impact the remainder of her tense journey because her life and her body are both in the hands of her stoically rough and sexy companion.

One-night stand: A character who didn't want to spend the night alone and chose to spend it with a stranger may never again be able to go to sleep without wanting someone beside her. She may find she's made a mistake and has a stalker on her hands, causing her to spend every waking moment looking over her shoulder.

Bargaining chips: A character who traded sexual favors to seal a business venture may wake up the morning after with a newfound enthusiasm for what lies ahead. She knows she's come out on top with the agreement she needed and no longer has to worry about struggling to make ends meet. Or … she could continue to worry until the paperwork is signed, and the only change she experiences is even more worry.

Scorchers

Look to your story's theme and premise—and to your characters' backgrounds and current goals—for the best ways to bring about change through sexual activity.

Killer stress: A character realizing she's blown off stress through repeated orgasms at the hands of an inappropriate and really bad boy may berate herself for having lost her mind, her self-control, and her sense of taste. She may take things one step further and vow to change her bar-hopping ways. Then again, she might change her mind about inappropriate bad boys!

The last remaining virgin: A character seeking to lose her virginity is probably faced with the most obvious change; she's no longer a virgin. Beyond the physical transformation, however, consider her emotional state and the changes wrought internally. She might be left feeling physically satisfied but emotionally cold and wish she could turn back time. Depending on who she gave herself to, she may hide the truth from her best girlfriend, creating the conflict of a lie between them where previously there had always been truth.

Hooked On a Feeling

Next to showing the physical pleasure shared by a hero and heroine, demonstrating the emotions they experience is a major purpose of the sex scenes in any story. Whatever emotion has brought your characters to the point of seeking out sexual intimacy, it must be a palpable thing hovering between them as they make love. One character may be experiencing fear while her partner is experiencing loneliness, and together they struggle with feelings of remorse or anger at needing one another the way that they do.

Additionally, sex will expose the tender and revealing underbelly many characters keep hidden from everyone—even from themselves. This could be their greatest weakness or a flaw they consider fatal. Perhaps they've been nursing guilt or regret over a past action and have never had the courage to seek forgiveness. Opening themselves up emotionally through a sexual encounter may be the impetus they need to do so.

Can You Keep a Secret?

Unguarded moments of intimacy are often times when characters find themselves revealing secrets to one another. These may be painful events from their past they've never before shared but that have haunted them with an emotional weight they've long wished to unload. A secret may be what's holding a character back from making a commitment, or from making a career change, or from making a run for public office.

Scorchers

Don't overlook secrets that could also be related to the story's plot as much as to the characters themselves.

If your characters are on the run for their lives, your hero may be aware of the villain's motive for giving chase and finally recognize he's doing your heroine a disservice by keeping her in the dark. The tender moments between them not only have him in a thoughtful mood, but also have him considering someone other than himself.

Ho-Hum

You know you've heard it. Complaints by readers that they skip over sex scenes because they find them boring and filled with the same ol' same ol'—clichéd descriptions, implausible choreography, *purple prose*, etc. Or even worse, that every sex scene they read is interchangeable, with every tab A and slot B the same as the last.

Boring sex scenes can result from several things:

- The author's discomfort with writing sex.
- Lack of immersion in character point of view.
- Incompletely developed characters.
- No clearly motivated reason for characters to have sex.
- Scene's stakes are not high enough or clear to reader.
- No change is evident.
- No emotions are obvious.

def•i•ni•tion

Purple prose is a style of writing in which the author uses an overabundance of flowery or extravagant language to create evocative passages.

Look at scenes you've read that may not have worked for you—as well as ones you've written that you felt may have fallen flat—and see what other reasons you can come up with. Then study those craft basics, or do a second pass through the scene to add the necessary elements to turn it from boring to evocative.

I Should Have Known Better ...

In the next chapter, I bring up a lot of questions that a character may ask herself when she wakes up the morning after—questions that are designed to increase post-coital tension and keep the flame of sexual heat burning high. Right now, however, let's look at questions that dig even deeper—right to the heart of who a character is.

These questions work away at a character's self-perception, as well as impact his motives and goals. Also, similar to the changes he experiences, the things he asks himself are often rooted in his reasons for having sex. Basically, he wants to know why he chose to do what he did and to figure out how his actions are going to cause him problems. For example ...

- Did I just jeopardize the career advancement I've been working toward for months by having sex with a co-worker?
- Was I stupid enough to blow two years of undercover work by having sex with a possible witness?
- The sex was great, but what was she really after—and why didn't I figure it out before taking her to bed?
- How could I have put her life at risk by getting intimately involved when she's under surveillance?
- Does she think I'm going to allow her to write off nonbusiness expenses because we've slept together?

Depending on the needs of your plotlines and those of your individual character's journeys, questions similar to these will need to be raised following sex.

When a hero questions his actions, this …

- Shows the opposition between his internal and external goals.
- Ups the stakes of his story's outcome.
- Adds new motivation driving him toward his goal.
- Increases the sexual tension between him and the heroine.

Scorchers

Look to your story premise to discover what direction you can take the forward motion with the answers your characters give you to the questions they ask after a sexual encounter.

Achilles Was More Than a Heel

Many times it takes a situation where a character lowers his defenses before he's in a position to be made aware of his own vulnerabilities. I can't think of anytime a character is left as unguarded as while making love. He is literally exposed, an open book, and he has nowhere but the bathroom to hide.

A heroine could do several things in such a situation. If she wanted to do nothing but soothe him, she could talk him through his angst. If, on the other hand, she was an undercover agent seeking classified information, she might try to get him to talk without him being aware of what he's telling her.

Exposing your characters' vulnerabilities during sex and then using those vulnerabilities to cause additional conflict is a great way to be sure your sex scenes are not just about sex.

Where Do I Go from Here?

In an earlier chapter, I talked about plot reversals where the action a character takes based on a decision he's made triggers an outcome opposite of what was desired. Sex can do that, too.

A character may go into a sexual encounter looking to expose his new female partner as a fraud and come away with a newfound respect for her instead. This unexpected revelation will take the plot in a new direction. The characters may team up to discover who planted the false information about one of them in an effort to bring both of them down.

Another character may realize that she can no longer face her business partner after sleeping with the very man who broke the other woman's heart. If the plot was the story of the two best girlfriends getting their business off the ground, something is going to have to change. The guilt-harboring character can claim cold feet and allow her partner to buy her out … but then what happens to their friendship?

Before sex, a character may have been 100 percent certain where she was headed. After sex, she may feel as if she's spinning in circles as the choices she's forced to make following sex take her in new directions.

Slip of the Tongue

Author Sylvia Day shares her thoughts on the importance of the sex scenes in erotic romance: "I write exclusively erotic romance. In my stories, the pivotal turning points of the romance happen during the unguarded intimacy of lovemaking. Afterward, the increased sexual tension between the characters as they struggle to stay emotionally distant while physically craving each other is powerful, and oftentimes heart wrenching. That's where the joy of writing romance comes into play for me. Those moments in a love story are what make this job my dream career."

Is This Really What I Want?

Not only will sexual contact cause your characters to examine how they think and feel, they will also look anew at their story goals. Whatever knowledge they've learned about themselves due to this newfound intimacy will have an impact on what they want. Whether they change their minds or renew their efforts, they won't approach their goals in the same way they did before the sex. How could they? They're no longer alone on their quest.

A career-focused character who had been pursuing a promotion or putting in copious hours to make partner may look at his future and wonder if obtaining the goal is worth it—especially if it means he'll be spending the rest of his life working at the same breakneck pace and never having time for a real relationship.

A character who seduced another, hoping to obtain information on a treasure she is hunting, may be forced to reconsider the intricate plan she had to obtain it. Doing so might just save her life, as one of the secrets her lover revealed is that he was hired to protect said treasure from poachers like her.

There are any number of reasons characters may rethink their goals based on a sexual encounter. I've given you two examples here. Now it's your turn to do the same for your story!

Why Am I Doing This Again?

Now that your characters have made love—or had sex if another emotion drove them to sexual intimacy—they'll be in a new place and may find they have new motivations spurring them on. Such motivations could be related to the person they've slept with or be the direct offshoot of accepting the changes foisted upon them.

A character whose goal was to become pregnant will now be motivated by all things related to motherhood. The health of her unborn child will now be an issue and will motivate her to avoid risky situations and take even better care of herself. A character who sealed a business deal with sexual favors may be motivated to seek revenge or payback because the ball is now in her court and she's experiencing unexpected guilt.

Scorchers

The more elements of your story affected by your characters' sexual liaisons, the better. This wraps the sexual content inextricably within your plot and allows it to do double or even triple duty as a plot device.

The Least You Need to Know

- Adding sex to an existing story does not guarantee it will work as an erotic romance, where the sexual content must be intrinsic to the plot and character development.
- The changes a character experiences following sex may be tied to the emotional reason that drove her to the encounter.
- Emotions are equally important to sex scenes as the physical act of making love.
- Look carefully at the elements in your love scenes—as well as the language used—to be sure your reader understands what's at stake and won't be bored with what would otherwise be a scene no different from any other.
- Revisiting your characters' goals and motivations following sex will help up the stakes of your story.
- Make use of your story's sexual encounters by using them to add new twists to the direction of your plot.

Chapter 14

The Morning After: Postcoital Tension

In This Chapter

- Tension-increasing questions
- Using distance to your advantage
- Emotions in upheaval
- Revisiting conflict following sex
- Subtly sexual thoughts

In a traditional romance novel, the sexual tension between the hero and heroine continues to heighten until it's relieved by an emotional commitment and their sexual expression of love. In an erotic romance novel, the author must maintain the same level of tension even after the couple has indulged in sexual intimacy.

I talk more in Chapter 16 about the basics of writing good sexual tension, but for now, let's take a look at how the tension in an erotic romance differs from—and is similar to—that in a traditional romance, and how to be sure you don't lose the sizzle!

Not Losing That Loving Feeling

As I discussed in Chapter 12, the sex in an erotic romance is not always about love. Just because your characters have taken that all-important and physically intimate step doesn't mean they've reached the end of their emotional journey—or that they've even admitted to the possibility of falling in love. In fact, many times readers will be aware of love happening long before your story people are ready to admit it to themselves or to each other.

You may hear authors argue that a story loses its potential for sexual tension after a couple has consummated their relationship. I'm here to argue the other side! I'm a firm believer that sexual tension can be maintained—and even increased substantially—following every act of making love.

Scorchers

Don't forget! Readers still want to feel the same taut push-pull between your characters after the deed has been done as before—no matter if it's the first, second, third, or fourth time!

Accomplishing this may sound daunting or even impossible, but it's not difficult at all when you get into your characters' heads and start by asking all the questions they would be asking themselves the morning after.

Questions, Questions, Questions

There's possibly nothing that challenges a character's self-perception more than the reasons she chooses to have sex. This is especially true when said sex is with a new partner for the first time and for reasons having nothing to do with love.

And yes, I said *she* on purpose. Most men are physical beings. That's not to say they don't make love with their partners for emotional reasons, but they rarely come to that first sexual encounter with the same anxiety or concerns as most women will, or with more on their mind than having a good time and giving the same in return. (Not all, of course, but the genders are not engineered the same, resulting in conventions that often prove true!)

Men, for the most part, are biologically designed to get in, get out, and continue with their hunting and gathering, while many women will ponder the sexual experience and what it means in the scheme of their days. That is, of course, only one version of the gender dichotomy—and a very generalized one at that. And in an erotic romance, a heroine is just as likely to be the one to initiate that first sexual encounter. Even so, psychologically she will more than likely be the one to court the most doubts simply because of her unique female perspective.

And yes. We're writing fantasy fiction read primarily by females, and we do have the freedom to portray our fictional men any way we want. We can write real men, fantasy men, pure alphas or betas, or we can create gammas with the best traits of alphas and betas combined. (Our readers won't be shy about letting us know what they want in our story men!) However you choose to depict your heroes, don't forget that they, too, need to wake up the morning after wondering what in the world has happened and what's going to happen now!

Scorchers

For every female author whose experience with men runs to the alpha stereotype, another author will draw on a different personal experience as she writes. Our unique situation as women writing emotionally charged, sexually explicit stories with leading male protagonists means we will occasionally run into readers who may not buy into our heroes as what they deem to be "real men." Luckily, our diverse readership means that as long as we stay true to our characters, we'll find readers looking for the type of men—and women—we write!

What Have We Done?

What your characters have done is obvious—at least physically obvious. But that's not the question they're asking. What they're wondering about are the ways this one act is going to change so many things in their lives. Think about it like this: have you ever wished to undo something you've done? To get back the last 24 hours to make a different choice?

This isn't to say your characters are going to want to reverse their decision to have sex, but they will be in that situation of nothing ever being the same again and trying to imagine—whether nervously or anxiously or breathlessly—what to expect next. Play up that uncertainty, and wring all the tension from it that you possibly can!

Are We Going to Do It Again?

Not only *are* we going to do it again, but do we *want* to? If so, is it simply because it was so very good, or did we make a deeper-than-physical connection we want to explore further?

These are only a few of the postcoital questions about future sexual liaisons that will be running through your characters' minds. The answers they give will determine much of the direction your story takes and help set the stage for their character growth. This is where some of that advanced planning you've done can come in handy and keep you on the right track.

Then again, you might want to let your characters surprise you and send your story in a direction you hadn't anticipated. Doing it again because it feels good might imply a fun, light-hearted and sexy romp, while exploring the deeper connection might indicate a story with a more serious tone. It's all about giving your characters hard questions to answer, staying true to who they are, and letting them be the ones to give *you* the answers!

Does This Mean We're in a Relationship?

In a traditional romance, one in which sex is a demonstration of love and emotional commitment, that's exactly what it would mean. But this is erotic romance, in which sex is often initially about nothing but the pleasure, relief, etc., the act brings. The relationship question can still be raised, however.

Think of the conflict when one party equates intimacy with monogamy while the other feels the need to reach out and touch someone anytime they've had a bad day. Consider the uncertain hesitancy in doing it again if neither participant knows where they stand and fears making a misstep. Use any and every opportunity you can to keep the tension high!

Is It Love, or Is It Sex?

Whether your characters' sexual intimacy occurs early in your story before they know each other well, or whether they've established a relationship of sorts before doing the deed, this possibility will eventually run through their minds. Even if they've set up guidelines or made an arrangement based on nothing but their physical needs, your story will demand that the question be raised.

So raise it. Make them think. Make them worry and fret. Make them realize how easily a single question can upset their comfortable situation. After all, putting characters through the wringer is your job as an author!

Scorchers

Don't think your heroine has to be the first to fall in love. Readers enjoy seeing a strong man tumble, and his battle with emotional uncertainty endears him to them even more.

Is It Going to Be This Good Every Time?

That's assuming it was good the first time, that it wasn't a bumbling case of nerves and apologies and no one having any fun … which doesn't sound very appealing, does it? Thing is, bumbling nerves are very much a part of real life. Getting naked and intimate with someone for the first time, especially if the someone is a person we don't know well, means offering ourselves up as an open book. That vulnerability is what makes us human, and characters who are truly human are the ones readers love most.

First times are awkward. We don't know how our bodies will fit, where our hands should go, if touching here is better than touching there. Think of how much can be revealed by characters forced to deal with an unsatisfying experience. Then think of all the ways they'll wonder how they could have made it better … and how they'll be looking for an opportunity to do just that! Of course, if the earth did move, they'll still be looking for that opportunity, which puts sexual tension right back into play. See how easy that was?

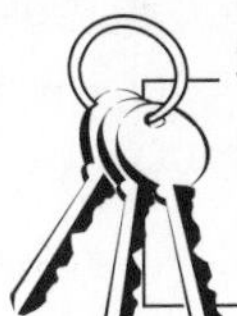

Scorchers

Not every sexual encounter needs to make the earth move!

How Did I Compare?

Unless your characters are virgins, they'll both have previous partners to use as a basis for sexual comparison. This reality can cause distress, even in the most sexually confident characters. She wonders if she's met his needs as fully as the women in his past have. He wonders if he's pleased her as well as her previous lovers did.

The flip side is a character determined to make her new man forget any other women existed before she came into his life. Or one whose goal is to wipe away his new woman's every memory of previous loves. Don't just assume a comparison is a bad thing. Make it work for your story by ramping up the postcoital tension!

What Does He Think of Me?

Was I what he was expecting? Is he regretting anything about what we did? Did I shock him, frighten him, please him, bore him? Like those of us living in the real world, characters are bound to wonder what others think of them. It's a natural response—especially when the other is someone with whom they've been as intimate as two human beings can possibly get.

Whether based in insecurity or simple curiosity, play up these questions. Maybe the answers—or absence thereof—will spur your inquisitive character into action of an unexpected sort. This could pump up not only the internal conflict but the external as well, while keeping the sexual tension at a fever pitch!

Is He Going to Call Me Again?

Even if your heroine is wondering such a thing, she's not sitting beside the phone waiting for it to ring or checking her incoming log every 5 minutes to see if she's missed your hero's call. Your heroine, remember, is smart and confident. Wondering is fine, but she still has her dog to feed and her laundry to do. Life doesn't end or grind to a halt while she waits. She goes to work. She meets her obligations. She lives up to her responsibilities.

> **Naughty, Naughty**
>
> No reader wants to read about a heroine who is so needy that she drops out of life while waiting for a man to call!

Of course she can fret—but just don't have her doing so to the exclusion of living her life. And besides, there's a whole lot of tension to be had while waiting!

Does He or Doesn't He?

Separate from wondering whether or not sex equals love is having one character wonder if her partner feels the same emotional attachment or if her feelings are one-sided. We don't all fall emotionally at the same time, even if we made the perfect physical connection. One couple may experience love at first sight, while another may find themselves on an uneven keel, rocking back and forth to find a balance. Dealing with such a major uncertainty presents a great source for continuing conflict—and continuing sexual tension!

So Far Away

Another sure way to keep tension high is to keep your characters apart for reasons beyond their control, such as work, travel, or busy lives that have them passing like ships in the night. Now, tell me that any of those situations won't result in sexual tension even if your characters have experienced an orgasm or two together!

Say your couple can only meet for a quick lunch before one is sequestered for a trial and the other is off to Tokyo. And say said lunch provides no time for anything but eating—if either has an appetite—and holding hands, sharing heated glances, and playing footsie under the table.

Tension, tension, tension. Keep your characters apart and watch the sparks fly as they struggle to get back together. Just don't keep them apart for too long; romance readers aren't big fans of extended separations!

> **Scorchers**
>
> For sexual tension to be effective, your reader must feel what your characters are going through physically and emotionally. The best sexual tension occurs on both levels for your characters and will work best for your readers when it does the same for them.

Turn Down the Volume

A sure-fire way to increase sexual tension after consummation is to keep your characters from doing it again—or from getting the same sort of satisfaction out of it if they do. I've talked previously about using bad sex as a tool for character growth and about the bonding that might occur between a couple laughing their way through getting it right.

This is a different sort of tension. If their first encounter was romantic and tender, the second might be the result of an angry confrontation. Even though both may reach orgasm, the connection may be nothing compared with their first time together and cause one or the other—or both—to feel conflicted in an entirely new way.

Ramping down the pleasure a notch—or turning it in an unexpected direction by forcing your characters to work to get back the joy of that first time—can do a number on the sexual tension between them.

Don't Even Think About It

Why not look into increasing tension by refusing to give a character what he or she wants? If one partner is looking to sex for intimacy, have the other partner back away emotionally—or go even further and back away physically because they're not ready to give that much of themselves to the relationship.

Scorchers

Using sex as a weapon—a well-motivated and believable weapon—can provide ongoing sexual tension following an initial consummation.

Maybe your heroine will let your hero get to first or second base but no further until he realizes how his workaholic tendencies are driving her away. Maybe your hero will bring your heroine to orgasm with his hand but won't offer pleasures of any other sort until she stops booking her social calendar and failing to leave time for him.

See what reasons you can come up with for one character to withhold sex in order to drive the other crazy, and make your sexual tension crazy, too!

No Going Back

That wishing-to-turn-back-time thing I mentioned a few paragraphs ago? You got it. After the deed has been done, there's no such thing as going back to the beginning, starting over, doing take-backs. Sure, a character can experience second thoughts and wonder over what might have been had there been no change to the status quo. But that status quo has been flipped end over end. From here on out, nothing will be the same. And that can cause all sorts of tension—including sexual.

Consider a character who remembers her lover's hands on her body every time she dresses for work. He's now with her all the time, even while she's uncertain when or where she'll be able to see him again. When they do finally hook up, those thoughts and feelings will be with her. She won't be able to shake them. They leave her short of breath, swallowing hard.

Consider a character who found the earring his lover lost in his car and now keeps it in his pocket with his keys and his change. Every time he reaches in, he feels it, he strokes it. He relives the touch of her fingers on his skin. He remembers her scent, and he grows hard as he picks up the phone to call her.

Lust? Certainly. But don't overlook the sexual tension inherent to characters thinking about one another, remembering one another, and realizing they'll never be able to shake the other person from their mind and can only go forward from here.

Uncharted waters, anyone?

Scorchers

The best guarantee for keeping sexual tension at a fever pitch is to have your characters thinking about one another at unexpected moments—if not all the time. You don't want them to appear stalkerlike or possess an implausible fixation, but there's a lot to be said for a constant craving where fleeting thoughts remind a character of what he's missing—and what he hopes to have again soon!

So Much for Smooth Sailing

Sex is not a true solution to the obstacles your characters face as they make their way through your story—even if they try to use it as one! Indulging, however, definitely provides an ongoing source of tension until they've admitted their love and made an emotional commitment. In fact, sex should ramp up what conflict already exists and add another layer on top.

Conflict is the basis of tension; ergo, there's absolutely no reason consummation should put an end to that tight push-pull of attraction between your characters. They still have to deal with whatever it is keeping them apart. Perhaps it's falling for a totally inappropriate person, wanting what they know they can't have, or giving in when they know they shouldn't. Perhaps they are competitors, bidding on the same job, courting the same client, and fighting off an attraction that keeps both up nights and interferes with their work.

Whatever previous conflict was standing in the way of your characters' romance—or in the way of their reaching their individual goals—will now cause them even more grief. Adding sex to the mix might do one of several things:

- Exploit a character's vulnerabilities
- Divide concentration between business and pleasure
- Threaten professional reputation if made public
- Require secrets be kept to avoid hurt feelings or rumors

The focused, believable conflict you've developed (that I described in Chapter 7) will help guarantee that the tension between your characters sizzles until the very last page—even more so now that intimacy has been added to the mix!

That Ol' Gut Response

The sex in our books, no matter how graphic, explicit, or steamy, no matter if engaged in for nothing but pleasure, always results in emotional ramifications. Those emotional ramifications are a natural source of sexual tension.

> **Naughty, Naughty**
>
> Characters who walk away from a sexual encounter with no sense of emotional upheaval won't ring true to the readers of erotic romance.

Uncertainty, wonder, disbelief, delight … any of these can create new sexual tension or build upon that which already exists. Remember, while your characters are enjoying themselves physically, there are too many things unsettled between them for either to relax completely.

The Least You Need to Know

- Having your characters question what their new physical intimacy means will keep the sexual tension high.
- Characters forced apart by circumstances beyond their control will give you an opportunity to ramp up the tension between them.
- A character who realizes the full impact another has had on his life experiences a whole new level of sexual tension.
- Revisiting the conflict that is already keeping your characters apart and notching it up postcoitus is a sure way to add to the existing tension.

Chapter 15

No Room at the Inn for the Shy and Retiring

In This Chapter

- Exploring a broad range of sexual experience
- Having fun with sex
- Seeking perfection in sexual encounters
- Keeping sex hot yet simple

Can an erotic romance feature characters who are sexually inexperienced? What about characters who've been around the block a time or two? The story people in an erotic romance are not shy and retiring; they're all about experimenting, learning, exploring, and feeling.

Your characters are people with pasts—whether checkered or plain is up to you. It's how you use their sexual history in your story that defines who they are now.

Too Experienced? Say It Isn't So!

Every sexual partner a character has (or has had in the past) brings something unique to the table for that character. It can be a new physical experience or an increased enjoyment of a tried-and-true favorite. It can be an emotional self-realization. Perhaps a character abandoned early in life has looked to sex to feel loved and wanted. That doesn't mean she doesn't know the difference between the two or that she isn't well aware of what she's been doing and why—or that she's not ready for one special man to fill that void.

Scorchers

Characters are human. They don't appear in your stories without a history, and that includes a sexual history filled with both pleasures and disappointments, good choices and bad.

The reasons for your characters' sexual experiences say a lot about who they are now. Explore those reasons. Use them to your story's advantage. You'll be taking your characterization to a level you might not have reached before!

Author Pamela Clare shares these thoughts on a character's sexual experience: "Writers have to know their characters on the deepest level to write convincing sex. No two couples are going to have sex the same way, and different people will have different experiences when paired up with someone else. Understanding how this particular couple expresses itself sexually is the key to writing authentic, convincing, hot sex. Sex scenes need to incorporate the character's entire personality, including his or her sexual past, just like any other scene. Whether the heroine is a virgin or a former porn star, the reader needs to see how the person's emotional and sexual history has led to this point and needs to see the impact of her sexual history at work in the scene.

"For example, a virgin might be really turned on and ready to go because she's been waiting so long to have sex and wants desperately not to be a virgin any longer. Or perhaps she's a virgin because she was raised in a religious family and feels shame about sex. Perhaps the porn star is very turned off by sex because she had such degrading experiences before the camera. Or maybe she's so at ease with her body that sex is like breathing for her. All of these extremes can be real and convincing if the writer has done her characterization well."

The Very First Time

A virgin in an erotic romance? Why not? Being a virgin does not mean a character is uninterested in sex. All it means is that he or she has not engaged in sexual intercourse. That state of physical inexperience does not prevent said character from having a sexually adventurous nature. As long as he or she is confident, mature, and ready—even eager—to take that step, there's nothing wrong with giving him or her a starring role in an erotic romance.

Of course, the reason a character has retained his or her virginity will play a part in the story—especially if you're writing a contemporary erotic romance. Living in the society we do, where we are inundated with sex columns in magazines and sex scenes in movies and sexually evocative commercials on television, it's hard to believe any contemporary character wouldn't know the basic workings of Tab A and Slot B.

Maybe a character who is searching for Mr. Right has never found a man she feels comfortable enough with to give herself to. That doesn't mean she's not interested. She's simply been waiting for the hero you've created to come along!

Here are a few more reasons a character might not have taken the sexual plunge:

- Moral convictions
- Isolation
- Illness or physical ailment
- Wanting the first time to be for love
- Overly cautious about disease and pregnancy, perhaps due to a friend's bad experience
- Prefers to take care of her own needs with a vibrator than deal with the man-grief her girlfriends have had

Scorchers

Remember, our characters are inherently sexual beings. They are curious, open-minded, and imbued with a sensual spirit. They are also willing to experiment and explore that part of their personality. A character does not have to be a skilled or experienced lover to possess the attitude befitting an erotic romance protagonist!

Any of these scenarios still allows for a character to have a sexual nature; it's just one she hasn't yet found a reason to fully express or discover. That's what you'll do for her by writing her story, and she'll be grateful forever!

The In-Betweener

Between the virgin and the old pro is the character who is more than ready to expand on her limited experience but just can't catch a break. Maybe she's never been able to get it right physically and is beginning to wonder if a long-term commitment to her dependable battery-operated boyfriend might not be a bad thing. (Oh, is this character in for a ton of fun when she meets the right guy!)

Then there's the one who knows exactly how much fun she could be having—except every time she gets a chance to play, she also gets a call from the office and ends up with hours of overtime. Maybe those hours are spent on her graduate studies when she'd rather be getting a more intimate education. What if she's in a relationship with a workaholic who's never awake at the same time she is? Sounds like the perfect candidate for a role-playing kidnapping, don't you think? Or maybe she's grown pickier after a series of bad encounters and is saving herself for something bigger and better.

> **Scorchers**
>
> I love the in-betweener character. There's a chance to fulfill the romantic fantasy of a sexual education obtained at the hands of the perfect man and partner, and there are no physical (or possibly emotional) issues of virginity to deal with.

That's just a handful of reasons a heroine might not be getting the sex she wants. There are so many possibilities that all you have to do is let your imagination run wild!

A Lion or a Lamb?

The title of this chapter is a bit of a misnomer, as it implies anyone who is shy could not be the hero or heroine of an erotic romance. Why am I correcting myself, you ask? Well, being shy or introverted hardly equates with a lack of interest in sex, or with a lack of willingness to explore, or even with the lack of an innate curiosity.

Ingrid Bergman was once quoted as saying, "I was the shyest human ever invented, but I had a lion inside me that wouldn't shut up!" And that about covers it. It's the lion inside roaring and clawing to get out that determines whether or not a character has what it takes to work in a story with a high emphasis on sexuality.

Curiosity Only Kills Cats

Girls talk. (Guys talk, too, but for now I'll focus on the girls.) They read the sex advice columns in women's magazines. They read erotic romances! They huddle together at lunch or get together after work and talk about the guys they've been seeing and what those guys can do, uh, down there … and do well while they're down there! Then these girls go home and convince their lovers to give it the old college try because they don't want to be missing out on anything! (Anyone remember the "Venus butterfly" from television's *L.A. Law?*)

Characters who are curious about sex and eager to try new things are great for spicing up your story. They bring an exciting perspective to the tried and true.

Give It to Me, Baby!

Going after what she wants is one of the trademarks of our adventurous heroine. Whether she plays the ingénue and wraps the hero around her little finger, or takes on the role of seductive vamp and wraps him up in her satin—or flannel—sheets, no one is going to accuse her of being a bad girl—and get away with it!

Our heroines are confident in who they are, know what they want—even if they've never had it before—and have no qualms about being the aggressor. That said, they still have to be women who appeal to our readers. Many readers need to be able to identify with or relate to a fictional heroine's actions. Others simply need to understand and respect the same—even if they don't approve. Characterize your heroines fully and honestly, and you'll never lose a reader because of issues with plausibility when it comes to sex.

Scorchers

An erotic romance heroine who is interested in a man does not have to wait for him to make the first move. And even if he does, she can easily be the one to make the second.

The Places You'll Go

About that curiosity … one of the things to consider with your characters is where they are in their relationship. Is it a purely physical arrangement, or is it on the verge of blossoming into a full romance? Is your heroine's lover a new man in her life, or is he someone with whom she's been making whoopee for a while?

Taking a character places she's never been before sexually can result in all manner of changes and growth. Exploring not only her comfort level, but also the measure of trust she shares with her partner gives you many opportunities to increase conflict and characterization. While she might expect her long-time lover to be receptive to trying new things, her request might instead cause him to back away because he questions her motives or fears he no longer pleases her.

Sex in a loving situation is not always perfect any more than it is in a new one. Bringing sexual doubts or difficulties into an ongoing romance presents your characters with challenges in the same way introducing uncertainties into a new one does. And overcoming these intimate conflicts makes even fictional people stronger!

The People You'll Do

One thing erotic romance allows for is the expanded sexual lives of its characters. Many readers still prefer that a story's main protagonists have sexual contact with no one but their romantic partner after the two have met. Other readers and authors don't mind—and will easily forgive—a character who strays outside the bounds of a relationship if properly motivated.

Perhaps as a couple, your story's hero and heroine enjoy bringing another partner into their bed. Perhaps one is turned on by the voyeuristic thrill of watching the other seduce a stranger. Perhaps with your hero unavailable, an emotional tragedy sends your heroine into the bed of an old friend, ex-love, or even a stranger. She's not thinking straight and is desperate for a human connection in her time of grief. Perhaps her continued grief causes her to freeze out the man she should turn to, and he weakens and turns to someone else to ease the sting of her rejection.

Naughty, Naughty

Not all publishers are accepting of characters who have multiple partners in their erotic romance releases. Be sure to study the guidelines and preferences of any publisher to whom you're considering submitting.

Be aware that not all romance readers will stick with a book after running into scenarios of infidelity—even if the setup is one your characters have agreed upon jointly, or is one that is emotionally convincing. On the other hand, if you write a compelling story of two very real and fallible human beings working through their problems, you can't help but find an audience to relate.

Swinging Chandeliers and Trapeze Artists

Erotic romance offers authors the perfect venue for giving stories to characters who love to push their personal sexual boundaries. Not all do; many are content with getting it on the old-fashioned way! However, whether it's trying out new positions or paraphernalia, looking for excitement in exotic locations, or even dipping a toe into alternative lifestyles, experimentation plays a big part in many characters' lives.

The freedom in writing erotic romance enables you to fully explore the fun your characters might have when hanging by a chain from the hooks on their bedroom wall! But consider what happens when a hero walks into a heroine's bedroom for the first time and comes face to face with her jungle-gym apparatus? Is he raring to go … or backing out the door? And how does your heroine react to his reaction? Does she blow him off … or wonder if he thinks there's something wrong with her?

These circus-trick scenarios, or the urge to work through every page of the *Kama Sutra*, give you occasion to learn much about who your characters are sexually—what drives them, what are they looking for, how do their partners feel about their need for wild sexual theatrics? It could be an adventurous spirit's search for pleasure, but it could be more. Figuring it out is between you and your characters!

Naughty, Naughty

As with all sexual content in erotic romance, experimentation should never be included simply for another chance to let your characters have sex! It must mean something and be as inseparable from the plot as every other element.

The important thing to remember is that there are deeply seated reasons for these wants and needs, and they'll have an impact on your story as a whole. While one character might be looking for nothing but increased pleasure, another might need an emotional release he can find only in bondage, and yet another might want to be pushed to the edge of her comfort zone by a stranger. As I've said before, the characters in our books are sexual beings, and having them learn about themselves while having fun is a very good thing!

Naughty, Naughty

When writing sexual gymnastics, avoid making your reader roll her eyes in disbelief. This is especially important in erotic romance where sex is described in graphic detail. If a scene makes a reader cringe in fear or, even worse, laugh at the prospect of body parts breaking, she'll be pulled out of the story, and that's the last thing you want to happen!

You Can't Go Wrong with Vanilla

Just because you're writing an erotic romance doesn't mean your story must be filled with the aforementioned sexual gymnastics, experimentation, or multiple partners. There's not a thing wrong with plain-vanilla, missionary-style, monogamous intercourse. This is all many readers need. In fact, the only thing they find missing in traditional romance is explicitly detailed descriptions of romantic lovemaking. And that's the reason they've turned to the erotic subgenre.

Don't feel your characters have to bring toys or food or kinks of any kind to the table—or the bed—for their sex to be hot. There are any number of authors writing today whose books sizzle and burn while depicting only the most basic encounters of oral sex and intercourse.

If that's your comfort zone, no worries! Vanilla is timeless and classic. It's all many readers want or need ... well, with the added erotic cherry on top!

What Happens If ...

In Chapter 14, I discussed the emotional aftermath of a sexual encounter. But let's not forget the possibility of a physical aftermath as well. What happens if a character decides she *never* wants to do that again, while the man she's with thinks it's the best thing ever? Well, for one thing, you've got a great new source of conflict!

> **Slip of the Tongue**
>
> Author Lydia Joyce says, "I like working with main characters of different pasts, but whatever their histories, they must have shaped and been shaped by their personalities, insecurities, etc., and must continue to influence their present relationship. I've written about virgins and ex-streetwalkers and everything in between. My advice is quite simple: Keep it real."

Maybe what they did together caused her pain or brought her absolutely no pleasure. Does she tell him? Does she avoid him? Does she go along, hoping things will get better?

What she does will mostly likely depend on where they are in their relationship—and where she's wanting it to go. Sexual communication is a big must in erotic romance. The sexual intimacy between your characters is vital to their story, making it doubly important that they deal with that part of their relationship honestly.

If at First You Don't Succeed ...

Not every sexual encounter is magic, and readers of erotic romance know that. When writing our sex scenes, we need to remember this: realism beats out unbelievability every time. I'm not advocating we write books filled with bad sex; no one wants to read that! I am suggesting that, by giving characters less-than-perfect experiences, we're giving ourselves even more opportunities to deepen our characterization.

Maybe a couple who's been together for a while needs a bit of spice in their love life to chase away the converging boredom. Maybe a couple hooking up for the first time just can't get it right and ends up laughing through every failure and growing closer because of the emotional bond they develop. Oftentimes, it's the not-so-good sex that shows the truth of a character's nature—not only in how she deals with the failure on a personal level, but how it influences her relationship with her current lover.

Making a character work for what she wants—even if that something is good sex—is another way to push her into discovering more about herself. It's all about the character arc, baby!

The Least You Need to Know

- A character's sexual experience or lack thereof matters less than his or her attitude or sexual nature.
- Toys and other experimental games are not required for sexual encounters to be hot.
- Whatever type of sexual escapades your characters share, be sure the activities are believable to your readers.
- Characters who are sexually adventurous must still face emotional challenges.

Chapter 16

Writing 101: Sexual Tension

In This Chapter

- Writing seductive conversation
- Sex on the brain
- Understanding what nonverbal communication reveals
- Looking at a number of sensory perceptions
- Taking chemistry out of the lab

Sexual tension is the spark that brings your characters and their love story to life. It flavors every word spoken and fuels every response from your hero to your heroine and vice versa. It's the taut push-pull of wondering if they will or if they won't, and it's there in your book from beginning to end.

Sexual tension is not sex. Sexual tension is not blunt lust. It's the foreplay of foreplay. It's the testing of waters before taking the plunge. It's a rising awareness of sexual attraction that your characters experience emotionally as well as physically, and you can express it in your writing with specific tools of craft. Let's take a look at getting that fire started!

The Art of Innuendo

In common usage, *innuendo* often has a negative connotation and insinuates something derogatory or disparaging. In romance writing, however, innuendo is more about being suggestive or alluding to something sexual in nature that will further the attraction between two characters. When done well, it can leave a character speechless, never insulted, and searching for a response while calming her fluttering heart.

> **Scorchers**
>
> A very common use of innuendo is in flirting. Characters working to get a rise or reaction out of one another often dip into the bawdy, provocative territory they would avoid in a more professional situation for fear of being accused of harassment.

Well-done innuendo adds the perfect sexual seasoning to a conversation; poorly done, it comes across as rude or even lecherous and insulting. Be sure to avoid the latter!

Banter, Don't Bicker

Good banter is hard to come by. Too often, it comes off as bickering or even rude sniping. Banter is a big element in comedic situations, and television sitcoms provide some of the best examples you can study. Watch a few episodes of *Will & Grace* to see what I mean. The quips and quick-witted repartee are brilliantly written and delivered.

A Double Order of Entendre, Please

A *double entendre* is like manna from heaven. It's rarely a conversational element that can be planned, but often it pops up unexpectedly when you're writing and is based in the context of what your characters are saying. For example:

> **def•i•ni•tion**
>
> A **double entendre** is a comment or phrase that has more than one meaning or interpretation, one of which is usually suggestive or risqué and often used to induce comic irony.

Brandon rushed into the office. "Sorry I couldn't get here any sooner. Dad had us up to our knees cleaning Mom's koi pond."

"I wasn't sure you got my call." Rachel crossed her arms and moved to stand behind her desk. "I figured you'd left your cell in the car."

"Nope." He reached into his pocket and pulled out the phone. "Had it right here."

> Rachel shook her head and smiled. "So it's true. You *do* keep it in your pants all the time."

See? The "keep it in your pants all the time" can be taken to mean something other than a cell phone! Obviously how it's intended will depend on who's saying it and in what context.

Slip of the Tongue

Author Jo Leigh is a master at writing banter. I particularly enjoyed the scenes between Margot and Daniel in her 2005 Harlequin Blaze, *A Lick and a Promise*.

The Truth of Subtext

When it comes to *subtext*, you can't apply the old adage of, "Say what you mean, and mean what you say." Subtext in conversation is the unspoken meaning beneath what is said aloud.

def•i•ni•tion

Subtext is the underlying or implicit meaning in text or spoken dialogue.

Let's take the same dialogue exchange from earlier and turn it from a flirtatious double entendre, giving it a more bitter subtext. If you could read dialogue and see the subtext, it might look like this:

> Brandon rushed into the office. "Sorry I couldn't get here any sooner. Dad had us up to our knees cleaning Mom's koi pond." *(Meaning: I wasn't in the mood to spend Saturday inside doing taxes.)*
>
> "I wasn't sure you got my call." Rachel crossed her arms and moved to stand behind her desk. "I figured you'd left your cell in the car." *(Meaning: don't even try to fool me. I know you'd do just about anything to get out of taxes, including mucking around in a pond and leaving your phone on the car.)*
>
> "Nope." He reached into his pocket and pulled out the phone. "Had it right here." *(Meaning: I wish I'd left it in the car.)*
>
> Rachel shook her head and smiled. "So it's true. You *do* keep it in your pants all the time." *(Meaning: you know, at times, you can really be a jerk.)*

Of course this works much better in the context of a true scene, but you get the general idea. No matter how outwardly civil the conversation is between Brandon and Rachel, the subtext reveals the truth of what they're saying to one another.

Slip of the Tongue

On writing banter, author Jo Leigh offers the following tip: "One thing to remember when writing banter, or any dialogue, is to use contractions! Unless you have a darn good reason not to, you want your dialogue to sound natural, the way you and your friends sound. Even if you're writing characters from another planet or foreign speakers, make it easy for the reader to get lost in the words say, by using one or two formal phrases, then get right back to natural-sounding speech. When you don't use the contractions, the reader pauses to mentally make the contractions, which automatically (and subconsciously) takes them out of the moment."

What Dialogue *Doesn't* Say

Aside from any inherent subtext, a dialogue between two characters is often rife with emotion and even physical evidence of what one may be holding back. All these things are conveyed with the words they use as well as their tone of voice, and any hedging or conversational shortcuts they take. Think, too, of an unsteady voice or one that cracks. Each of these clues offers a true indication of a character's state of mind.

Actions Speak Louder Than Words

This adage is as recognizable as the Golden Rule and is as applicable in fiction as in real life. A character who doth protest too much that he isn't interested in a particular woman will prove his own words wrong when he's constantly seeking her out. Likewise, a character who proclaims she doesn't care whether or not a particular man is going to be at a party reveals the truth when she obsesses for hours over her clothes and makeup.

A Comprehensive Look at Conversation

Action speaks louder than words, so here's an example of innuendo, banter, double entendre, and subtext all rolled up into one scene. This is from my 2002 Harlequin Blaze, *All Tied Up*.

I'll give you a quick setup: Macy Webb is a free-spirited webzine editor, and Leo Redding is an uptight attorney. Along with several other couples, they're testing a couples' scavenger hunt. The results will help Macy decide whether or not to include the game on her company's website. Prior to this encounter and as part of a game of

Truth or Dare, Macy had been sitting in Leo's lap, trying to get him to smile. Now that the rest of the crowd has gone, he's returned to her loft and finds her in the middle of folding laundry—bras, specifically, which are hooked over her arm by their straps.

> Macy nodded an acknowledgment and then moved back into the loft, sensing this conversation was not long for turning to the weather. Leo wasn't here for that any more than he was here to discuss the city's real estate market.
>
> She wanted to know why he'd come. What he wanted. If he intended to stay. Why she wanted him to do just that when she should be showing the arrogant beast to the door.
>
> He walked out of the balcony's darkness and into her light. The stars in the night sky behind him winked with but half the sparkle in his eyes. Macy forced herself to breathe.
>
> She couldn't let him get to her this early in the game. She had to avoid this plaguelike attraction. The man was too logical, too seriously uptight and sensible. She doubted she'd find a spontaneous bone in his body.
>
> Then again, that depended on what one considered a bone, didn't it?
>
> "What's the frown for?"
>
> She glanced up at his question and frowned. "I'm not frowning."
>
> Sliding the balcony door shut behind him, Leo responded to her denial with the bold arch of one brow.
>
> "Okay. I'm frowning. But only because you said I was." Yes. That made a world of sense. But it was certainly better than confessing her previous ponderings.
>
> "Then, you admit to the charge. And I rest my case."
>
> Macy once again crossed her arms, sending the clothesline of under things swinging at her waist. "Tell me, Mr. Redding. What's the difference between a lawyer and a prostitute?"
>
> "A prostitute won't screw you when you're dead."
>
> She snorted. He hadn't even hesitated long enough to blink. "I suppose you've heard them all."
>
> "It comes with knowing the territory." He took a predatory sort of step farther into the room. His mouth crooked with a predatory sort of grin. "And I'm very good at what I do."

> Maybe so, but Macy Webb was no man's prey. "Yes. I remember you making that boast."
>
> "I wondered about that. If you remembered."
>
> "I don't forget much of anything. Unfortunately."
>
> "Except where you keep your lingerie?"
>
> "Funny." She glared, draped the lot over the back of the sofa. "Okay, I forgot to do my laundry until this afternoon."
>
> "So I noticed."
>
> "That I didn't do my laundry?"
>
> "That you weren't wearing your laundry." Her expression said, 'Excuse me?' and he added, "When you were in my lap."
>
> "And I guess I should be flattered?"
>
> He offered the shrug of one shoulder instead of a simple yes or no reply. "It wasn't like I went out of my way to look. Your chest *was* in my face."
>
> "I see. So, what you're saying is that when my chest isn't in your face you don't notice it?"
>
> "No. That's not what I said. But, now that you mention it …" He let the sentence trail.
>
> Macy picked right up where he left off. "Mention what?"
>
> "Victoria's Secret? I think she shared it for a reason."
>
> He was *so* going to pay for that one.

As you can see, the dialogue is fast-paced with very little introspection or action hindering the zing of the banter. Leo's comment about being very good at what he does serves as a double entendre, as it could refer to his profession or to his skills in bed. The exchange also includes sexual subtext necessary to the scene as Leo reminds Macy of how close their bodies had been earlier when she'd sat in his lap. Of course, all this is much easier to see in context of the whole, serving as the sort of back and forth that increases the sexual tension!

Intimacy: A Twelve-Step Program

In his book *Intimate Behavior: A Zoologist's Classic Study of Human Intimacy* (Kodansha Globe, 1997), author Desmond Morris discusses the steps human beings go through, from our initial visual connection to full sexual contact. Each stage heightens the degree of intimacy between two people as well as increases the sexual tension.

Where holding hands may have once been enough to start your couple's hearts racing, soon they'll want and need more. A hug, a caress, a kiss. Moving slowly through each of these steps will give your story a constant sense of rising sexual tension. Skipping a step or two will do more.

In erotic romance, skipping these steps is a matter of course. We aren't usually writing about first dates and courtship and progressing one step at a time toward the marriage altar. Note that I said "usually" because there are, no doubt, erotic romances that do just that! For the most part, however, we're writing stories where eye-to-body contact is followed by a kiss or a heated embrace.

Moving toward intimacy can be done slowly or at supersonic speed. The pace you use to get your characters there will determine whether your sexual tension heats gradually from a simmer to a boil or blasts into the sky like flames from a furnace.

Scorchers

New York Times best-selling author Linda Howard presents a wonderful workshop, *The Twelve Steps of Intimacy,* based on the work of Desmond Morris. Check it out if you get a chance!

Sensuality vs. Sexuality

The characters in erotic romance will be both *sexual* and *sensual* creatures. Although there's a lot of crossover, as sexuality involves sensuality, the two are not interchangeable. Sexuality is a focus on sex, sexual activity, gratification, etc., while sensuality is about sensual pleasures—including but not limited to sex. (I discuss the use of the senses to evoke sexual tension and to add the oomph to your story that results in reader involvement later in this chapter.)

Does either element need more emphasis than the other? I'd have to say that's totally dependent on the type of story you're writing and the characters who populate your story world. A heroine who is a sensualist will enjoy the tangy aroma of a spoon of lemon sorbet; the feel of the icy-cold dessert melting against her hot tongue; and the zesty, zingy-sweet tang that causes a shiver to run through her. Her dinner partner, on the other hand, a captive audience, is a slave to his physical nature, enjoying her sensuality from a viewpoint centered in sexuality.

Do both elements have a place in erotic romance? Yes, of course. I'd go so far as both *need* to be included. Even though sexuality is a more carnal condition, it's rooted in the sensual enjoyment of touch and corporeal sensation. And when the two are blended together seamlessly, they give a love story the eroticism that can make or break it as an erotic romance.

Slip of the Tongue

Author Jordan Summers looks at sensuality and sexuality this way: "For me, the difference between sexuality and sensuality is that one is a solo journey, taking place internally, while the other is external. Sexuality is explored by the individual—for the individual. Everything that you learn on your journey brings you one step closer to understanding yourself. Sensuality, on the other hand, allows the individual to understand the world around them via the senses."

Brain Sex

Men and women share the most important sex organ of all: the human brain. Inside this single organ, both imagination and fantasies are born—those that offer sexual fulfillment and those that allow us to relive past sexual encounters complete with the sensations of arousal.

When a woman says she's attracted to a man with a good sense of humor who can make her laugh, or to a man who's a good conversationalist and can make her think, she's experiencing the flying of intellectual and mental sparks. That connection is important to women. As physically sexy as a woman may find a man, she is looking for more in a mate. She may enjoy a little boy toy time now and then, but when she's ready to settle down, she'll be more interested in a man who is a good provider and father for her children.

A man, on the other hand, does not want to be fixed up on blind date and told the woman has a good personality. That's a code that signals she may not hit any of his physical buttons. The male brain—and sex drive—is wired to respond in a more carnal fashion. That's not to say men don't bond emotionally with their mates; not at all. But that's rarely their first response upon meeting a new woman.

This reality isn't one that many romance novelists or romance readers want depicted in their books. We're writing female fantasies, and the female fantasy is about bonding on more than a physical level. But because we're writing erotic romance, we know that bond will be made and it will be strong—both emotionally and physically!

Body Language

I attended a writing workshop early in my career—one of several that have stuck with me—where the speaker used audience participants to visually demonstrate how clearly our bodies talk. Body language is often more instructive than the words a character speaks. In fact, body language may be more instructive because bodies rarely lie.

Scorchers

For a great in-depth look at body language, check out *The Complete Idiot's Guide to Body Language* by Peter Andersen (Alpha Books, 2004).

Here's a perfect example. I recently watched a movie that opened with a husband and wife in couples' therapy working through marital issues. They sat in their respective chairs facing the counselor. Both had their legs crossed away from each another. Both had their arms crossed tightly over their chests, their bodies turned slightly to the side. Basically, each was closed off from the other, having left no opening for the other to get close.

On the other hand, think of movies or television shows you may have seen where a woman leans close to a man with whom she's having drinks, where a man reaches across the table to touch her arm. Perhaps they are sitting side by side and the woman crosses her leg toward the man and lets her shoe dangle from her foot. This is an inviting, open pose. Her body is telling him that she's approachable and receptive.

Look at your characters and how you use their body language to increase the sexual tension between them!

Senses: A Set of Five—or Six

Nothing brings a story alive for a reader more than an author's skillful use of the senses. We all experience life through sight, touch, scent, sound, and taste. Our characters are no different—at least they shouldn't be! Their senses play an especially important role in establishing sexual tension because they actively show (rather than passively tell about) one character's awareness of another.

Giving sufficient attention to the senses in any given scene will bring your writing to life and guarantee reader involvement. Let's take a look at ways to use each of the five senses in sex scenes and beyond!

Sultry Looks and Heated Glances

Unless they find themselves touching in the dark, eye contact is the first external connection two characters will make and is often the initial method of determining physical attraction. Characters may have met over the phone or via a means of electronic communication and established a bond or a friendship, but they may be hesitant to fall sight unseen into anything more.

Scorchers

Using the senses is what makes a work sensual. The word *sensual* means "to pertain to the senses."

This isn't to say a character wanting to see another is shallow or looking for a relationship based on a purely physical attraction. There is, however, that thing called chemistry that can't be denied, and about which we'll talk more in a bit.

Touch Me, Feel Me

In erotic romance, the sense of touch is vitally important. Our characters are sexual, sensual beings, involved in activities that are all about feeling. A heated glance from across a crowded room can cause skin to pebble, nipples to harden, shivers to run down a spine—all clichés, but all very real sensations.

In addition to those, we employ the sense of touch to show arousal. I mentioned in Chapter 18 the importance of the skin as a sex organ. Hugging, holding hands, even playing footsie while naked in bed are all ways to use the sense of touch. Sensation play during bondage scenarios—or even without the bondage—are also perfect opportunities to evoke sensory identification in readers while raising the sexual tension between characters.

Breathe Deep

Aromas and scents are very closely connected to tastes. So many of the things we eat have smells that entice us to try them. Characters can be drawn to one another the same way. Take perfume, for example. A woman walks by a man and he catches a whiff of the designer fragrance she's wearing. Or better yet, he catches *her* scent and her pheromones.

In addition to the aromas characters will notice day in and day out, the sex act itself gives an author any number of opportunities to evoke the sense of smell. Soap and shampoo, sweat, the musky sweet odors of skin and especially genitalia. Does your heroine burn incense or candles in her bedroom or bathroom? If your hero works with motors or machines, does he always bear a trace of a chemical odor? If he's a chef, maybe his hands smell like lemon or vanilla with a lingering bite of onion or garlic. Look to your characters for scents distinctive to them to add a unique twist to your story.

Do You Hear What I Hear?

The sense of sound is not limited to conversation and listening to a lover snore—although our characters will of course do a lot of the first! Getting-to-know-you conversations, a quiet intimate tête-à-tête while making love, even arguments and heated discussions will be a part of our stories. Characters will pick up on the tone and timbre of one another's voices, as well as nuances of hidden meaning, mood … the list goes on and on.

Characters will also be in tune to other sounds around them. The rustling of bed sheets, running water, a lover's deep breathing, the sound of the wind through the tree branches overhead, the roar of the ocean. And don't forget the sounds of making love; the gasps and groans and snicks of sticky skin all bring your characters to life and the reader into the room!

Lip-Smacking Good

During the days when I met regularly with a critique group, I was constantly teased about my chapters making my critique partners hungry. I have a thing about putting food into my books and describing in great detail what my characters are eating and drinking. And then there is that oral fixation thing … oh, wait. That's best saved for another confession.

Think about the tastes your characters will experience in a love scene: the salt on one another's skin, for example, along with others that are more earthy. There are flavors with zest, with tang, ones that are your basic bitter, sour, and sweet. Use all of them to give your readers a true taste of your scene!

Scorchers

If you can make a reader's stomach rumble by doing no more than describing the meal a character is eating or by giving a play-by-play complete with sensory detail as a couple flirts and banters their way through cooking dinner, then you've got a solid handle on using the sense of taste.

The Unexplainable

This is my version of that psychic sixth sense. The way a wife is able to finish her husband's sentences or how a husband knows what a wife is about to ask before she ever says a word. That connection, that *knowing*, offers yet another level of sexual tension between your characters.

This isn't necessarily a "sensual" sense, as it's not determined by sight, sound, smell, taste, or feel. It's a gut feeling or an intuitive vibe—a sense that's internal, mentally, emotionally, or psychologically based. If you've experienced it, you know how hard it is to define or describe. It's just … there!

Slip of the Tongue

Author Lydia Joyce shares a wonderful explanation of the differences between sensuality and sexuality: "Sexuality is a miniskirt and a hot car. Sensuality is dinner on the Riviera at dusk. Or rock climbing in Arizona. Or being trapped in a broken-down Volvo thirty miles outside of Cedar Rapids, Iowa. Sexuality is always aimed at the final goal—sex—and the fastest and most sure way of getting there. Sensuality is an awareness between two people that can charge virtually any situation with electricity. While the sexual element is the required foundation, the emphasis is on savoring the voyage at least as much as enjoying the destination. Sensuality is to sexuality what an incredible dessert is to granulated sugar."

Chemistry 101

An intellectual or emotional attraction, one established online via written communication or even over the phone via voice, does not guarantee a couple will experience the chemistry that makes a relationship work. Chemistry is about endorphins. It's that sizzle one person feels for another that has its basis in their unique compatibility, and it's totally unexplainable.

Scorchers

Chemistry isn't necessarily as immediate as sexual tension and attraction, and two characters who share an initial sexual attraction may end up having no chemistry at all—or vice versa!

Consider those who've known one another as friends long before falling in love. Something there drew them together, and a deeper bond was made without either being aware of it happening. Chemistry then began its chain reaction, and the result is love!

The Least You Need to Know

- Conversation provides many opportunities for sexual tension, including innuendo, banter, and double entendres.
- While sexuality is a more physical condition, balancing it with sensuality helps increase a story's eroticism.
- Characters can experience sexual tension both mentally and physically, and their body language is a good indication of their feelings.
- Using the five senses will bring your love scenes to life and add an evocative realism to your prose.
- Chemistry between two people is conveyed through their sexual, emotional, and intellectual attraction.

Part 5

Talk Dirty to Me: Writing Explicit Sex

When applied to a romance novel, the word *erotic* means the intimate scenes between your couple will be explicitly detailed as well as highly charged with both emotion and sensuality. It's a demanding task, one requiring an understanding of the sexual workings of the human body in addition to subtle tricks of the writing trade.

It also requires an author never forget she is writing a love story for a primarily female readership. In Part 5, I get down to the nitty-gritty of writing about sex—finding your own comfort zone, putting body parts into action, the wilder side of the sexual life—and writing it all while using the words erotic romance readers want.

Chapter 17

Lose Your Comfort Zone? Let's Find It!

In This Chapter

- Writing with sexual authority
- Ways to go about researching sex
- Getting in the mood to write the hot stuff
- Dealing with critics and naysayers

Writing erotic romance is not for the faint of heart! If you're antsy when you sit down to write detailed scenes of explicit lovemaking, your discomfort is very likely to show in the finished product. If you're embarrassed at the thought of people you know—as well as those you don't—reading sex scenes you've written, you may not need to be writing erotic romance. Don't give your readers a chance to see the nervous author behind the words on the page. You are your story's expert. You know your plot. You know your characters. Be sure you also know your sex and you don't have a problem writing those pivotal scenes!

The good news is, expanding your personal library of sexual knowledge doesn't require a road trip to your local red-light district. It can be accomplished with the same research methods you use for the rest of your subject matter.

Write What You Know

In Chapter 2, I discussed writing what you know when it comes to choosing the subject matter, theme, setting, careers, etc., for your story and your characters. Now I'm talking about writing what you know about S-E-X. If you're writing sweet or even sensual romances, you can write love scenes with very little description of the physical nitty-gritty. The connection between the characters in such books has a more emotional focus, one that concentrates fully on the internal changes wrought by two people falling in love. The love scenes will be more about feelings and sensations and less about the alignment of body parts.

Erotic romance is different. Yes, our stories also delve deeply into the emotions and character growth of our story people. But the subgenre also requires that sex scenes be explicit while still being vital to the forward motion and dramatic tension of the overall story. If the sex scenes can be removed completely from your novel, or if they can be reduced to a one-sentence synopsis of the act, they wouldn't require this sort of detailed attention. But because the sexual content in erotic romance is necessary for exploring changes in character, maintaining conflict, and advancing the external plot, they require just that. This is why being a "sexpert" is such an important part of your job as an author!

Bottom line: writing about sex is no different from anything else. The larger your base of knowledge, the more authenticity and authority you bring to your work. This subject just happens to be the one that's the most fun to study!

Naughty, Naughty

One thing you never want to do is write an envelope-pushing sexual encounter to impress a reader with your daring or to show off your sexual expertise. Writing erotic romance is not a competition. No prizes are given for the hottest, kinkiest, or most explicit sex scene. Remember, because sex is so incredibly personal, eroticism is in the eye of the beholder. What you or your reviewers may consider sizzling hot may be nothing but sweet to a reader!

If You Don't Know, Ask!

If you want to write about more than what you have personal experience with, you're going to have to get the information somewhere. Yes, we all have wonderful imaginations or we wouldn't be doing what we do. But in some cases, imagination only goes so far!

For example, most of us writing erotic romance are women, and we can only imagine the physical sensations that occur in the male body. That doesn't stop us from writing sex scenes from the male point of view or from describing male body parts that heat and throb without knowing if that's what a man feels when aroused. Instead, we may be resorting to long-accepted descriptions we've read in romances for years without knowing whether or not a man's penis actually does heat and throb. Maybe that's only what sex feels like when on the receiving end!

Men's responses will, of course, be as individual as those of women, but you don't want your male readers to roll their eyes during a sex scene written from the male point of view if it rings false. The same goes for writing from the female point of view should you include sexual acts that might not be up your personal alley but are your heroine's favorites! Being comfortable with writing sex plays a big part in determining your story's authenticity and your reader's ability to identify with your characters' experiences.

Slip of the Tongue

Author Sasha White takes this approach to sexual research: "When I have a list of the exact questions I need answered, I find a chat room and talk to someone. Most people are willing to answer questions when they know I'm honestly interested. Sometimes I give out my Website, or offer up a short story or book as proof I'm for real, and I get very good sources that way. They often read my scenes when I'm done as well, to assure me that I've got it right."

When thinking about who to ask for advice or feedback on your sex scenes, turn to those closest to you such as your significant other, your best girl friend(s), or your best guy friend(s). If you're too embarrassed to discuss the technicalities of sex with your partner, then putting those same technicalities on paper for complete strangers to read may be outside your personal comfort zone, too. If you're completely at ease and can coax the information you're looking for from your significant other, then who better to offer sexual advice!

Scorchers

No best guy friend? No significant other? Drag a family member into service then. Remind him that it's nothing personal. Explain it to him this way: you've been given a machine to operate but you don't have an owner's manual. Can he please help?

If the HBO television series *Sex and the City* did anything, it showed us girlfriends discussing their sex lives as openly and in as much detail as they discussed buying their Manolos. If you have a group of supportive female friends, invite them in for a night of Tex-Mex and margaritas and pick their brains. Just think of all the inspiration to be had in their collective experience!

You say you don't have a significant other of the opposite sex? What about a male friend who knows what you do and would be willing to help you out? If discussing the mechanics of sex and the workings of the male body in person make him uncomfortable, get him alone in a chat room or carry on an e-mail conversation. Do whatever it takes!

If You Can't Ask, Research!

I know what you're saying. Most of us know enough about sexual activity to describe the ins and outs. The information is everywhere—online, on television, on every page of lifestyle and gossip magazines. But nothing in anyone's life is more personal than his or her sexual experience.

And therein lies the rub. Our experiences may be limited and will rarely mirror those of others. To be able to write convincing love scenes, ones that aren't interchangeable from fictional couple to fictional couple, not only do your scenes need to spring from your characters, you as the author need a varied wealth of information and anecdotes on which to draw.

If all you require is your imagination, then good for you! Not everyone is so fortunate. For the rest of us, here are a few research avenues to turn to:

- In-person interviews
- The Internet
- Books and magazines
- Television and movies—even porn!

If you need information on the psychology behind fetishes, find and interview a psychologist who specializes in such. If you need information on the workings of the female body, a gynecologist is the perfect person to ask. If you need information on the BDSM lifestyle, talk to those who live it. Don't think you can't research sexuality by talking about it with experts. It's just like any other story element!

If you can't find someone to interview, the Internet can be a wealth of information. If you've never researched sex on the Internet, you may be in for a surprise. Not to mention a shock. There's absolutely nothing you can't find. I recently came across an online manual developed for a health organization's sex workers that was an invaluable resource. Yes, you often have to dig for what you want, but if you're not put off by pop-up ads displaying naked body parts, there's a good chance you'll find exactly what you're looking for!

Slip of the Tongue

Author Jordan Summers has this to say about research for writing sex scenes: "Primarily, I use the Internet. You can find just about anything on the web. I also read a lot of animal behavior books and non-fiction pieces. A couple of good books on writing love scenes are *The Joy of Writing Sex* by Elizabeth Benedict and *How to Write a Dirty Story* by Susie Bright. Nancy Friday's *My Secret Garden* is a must read, too. There's also Emma Holly's website (www.emmaholly.com), which has wonderful advice for writing steamy scenes."

And don't forget books—those things we had to use for research before the Internet! (Here I'll plug one of my own favorite "how-to" books: *Sex Tips for Straight Women from a Gay Man* by Dan Anderson and Maggie Berman.) There's no end to the articles and books available you can use to research sexual subjects. Of course you can check with bookstores and libraries, but don't forget another great resource: other authors. See what books they're reading and using for their research. The same ones might have the very information you're looking to find!

Just as romantic movies can put us in the mood to write romantic encounters, explicit movies can serve as research by giving us a visual depiction of a sex scene, helping us block out the physical action. If that sounds too analytical, then remember a scene you may have read where instead of wrapping you up in what's happening, the author loses you because you can't figure out or imagine what her characters are doing! A scene in which a man who is 6 feet tall takes a 5-foot-10 woman up against the wall will require different mechanics than a scene where the man is 6-foot-4 and the woman 4-foot-6! Watching it in action is oftentimes the best way to figure it out.

Whether via pornographic movies or fiction, the sex industry can provide a definite education in the technicalities of any number of sex acts and the workings of body parts. Pornography may not portray romantic entanglements, but as authors of erotic romance, we've got that part covered. What we're doing here is researching a major—and required—element of our subgenre; why not take advantage of adult entertainment on which, according to a 2004 story on CBS' *60 Minutes*, Americans spend close to $10 billion a year?

Slip of the Tongue

Author Pamela Clare offers another print resource: "My favorite book on sexuality is *The Guide to Getting It On* by Paul Joannides. It's a sex book that's for women as much as it's for men, and it makes sex fun while at the same time communicating literally everything you want to know—plus some things you didn't know you wanted to know."

If you have several friends also writing erotic romance, you could start your own research swap program. Each of your group could provide one new book to your library every so often and build an enviable set of references!

Boas and Bonbons: Getting in the Mood

For many, writing sexy scenes is a matter of course, as natural as writing dialogue, action, introspection, or exposition. They write their love scenes in a white-hot heat, getting down every nuance the first time through. For others, such scenes start out as somewhat perfunctory, similar to blocking action on a stage. Adding in the emotions and sensory details follows the initial run-through.

I've heard many authors admit that love scenes are the hardest scenes for them to write because of how much has to be conveyed. Beyond the physical pleasure and that intimate connection, we have to include the emotional component—whether the scene is about love, fear, loneliness, etc. And then there's the forward motion of the plot to consider. That's a lot for any author to manage in a scene, but as authors of erotic romance, we also have to place a high emphasis on the eroticism. In the following sections, I offer a few suggestions to help you get in the mood to write some steamy sex scenes!

Use Your Senses: Scents and Mood Music

Aromatherapy helps many authors get into the mood. Scents such as lavender and chamomile provide a relaxing effect. Other aromas offer an uplifting sense of well-being, while others work as aphrodisiacs. If you've never considered aromatherapy as a writing aid, now you have the perfect reason to do so. In fact, why not burn those candles in a softly lit bathroom while soaking in a tub of scented water and make the aroma do double duty?

Before you hop in the tub, be sure to put on some music! I've listened to author friends talk about writing to the beat of hard-driving rock 'n' roll, while others describe how their best writing is done to soft jazz or Celtic music or even Gregorian chants. Many even compile soundtracks for each book they write. Whether it's music to fit a particular scene, music to set a mood, or simply music to help you focus and block out surrounding distractions, you'll never know what works until you give it a try!

More Research: Read a Good Book or Go to a Movie

More than a few authors I know get into the mood to write love scenes by reading erotica. If you need the emotional stimulation, why not watch your favorite romantic movie? Say, *Last of the Mohicans* with Daniel Day-Lewis and Madeleine Stowe? Or *Jerry Maguire* with Renée Zellweger and Tom Cruise? Maybe *Shakespeare in Love* with Gwyneth Paltrow and Joseph Fiennes? Pop your favorite romance in the DVD player, one that gets you in the mood to put your characters in the mood, and get ready to write!

Silence Is Golden

While some authors enjoy or even need music to relax, set a mood, or help them focus, others want complete silence. During the years I wrote while still working full-time, I used to get up around 4 A.M. and write not only in silence but—except for the glow of the computer screen—in total darkness, too. In fact, I still do my best writing under those conditions. Perhaps it will work for you!

Many of us don't have the luxury of complete silence or even solitude when writing. We're sneaking in writing time between homework time, dinner time, carpool time—even putting off husband time and bed time to get in our quota of pages. Even if you've learned to write amidst all those distractions, there are still times when nothing enhances creativity like being alone. Grab every moment you can.

Slip of the Tongue

When talking about getting in the mood to write sex scenes, author Shiloh Walker says, "The biggest help for me is not having anything around to distract me … kids, a lot of noise going on, the TV. I work best with just quiet or some music playing. It's very hard to stay focused on a hot, steamy love scene when your four-year-old is in the bathroom, shouting, "I'm done!"

Chocolate: Nectar of the Gods

Finally, if nothing else works or is available or possible for you, try chocolate! If not chocolate, then drink some wine to relax, tea to soothe, coffee to stimulate … anything to calm you down, jump-start your imagination, or get your juices flowing. Whatever your personal poison or your favorite aphrodisiac, if it helps, indulge! No guilt allowed!

Everyone's a Critic!

We get it from all sides—friends, family, co-workers, neighbors, even complete strangers. Dealing with the fallout (and I don't know anyone who hasn't experienced it at one time or another) can be stressful. The stress we feel as a result of others' opinion of our work or what we do can cause doubts and misgivings as we balance our creative needs with familial and societal expectations. There may even be times when we're forced to choose between the love of our calling and the loves of our lives.

Dealing with the public perception—and misconception—of what we do isn't easy. It's worse when we find ourselves having to justify our work to those who know us best. In a perfect world, everyone would be accepting. But because the world is not perfect and acceptance not guaranteed, it can't hurt to have an arsenal of responses at the ready.

I Can't Face My Friends!

Sure you can! These are the people who know you as well as—or even better than—your family. They are the shoulders you've leaned on when the going has been tough. They know how much you want this, how hard you've worked. So what if you're writing kinky fantasies complete with explicit sex? It's not like they haven't entertained a few of their own! In fact, they would probably love it if you sought their input or picked their brains for story ideas.

What Will My Family Say?

Hopefully your family will be so awed by your creativity and thrilled by your success that they'll be telling complete strangers about your work. Not everyone, however, is lucky enough to have the support of those who are closest to them. At that point, we each have to choose whether to discuss our writing with our family members or to hold it close. In many cases, our work—and our muse—needs the protection.

On the other hand, no matter how supportive family members may be, there are situations where even they are unable to sing your praises or share their excitement over your success. Perhaps your husband works for an extremely conservative employer who would not be accepting of your writing focus. All of us have to make decisions in such cases. I've known authors who have taken pseudonyms to put distance between their personal and professional lives for this very reason. There is no blanket solution, no right or wrong answer. This is one we all have to work out for ourselves.

Strangers Say the Strangest Things

You think I'm kidding? For some reason, people we don't know often have no qualms about saying what's on their mind. Take a look at some responses other authors have received, and see if you're not in good company!

Author Pamela Clare shared: "I'm a journalist by profession and have won national awards for my work. The weirdest thing anyone has ever said to me is, 'If you leave journalism to write romance, won't you miss contributing to the world?' As if writing [romance] means no longer contributing to the world. Then there was the man who asked me if I masturbate while I write. It would be a hard thing to do since I need my fingers to type …."

Jordan Summers once had the following encounter: "She said, with the expression of someone who's just bitten into an unripe persimmon, 'I wouldn't want your sex life. It must be tiring to do all those things, and disgusting.'"

And embarrassing moments will happen, too, as Jaid Black notes: "I remember being spotted in the Atlanta airport. A woman ran up to me and asked if I was Jaid Black. I said I was and gave the very enthusiastic woman an autograph, then stood there while her husband snapped photos of us together. Of course, this drew other passengers' attention. Pretty soon everyone wanted to know who I was. The excited fan announced, 'She writes the greatest dirty books ever!' I about died."

And be prepared for comments such as this one Karin Tabke heard: "I was told by a married acquaintance that he was available as my research dummy. I politely declined. Mostly, when people learn I write erotic romance their eyebrows go up in surprise, then very quickly they come down in that sneaky, shady way, and always followed with the statement, 'Wow, I didn't know you wrote smut.' Then this inevitable question follows: 'Where can I get your book?'"

Church Ladies, Sewing Circles, and the PTA

What we write is not for children. I'm not about to argue that it is. But we *are* tapping into the same sexually prevalent popular culture kids are exposed to in movies, music, videos, games, and on television. The difference is that our novels are about the effort and care it takes to develop a relationship. We show the best things about the sexual experience—the way a man should treat a woman, the way a woman should treat a man. Explained that way along with the caveat that our books are adult reading material, what educator or parent could object?

Slip of the Tongue

"Obviously, I write for mature audiences, so I prefer for kids not to read my work, but it wouldn't be the end of the world if they did either. Parents will buy their kids violent video games, let them watch movies where people get hacked up left and right, but go into an uproar if a major network so much as hints at two people making love. Okay, sorry, but I don't get that mentality," says author Jaid Black.

As romance authors, we are writing about love, about romance, about couples giving one another security and comfort within the bonds of committed relationships. We are showing female readers that men will be there for them for more than just sex. We write about couples who communicate, who never purposely hurt each another, who kiss and make up when they do one another wrong. We write about healthy, positive sexual love, not abusive, humiliating, degrading encounters. How can anyone protest our writing of romantic love stories in that context?

The Least You Need to Know

- As with all your plot elements, you need to do enough research to be an expert on your story's sexual content.
- Don't overlook anyone you know as a possible source for answering questions about sex.
- Tapping into all your senses could very well help you get into the mood to write sexy lovemaking scenes.
- Having a plan in place to deal with critics of your fictional subject matter can get you out of the occasional jam.

Chapter 18

Say What? Flowery Language and Four-Letter Words

In This Chapter

- Becoming familiar with the human body
- Sexually appropriate content
- Emotionally romancing your readers
- The importance of choosing the right words

Authors of erotic romance often use explicit words, expressions, and phrases not found in nonerotic romance novels. Familiarity with the definitions and usage of these stronger terms, as well as with the workings of the human body and the differences between the genders from an emotional perspective is vital to an erotic romance author's authority.

Traditionally, romance novels are known for their soft, sensual, and often euphemistic prose. Erotic romance, while occasionally employing such conventions, often necessitates a sharper, grittier tone due to the edgy content of the stories.

Because of that, some language used in this chapter might be offensive to some readers. If you're a regular writer or reader of erotic romance, you probably won't bat an eye at such words, but for some, the information in this chapter might be a bit much, so proceed at your own risk.

And remember! The truth is in the details. Don't scrimp! Don't gloss over! Give your reader an eagle-eye view of the action as well as a mile-walked-in-the-character's-shoes emotional experience, and you'll have a fan for life!

Choose Your Words Carefully

As I mentioned briefly in Chapter 16, the most important sex organ shared by both men and women is the brain. The body may be what rises to the occasion, but without the brain to engage in lust and put the imagination to work, there would be no such thing as sexual tension—the driving force of romance.

Whether writing romantic or sexually intense scenes, always choose carefully the language for your characters' thoughts and dialogue. Their use of either flowery or four-letter words will reveal to your readers much about who they are. Think of the dichotomy between a character's deeply raw internalization and his external speech that's as sweet as it gets. Or one whose thoughts about his lover are beautifully poetic, but he can't put what he's thinking into anything but crude and suggestive words.

It doesn't matter if it's spoken dialogue or internal musings, the words your story people use are vitally important to their characterization. Don't reach for the first word that comes to mind or settle for overused clichés or meaningless expressions. Use only those that are appropriate to your characters and fit their unique vocabularies!

Writing Your Hero

Much the same way you need to understand that pressing down on the accelerator makes a car go and pushing down on the brake pedal makes a car stop, you need to understand the workings of the male body. The brake and accelerator are the stop-and-go mechanisms we use to operate the vehicle, but dozens of other parts beneath the hood must be functioning or else the pedals are useless.

It's the same with a man. We all know that the penis is the "Tab A" of the "Tab A into Slot B" expression referring to sexual intercourse. But because most of us writing erotic romance are female, and thus, don't own the equipment, we often forget about the rest of what makes the male motor run.

I hear you arguing already. Why do you need to know more than you already do about the male reproductive system? It's not as if you're writing a biology text. Well, there's a good chance you don't! But a lot of authors do want to understand the internal as well as the external workings. They may not put all of what they know on the page, but having it at the ready gives them a better handle on how to get their hero's engine started and keep it revved up. So stick around and find out what makes a man go!

Slip of the Tongue

When asked for his top five pet peeves about editing erotic romance, Virgin Books (Black Lace, Nexus) editor Adam Nevill gave me this response: "Dreadful description: overwriting during adult scenes, with a particular loathing for anatomical descriptions of genitals; or lazy description in which figures of speech and clichés are used—'It was a mind-blowing orgasm'. And don't send in any throbbings and pulsatings either."

What Do You Call It?

Penis and testicles. Cock and balls. Two turntables and a microphone. However you refer to it, it's best to avoid euphemistic references and call it what it is. This is erotic romance. We can take it. Readers would much rather read the word *penis* than to have the organ referred to as a purple-helmeted warrior of love!

Most important, consider whose viewpoint you're writing in. How would your hero refer to his genitals? A cock? A dick? Billy and the boys? What would his lover call it? If she's a contemporary heroine, she will most likely be as familiar with anatomical slang as your hero. If she is a medieval maiden, she may have witnessed the mating of livestock but be uncertain about or uncomfortable with making any reference to her lover's sexual organs at all.

Naughty, Naughty

Because your story people are the ones doing the thinking and speaking, it's your job to be sure their sexual references are in character. And really, do you know anyone alive, man or woman, who has ever seriously used the term "purple-helmeted warrior of love"?

How Does It Work?

I know an author who, to write accurately about the male sexual experience, once asked her husband what it felt like to have sex. His response? "Good!"

I said it in Chapter 17, and I'll say it again here: research. Talk to men; read about men; research and study men. Ask them about the tingles and the throbbing and the heat that have for so long been staples in romance novel love scenes written by women. Find out if these are the sensations men feel or if their enjoyment is of a totally different nature. If nothing else, you might come away with a new appreciation of the male body!

Pleasure Centers

If you think only women have erogenous zones, think again. What feels good to a woman feels good to a man. Neck, earlobes, nipples, lips, fingers, toes, the small of a back, the back of a knee. The skin is our largest sexual organ, and the nerves are highly sensitive to texture, touch, and temperature. Don't think men feel nothing except what goes on between their legs. They can be aroused by fingers stroking their neck or their chest as easily as by fingers stroking their driveshaft!

The Emotional Component

It's true that men are physical beings. That doesn't mean they don't experience romantic or loving emotions; they do. But they are not women, and their journey from sex to love is as unique to their gender as a woman's is to hers. I once had a man explain it to me this way: women make love because they are emotionally involved; men make love to determine if they want to become emotionally involved.

Of course, that won't be every man's (or woman's!) reality. An alpha hero may be more focused on a mate who is his match physically, while a beta may be looking for an emotional connection. In traditional romance, readers have come to expect the latter more often than not because romance is primarily a female fantasy. But we're talking about erotic romance, in which our female characters are just as likely to fall into bed for purely physical reasons and find themselves emotionally involved after the fact, er, act.

Scorchers

If you love reading about and writing real men in erotic romance, here's a tip to consider: a man fighting his emotions to the bitter end provides for great ongoing sexual tension!

For years there has been an ongoing debate among romance authors on writing real versus fantasy men and real versus fantasy romance. Many argue that romance is escapism and reality doesn't belong in the genre. After all, readers don't want to read about heroines turned into football widows by sports-obsessed heroes! Others prefer to portray men as close to the bone as they can. Fortunately, there are readers who love both kinds. As long as you're true to your characters and your story, you can't go wrong.

Women Writing Men

Getting into a man's head can be tricky business. All our people-watching and eavesdropping research won't do us a bit of good when it comes to figuring out how a man thinks. The one thing we can do, however, is be sure our fictional men don't sound like our fictional women. Read these two examples and decide which type of thoughts ring truest to you as an author:

> *Example #1:* Brandon stood staring out the conference room window at the street six stories below, pondering his partner's question. Was his relationship with Rachel serious?
>
> Right now, he couldn't even think about serious. Rachel was great. No doubt. But he was putting in eighty-plus hours a week and was due to spend the next month in Tokyo. It was going to be tough dealing with the language barrier in addition to the stress of getting the job done.
>
> Adding a woman to the mix would divide his already limited attention even more. Maybe one day when he didn't have to give so much to the job they could make what they had permanent. Now just wasn't the time. Rachel would understand.

> *Example #2:* Brandon stood staring out the conference room window at the street six stories below, pondering his partner's question. Was his relationship with Rachel serious?
>
> Without a doubt, she was the best woman he'd ever known. He loved the breathlessness in her voice when she answered his calls and the twinkle in her eyes when she caught sight of him entering a room. His heart sped up every time he thought of spending his life with her.
>
> He couldn't wait to get back from Tokyo so they could settle their future. Being with her was what mattered most in his life. Serious? Oh, yeah.

There's nothing inherently wrong with either example. The first shows a man focused on his career and establishing himself so he has more to offer a woman. The second example illustrates a man more in touch with his emotions. You can write either type of hero as long as his external actions are consistent with his internal thoughts. While a certain percentage of readers may prefer example #1, you still have a win-win situation because another percentage wants example #2!

Writing Your Heroine

If you think a man's body is a tough one to learn about, a woman's is even tougher. While most men respond similarly to physical (or visual) stimuli, women are highly individual. One woman may not be able to relax enough to achieve orgasm if her roommates are home, while another woman couldn't care less if her best girlfriend walked in on her during coitus. One woman may not be comfortable unless she is in a dark room beneath a sheet, while another woman prefers lights on, and still another wants a mirror on the ceiling. And then there are our bodies. A hard touch here for one, a soft touch there for another. It's a wonder men ever figure us out!

Sensational Sensations

You don't want to overlook the female erogenous zones any more than you do the male's. Yes, sex feels wonderful, the sensation of arousal, well, arousing. There is the release of moisture that eases the way, the rush of blood to the genital area, and the subsequent swelling that occurs. But the closeness of two bodies pressed together and the skin-to-skin contact can be an equally fulfilling part of intimacy for women.

These physical sensations often spur on ones that are purely emotional. Whether it's the fantasy of being forcefully seduced, the desire to feel needed by someone who seems to have it all, or even the empowering sense of control in an explosive situation, be sure to explore the connection between the sensations of your heroine's body and those of her mind.

Naughty, Naughty

All women are not created equal. Studies or surveys may show that the majority of women are easily brought to orgasm this way or that way, but women are individuals. What works for one heroine may not work for another, and it's your hero's job to find her hot spots without relying on what the experts say!

A Perfect Body

Body shapes and sizes may be more of a concern for contemporary heroines than for others simply because of our cultural obsession with appearance. That said, a heroine in an erotic romance comes to the table with a fairly high level of self-confidence. She knows what she wants sexually, and even if she's hesitant, she's not going to be stopped by a few extra pounds on her hips. Neither will she be stopped by a boyish figure that's not as lush as she might like. That sexual confidence is what matters to the hero. Give him honest desire, and he's there, ready to go.

Erotic romance heroines, just like real life heroines, come in all shapes and sizes. And sure, a heroine may have issues with one thing or another about her looks. But unless her body image is a major plot point in your story, it's best left out of bed.

Scorchers

Remember! Our heroines are sexual beings—whether experienced or not—and they aren't going to let a little cellulite get in the way of their having fun!

Women Writing Women

As well as we know our own bodies, one thing is certain: what works for one of us when it comes to sexual pleasure may not work for another. You can base your heroine's sexuality on your own experience, or you can experiment with what for you is the unknown and have your work vetted should you have any concerns about whether or not it rings true.

However you write your heroines, remember to …

- Keep the characterization consistent.
- Keep the sex true to the scene.
- Keep the author out of the equation.

Writing the Sex!

No, erotic romance is not all about sex. Yes, erotic romance is all about sex. How can I be so contradictory, you ask? Well, an erotic romance novel is a romance novel. As discussed in Chapter 1, a romance novel is no different from any other novel in its basic structure. It demands conflict; an arcing plot with subplots often woven in; well-developed protagonists and possibly antagonists, each with their own goals and motivations; and a setting your readers can visualize—all the elements of any good story. Because it's a romance novel, it also requires a romance and the genre's trademark sexual tension. And because it's an erotic romance novel, it also requires sex.

Scorchers

The sexual content in an erotic romance plays a vital role, perhaps more so than in any other fiction genre.

That requirement for sex is what defines the subgenre much in the same way the inclusion of paranormal elements define the paranormal subgenre. It does not mean the books are all about sex anymore than paranormal romances are all about witches and warlocks. The books are love stories. They focus on a couple's journey from their first meeting or first attraction or first awareness of romantic possibilities to happily-ever-after. Along the way, much of what they discover about themselves—whether individually or as a mated pair—is learned through their intimate encounters.

In the books we write, sex works as a vehicle for characterization, for moving forward the plot's dramatic tension, and for continually increasing the conflict. It demands attention for the simple fact that it's a driving force of the book. So let's look at sex!

Fore! Play!

Foreplay is more than a hero making sure a heroine is properly aroused before penetration. Foreplay begins with sexual tension. It can be as subtle as a heated glance filled with sexual intent, or as bold as a scorching kiss beneath the mistletoe at the company Christmas party. The hero and heroine of an erotic romance are headed to bed. That much is a given. The looks, the touches, the flirting, the want, and the wait—it's all foreplay. Every bit of it.

Don't wait till your characters are naked to get foreplay started. The earlier it begins, the more fun they'll have when they get there!

Self-Help

Whether brought on by frustration or fantasy, masturbation is a staple of erotic romance. I opened my Harlequin Blaze, *The Sweetest Taboo,* with Erin Thatcher in her bed getting herself off to thoughts of Sebastian Gallo, and Sebastian in his shower taking care of business with Erin on his mind. Additionally, one character masturbating for an onlooking character's pleasure can make for an arousing scene.

Whether as a shared or singular activity, don't hesitate to let your characters take matters into their own hands should the need arise.

In and Out

Missionary position. Doggy style. Woman on top. A hero backing his heroine into the shower wall. A heroine in her hero's lap behind the wheel of his car. There's no end to the situations we can create for our characters to engage in sexual intercourse.

But remember this: it's not the position or the location that makes the scene erotic or edgy. It's what's at stake for the characters, the risks they're taking, the conflict to which they're closing their eyes that sends such a consummation scene into envelope-pushing territory. Be fierce in forcing your characters to face what troubles them—even during sex. The end result will be worth it.

Scorchers

For many readers, no matter how much sexual play of other sorts has gone before, the first consummation scene is the most important sex scene of all. I know authors who work and rework this single intimate scene more than any other to get it just right. Keep that in mind when planning out when and where your couple will experience intercourse for the first time!

Open Wide!

How much of the reality of oral sex you deal with when writing is up to you. You can keep the act all about pleasure and forget the sore jaws, the threat of teeth, the gag reflex, the acquired tastes, or you can let your heroine decide on the spur of the moment whether to swallow or spit. How does she make her decision? Does your hero feel rejected one way or the other? Does he feel that he's failed as a lover if he can't bring his heroine to orgasm orally?

Sex is never simple. It's complicated and it's messy, and how your characters deal with the various acts as well as the aftermath can reveal much about who they are. Never pass up a chance to deepen your story's characterization through sex. And that's saying a mouthful. (Sorry. Couldn't help it!)

The Back Door

Anal sex, virtually unthinkable in traditional romance novels, is, if not *de rigueur*, then at least accepted as mainstream in the erotic subgenre. For many authors, the edginess associated with such an activity offers an opportunity to dig deeply into her characters' psyches and explore whether or not they have an adventurous streak, how far they're willing to go and why, the extent of their trust, or their willingness to experiment with what they may have long considered taboo. When written well, these scenes can run the gamut from raw and gritty to seductively arousing.

Naughty, Naughty

Just remember, as with all sexual activity, the choice to engage must come from your characters and be driven by their story, their conflict, their motivations, etc. The last thing they want is an author intruding in their sex lives because of consumer demand!

Watch Your Language! Or Don't ...

In erotic romance, there are few if any limitations on the language you use when writing your love scenes, as long as you are faithful to your characters, their world, and their story, and you have your editor's and publisher's support. But how you use that freedom in your writing makes the difference. Are you using slang or strong language to be derogatory or empowering?

One of the erotic romance authors I first fell in love with was Shannon McKenna. Her work is rich and dark, and she doesn't shy away from using strong language. She's also the first author I read who used the "c" word in a love scene. Yes, a love scene. It was spoken by her hero to her heroine during the heat of the moment, and it was nothing if not romantic. Shannon and I talked about the language she used, and she explained to me that she did so to reclaim the word and to rid it of its derogatory connotation, giving her characters—not the word—the true power.

I've experimented a lot with the words my characters use during love scenes. For example, whether my heroes are vocalizing or internalizing, I have a hard time with them using clinical or anatomical terms for the female body because I, personally, don't consider those words evocative or sexy. As a reader, they pull me out of the scene as much as metaphoric euphemisms involving flowers. As an author, I haven't yet found such terms to fit the heroes I've written. Your mileage will vary, of course. Just be sure to stay true to your characters with any word choices you make!

Scorchers

Authors of erotic romance are allowed more freedom with language than were our genre's founding mothers, but such freedom creates a bit of a paradox. Just because you can use the words *labia* or *vagina* in your text doesn't mean you should if it's not in character for your hero to do so. If he's more the type of man to use a slang reference or not to name body parts at all, then that's your number-one consideration when putting words into his mouth!

Purple Prose Don't Play Here

Romance novels have traditionally been written for women and by women, and over the years, authors have employed certain keywords and phrases to shortcut sexual descriptions. Earlier I mentioned the purple-helmeted warrior of love; I was only halfway kidding.

While the genitalia of the genre's heroes often seems to have been forged in a blacksmith's shop (steel, rod, sword, etc.), the genitalia of the genre's heroines seems to have been grown in a garden (petals, blossoms, buds, etc.).

For the most part, readers of erotic romance aren't big fans of these keywords and shortcuts. They prefer their authors use slang or anatomical terms and avoid purple prose. Still not sure of the difference? Take a look at these two examples:

> *Example #1:* Rachel spread her legs, her intimate petals opening and glistening with her sexual dew. Brandon leaned closer and pressed his lips to her bud of desire.
>
> *Example #2:* Rachel spread her legs, her sex opening, moisture slicking her folds. Brandon leaned closer and sucked her clit between his lips.

The thing is, you want each of your stories to be unique, fresh, and as individual as your characters. If you resort to overused phrases or clichés rather than searching for meaningful words or the perfect expression for your characters to use, that won't happen. You'll blend in rather than stand out, and that's not what any author wants!

Slip of the Tongue

Best-selling author Sara Donati says of overused words and expressions: "Genitalia, erogenous zones and specific acts aren't the only place where the unmotivated, uncomfortable or lazy writer will resort to clichés. There is a list of words that have been so overused that they should be retired, maybe permanently. Silken thighs, raven tresses, sensual anything—these phrases have been stripped of any meaning they might have once had. Now they are nothing more than placeholders, and funny placeholders, at that. When the author resorts to these terms, you really have come to the place where it would be possible—and preferable—to substitute 'and then they had sex' for the whole extended scene."

Expletives Can Make for Good Pillow Talk

Earlier in the chapter I mentioned reclaiming sexual slang that's often derogatory and taking away the power of such words by giving them to our characters to use in sexual situations. Readers of erotic romance understand this. They are only critical when such words seem to have no purpose but shock value or are out of character.

If, in the throes of passion, your hero uses the F word to tell your heroine what he aches to do to her, be sure you've set him up as a man for whom such language comes naturally. Don't throw sexual slang into your work simply because you can. If those words are coming out of your hero's mouth or filling his head, they need to fit the man you've painted him to be.

That said, if such language *is* in character, don't hesitate to let him speak his mind. Your heroine will believe crudely uttered raw emotion long before she'll buy poetry from a poser!

Give Your Reader What She Wants

What about your reader and her expectations? What does she want from an erotic love scene? Let's take a look at two examples. The first is written for a sensual romance, the second for an erotic romance. Both, however, are fully realized love scenes.

> *Example #1:* Standing in front of the bathroom mirror, Rachel caught sight of Brandon's impatience reflected in his gaze. She was getting ready for bed, and he reached up to help her, sliding the straps of her bra from her shoulders, baring her before taking her into his hands. She loved the feel of his palms skating over her skin, and she responded with a sigh and with a shiver when he pushed against her. She leaned forward, the breath of cool air against her thighs quickly replaced by the warmth of his body as he rid her of the rest of her clothes and entered her, loving her.

> *Example #2:* Standing in front of the bathroom mirror, Rachel caught sight of Brandon's reflected gaze. She was late getting to bed, and his impatience showed. He reached up to slide the straps of her bra from her shoulders and freed her breasts. Her nipples tightened when he palmed them, and she shivered with an almost surreal pleasure at the press of his hard cock between her cheeks. She wiggled, and he pulled her panties aside, wrapping his hand around his shaft, stroking through her slick folds, finding her entrance, and driving into her so fully that she wanted to die with the pleasure.

Although both versions reveal the same actions and emotions, the first leaves a lot to the imagination while the second offers the reader a more intimate involvement with the act.

Don't Forget You're Writing for Women!

Women reading erotic romance are open-minded about the portrayal of sex acts in their books. In fact, most would prefer their authors skip the euphemistic references and refer to body parts and describe sexual encounters if not clinically, then by using accepted slang. That doesn't mean you can skip the emotional component while you're skipping the smithing and gardening allusions! Although you may not be using soft prose or metaphors, you still have to touch your readers' hearts.

Earlier in the chapter I talked about the different ways each gender handles emotional involvement. These differences are to be celebrated. They are the differences that have kept our species going for centuries. They help define your heroes and your heroines as story people with whom your readers can identify, and they help you avoid writing interchangeable characters. These differences also make for wonderful writing tools. Whether you choose to play up the distinctions between the genders or focus on the individual diversity that makes each character unique, always keep your story's emotional component in high gear!

> **Naughty, Naughty**
>
> Don't write your book's love scenes with the critics looking over your shoulder. Write them from the characters, and write from the heart.

The Least You Need to Know

- While traditional romance often employs softer, euphemistic prose, erotic romance allows authors to use language with a grittier tone.
- The sexual language your characters use must reflect who they are and not be word choices you as the author make on their behalf simply because erotic romance allows you that leeway.
- In erotic romance, there are fewer sexual taboos than in traditional romance, but you must consider your characters when employing them.
- No matter how much explicit detail you include in your sex scenes, you must give the same attention to the emotional component.

Chapter 19

Intimacy: The Character/Reader Connection

In This Chapter

- Employing craft elements to draw in your reader
- Understanding how, why, and when to break the rules of grammar
- Tips for preventing your characters from becoming caricatures
- Another visit with sexual tension

As an author, you have several tricks at your disposal to create a bond between your readers and your characters, and each is accomplished with the craft choices you make while you write. Putting your writing tools to work behind the scenes guarantees that you give your reader what she's looking for on the page, and offering her every opportunity to connect with your characters will heighten her enjoyment of your story.

But being conscious of craft is too much like homework, you say! You don't like to think about what you do! All you want is to put your story on paper in your words as it comes to you!

Believe it or not, I want that, too. The funny thing is that many of you writers probably use these tricks as a matter of course, never thinking about employing them intentionally at all. I'm simply offering them here for those who might not be aware that there *are* specific elements of craft you can use to deepen the connection between your characters and your readers. So let's take a look at a few ways to put craft to work to create not only a compelling read, but to intensify that vital intimacy.

Going Deep with Point of View

Getting into your characters' heads as deeply as you can is essential in bringing them to life. It can make the difference between your reader feeling as if she's reading about her best friends or feeling as if she's reading about strangers she couldn't care less about. Obviously, your goal is to draw her in so she feels she's a part of your characters' lives. And one of the best craft tools for doing so is deep point of view.

def•i•ni•tion

Deep point of view is an intensely penetrating third-person viewpoint with a first-person feel. It is akin to being inside a character's head and experiencing only his thoughts and feelings.

Simply put, writing with *deep point of view* means your character is the one narrating the story. He (or she) is using his words, whether colloquialisms or urban slang, and his method of speaking, whether with a patois or a certain cadence, as well as injecting his outlook on life into what he says. You do this not only in his external dialogue, but in his internal thoughts as well. When in a character's viewpoint, you are writing the world as seen through his or her eyes, and your reader is reading the same.

Author Kathleen Nance explains deep point of view this way: "It means that when you are writing in a character's viewpoint everything comes from that character: word choice, what he notices in the scene (and what he ignores), thought patterns, opinions. It means not using big words if your character is simple minded or avoiding slang if your character is a stickler English language teacher. It means using jargon and similes and metaphors that have meaning to your character. It means, if you are in the viewpoint of your villain, he's not thinking about how evil he is, but rather how much fun it is to hear people scream. It means not having a character mull over things he takes for granted, even if that information is something the reader needs to know. Find another way to get it in."

Let's look at a few specific tips for pulling this off with almost no effort at all!

Pronouns Are Your Friend

I'll admit to one of my personal pet reading peeves: I hate being in a character's viewpoint and reading his or her name over and over again—especially when it's an introspective scene and the character is alone or having a conversation with only one other person.

How often do we think of ourselves by our own names? Never, right? Then why would a character do so when in his own point of view—and do so repeatedly? After you've established who your viewpoint character is (and it only takes one mention of his or her name to do that), move into his head and think with his thoughts—not yours.

Read these two examples:

> *Example #1:* The slam of the front door to his condo echoed, leaving Brandon alone with the emptiness he'd tried to leave at the office. Brandon was damn tired of thinking. He'd had two months' worth of thinking. Brandon was ready for action, for a battle, for a brawl.
>
> *Example #2:* The slam of the front door to his condo echoed, leaving Brandon alone with the emptiness he'd tried to leave at the office. He was damn tired of thinking. He'd had two months' worth of thinking. He was ready for action, for a battle, for a brawl.

See how tiring it gets in the first paragraph to read Brandon's name three times when we know full well who he is? Even if you've gone several paragraphs without mentioning his name, you haven't changed point of view. There's no way your reader has forgotten who's doing the thinking. Give her credit for being smart and keeping up. She doesn't need the constant reminders!

Scorchers

Take a look at books as you read them, especially ones in which you feel a distance between yourself and the characters. Check to see if the author has used pronouns or if she's overused her characters' names. Doing so can often push readers away, causing them to feel as if they're on the outside looking in instead of being involved in your story.

Keep Up the Internal Monologue

Our thoughts reveal so much about us. Fortunately, we're the only one with access to them! Not so with our characters. Everything they think is there on the page for the reader to know—or at least everything you want her to know is there!

Internalization can be used to reveal a number of things. Here are just a few examples:

- The process of elimination a hero uses to narrow down an important decision.
- The list of reasons a heroine comes up with to avoid returning a phone call.
- A hero's thoughts about booze, baseball, and babes.
- A heroine's feelings about cowboys, cats, and kissing.
- The moment a hero knows he's no longer single.
- The moment a heroine realizes she's fallen in love.

Internalization, along with action and dialogue, help us learn who a person is. That doesn't mean a character is 100 percent complete or even sure of who they are. It does mean we as readers get to make that discovery with them. And isn't that the best part of reading a book?

Grammar Purists Be Gone

Be honest. Whether in e-mails, casual conversations, or even when lost in thought, none of us use proper sentence construction or follow all the rules of grammar perfectly. So why would our characters? Short, choppy snippets or even single-word responses get the job done—especially when in deep point of view.

Don't believe me? Which of these seems more natural?

> *Example #1:* Brandon could not believe his boss had just asked him to work over the weekend when he had planned a romantic getaway with Rachel. "I'm sorry, Stan, but I have a conflict."
>
> *Example #2:* Unbelievable. Working over the weekend? So much for his getaway with Rachel. "Sorry, Stan. No can do."

See what I mean? Now, there's not a thing grammatically wrong with the first example. It's stiff in its grammatical correctness, though. The second example, filled as it is with incomplete sentences, gives more immediacy and a realistic flavor to Brandon's thoughts and dialogue, not to mention it reveals the frustration he's feeling. Don't be correct because it's the right thing to do. Do the right thing because it makes your story better!

Naughty, Naughty

I'm not advocating a total abandonment of grammatical rules. Not all scenes will be written in a deep third-person viewpoint. You may use an omniscient voice when writing exposition, or you may use a secondary character as a disinterested narrator. Save your rule-breaking for times you're using deep point of view to maximize the impact.

What's Your Hurry?

Pacing is a funny thing. First, there's the length of your sentences. Then there's the length of your scenes. There's rhythm: fast, slow, smooth, choppy. There are word choices. Languorous words. Dull words. Action-packed words. Pacing, believe it or not, can say a lot about your characters.

Here. I'll show you:

> *Example #1:* Brandon stared off into the distance, his lashes drifting down as he watched the rolling waves spill onto the sand like paint onto a canvas, picking up the same palette of colors the sun picked up in Rachel's hair.
>
> *Example #2:* Brandon's gaze snapped to the left. To the right. Monitor to monitor. NYSE up. NASDAQ down. Crap. Hell of a day. Hell of a night ahead. Rachel had bailed a week ago. She couldn't take his eighty-hour weeks.
>
> *Example #3:* Brandon scoped out the woman as she eased her very fine ass onto the stool at the bar and wasted no time making his move. He'd spent six months surrounded by heat, poverty, and bugs as big as his arm. It was time to surround himself with her.

Not only do those sentences establish the pace of your scene, the pacing in each says a lot about Brandon. He's an artistic daydreamer; he's a workaholic; he's a bad boy who needs to come to bed.

Scorchers

Don't discount pacing as a way to establish a bond between your reader and your story people.

Create Characters, Not Caricatures

The way you write your characters can make the difference in whether or not they come alive or just lie flat on the page. A flat character is fine if you're in grade school and folding up a construction paper person to ship around the world for a geography project. (And how many of us did that at one time or another!) But we're all grown up here, and we want our characters to be muscled, 6-foot-2, 210, with bright blue eyes and coffee-colored hair. Oh, wait. That's just me. Ahem. But you get my point.

I've already talked about developing characters by giving them fully realized back stories and active, meaningful lives complete with interfering and well-intentioned friends and family. But how can we use elements of craft to make them even more real for our readers? Let's examine several tools of the writing trade.

Let Your Characters Do the Talking

Say Brandon works as a member of a pit crew for a racing team. Which of these descriptions of Rachel would make more sense in his viewpoint?

> *Example #1:* The feminine heel that hit the concrete floor had to be at least three inches high, the leg above long and sleek. She stood in front of the car, soft feminine curves outlined against the metallic frame. A gold watch winked like Christmas tree lights where it circled her slender wrist.

> *Example #2:* The feminine heel that hit the concrete floor had to be at least three inches high, the leg above long, formula-sleek, and way out of his league. She stood in front of the car, soft feminine curves against aerodynamic lines. A gold watch winked like an amber countdown light where it circled her slender wrist.

See how the descriptors used in the second example are more in keeping with the way Brandon would think? Always, always, *always* let your characters do the talking, using words and phrases that fit the person you've created. A rancher might think of a woman as being as feisty as a filly. A sports nut might brag to his buddies that he scored more than a touchdown the night before, wink, wink. Think about the characters you're writing in your current manuscript. Are you letting them do the talking?

Idiosyncrasies: Learn to Love Them

I love the strange but true habits people have. I'll tell a tale on my husband, knowing he won't mind: he is right-handed and does everything with his right hand except eat. Why does he eat with his left? Because when he was a child and his mother set the table, she placed the fork on the left of his plate, and he thought that meant he had to use his left hand. Kids. Go figure. But this has stuck with him his entire life.

Giving quirks to your story people makes them real. We don't want to read about characters who are too perfect. We'll identify better with a hero who has a ridiculous fear of clowns than with a hero who has no fears at all. Giving unique traits to your characters will help them—and you—stand out in the crowd!

People-Watching *Is* Research!

One of my favorite things to do when I worked away from home was to take my lunch hour in one of the public areas in the city's underground tunnel system and people-watch. I would choose a table from any number of food courts or open-air restaurants and, with my laptop and paperwork spread out in front of me, pretend to be lost in thought instead of busy researching character traits! Seeing people in a hurry or taking their time, watching their expressions while they talked, and studying how some made eye contact and others stared at the ground kept my well of character traits filled to the brim.

Here's a tip: pay attention to people you don't know as much as to people you do. You already have an idea what to expect from your friends and family. Now it's time to observe and learn from strangers. Look for commonalities. Look for unique traits. Borrow—no—flat out steal anything you can. And if I see the left-handed eating thing in anyone's book? I'll know where you got it!

Naughty, Naughty

When saddling your story people with fun and quirky habits, don't assign them off the cuff or solely for effect. If the quirk doesn't fit the character but is, instead, an obvious case of author intrusion, your reader will be the first to point her finger and say, "A-ha!"

Eavesdropping Is Research, Too!

Listen to the way people talk. Not only the words they choose, but how they place emphasis on certain ones within a sentence—if they even use a sentence at all. Maybe they shortcut their thoughts or stumble over words until a friend fills in the blanks. Do they use contractions? Do they talk with their hands? What sort of cadence or rhythm do they speak with?

Now, write your dialogue just like that. Make your characters sound like real people sound. No reader wants to feel as if she's intruding on a stilted conversation. She wants to settle in for a night of good, juicy gossip. Give it to her!

Let Gender Do the Talking

When you're eavesdropping (it's okay—I just gave you permission to do so), I want you to pay special attention to how women talk and how men talk, not only in a one-on-one situation, but also in a group. Think about the following while you eavesdrop, er, do your research:

- Is one gender more animated than the other?
- Is there competition for the floor within a small group?
- Do women tend to huddle close and whisper more often than men?
- Are men louder when they talk about sports and more stern when discussing business?
- Does either sex focus on action more than feeling?

Scorchers

If you haven't already, read Deborah Tannen's *You Just Don't Understand: Women and Men in Conversation*. Even if you don't necessarily agree with her observations, the book gives a fascinating look at the differing approaches men and women take to engaging in conversation.

And no, I'm not stereotyping. I'm only asking you to stop, look, and listen. If you discover a prevalent trait among men or among women, chances are most people will find the same to be true. As I mentioned in Chapter 1, author Lynn Viehl reminds us that, "Men and women are biologically programmed to look, act and speak differently, and that's made our species successful. This is not something to mourn or homogenize; I think we should celebrate our differences."

Think about those commonalities and how to use them to create characters with whom we can all identify. After all, that's your number-one goal!

Take It to the Limit

Readers need to witness a character's struggles to believe in his growth and change. That intimate connection can be accomplished by pushing your protagonist to the limit. This exposes the deepest conflict possible and shows who your character is through his decisions and choices. Don't make it easy on him. Take away what he's worked for. Deny him what he wants. Put him in a situation he's not sure he's equipped to deal with, and watch him work his way out. Push, push, push! There's no such thing as pushing too hard!

The Character Arc

When planning your characters, ask yourself what they'll learn by the end of the story and then think about all those scene goals I mentioned previously. How your characters react to their success or failure at meeting those smaller goals will play a huge part in their character arcs. They can even take two steps forward and one step back—as long as they are moving and aren't stagnant.

The best and surest way to initiate character growth is to require your characters to make hard choices. These choices challenge your characters' beliefs, requiring them to defend what they stand for or to admit the error of their ways. Taking them to the limit of what they can endure, testing their emotional and physical strengths, will spur on the learning process that pushes them into change.

A character who reaches the end of the story still in the same condition as when he stepped onto the first page is rarely a character a reader can care about. Just as each scene advances your plot in increments, each scene will show your character growing through small trials and tribulations and reaching for the big change that comes at the end.

Sexual Tension Redux

Have I mentioned yet that I'm a firm believer in sexual tension being the most important element in making a romance erotic?

I talked in Chapter 16 about the brain being the most important sex organ of all, and how sexual tension starts there with a couple's initial attraction and the blossoming (or exploding) desire that follows. One thing that can't be emphasized enough (so I'll do so again!) is that there's no need to go overboard. Oftentimes beginning authors don't realize how subtle sexual tension can be and still be effective. Take a look at these two examples:

> *Example #1:* Brandon glanced at the memo lying on the table, his attention on the woman sitting in the chair directly across from his. Rachel's client was suing his client for divorce.
>
> The settlement offer was ridiculous. Yet all Brandon could think about was Rachel's mouth. Her plump lips. The wicked red of her lipstick. How he longed to feel her suck his cock into her mouth.

He grew hard and shifted in his seat. He wanted to bend her over the table, pull her tight skirt over her tight ass, tear away whatever she was wearing beneath, and shove himself inside her, show her who was the boss.

He looked up, arched a brow, shoved the memo toward her. "This is a joke, not to mention a waste of my time."

Example #2: Brandon glanced at the memo lying on the table, his attention on the woman sitting in the chair directly across from his. Rachel's client was suing his client for divorce, and the settlement offer was ridiculous.

He looked up, arched a brow, and shoved the memo toward her. "This is a joke, not to mention a waste of my time."

Rachel pursed her lips, the wicked red lipstick she wore this close to distracting Brandon from the purpose of this meeting. "I assure you. It is not a joke."

He swallowed hard, wishing their clients gone, wanting to get Rachel alone. The business of divorce could wait. He was more interested in the business of sex. And he could tell by the way she pressed the tip of her tongue to the edge of her teeth that so was she.

Naughty, Naughty

One thing you want to avoid is having a character act like a jerk in the name of sexual tension. A hero's thoughts can be as raunchy and raw as fits his character, but they should never be abusive, disrespectful, or dehumanizing. A hero does not harass or objectify his heroine as nothing but a sexual object.

There's nothing inherently wrong in the first example. It's sexy; it's raw; it's very human. The second example, however, although just as sexy, is less in-your-face while still conveying the same sense of urgency.

More than anything, the tone of your story will determine the style of scene and tension that will work for you. Just don't think that sexual tension is purely physical or that it demands gritty or coarse language. That works, but so does the earthier, subtler depiction of desire.

Put It in Every Scene

I know what you're thinking: *My characters aren't necessarily together in every scene.* Exactly! And they don't have to be. Remember the brain? Sexual tension can exist when one character is thinking about the other. It can be present in a telephone conversation. Rachel can mention to a girlfriend the way Brandon's gaze caught hers across the conference room table and feel her heart pitter patter in reaction to the memory. Brandon can remember the color of Rachel's lipstick when he's in the shower, alone, with a lot of steam and soap, and wish she was there to help him take care of business.

As long as your characters' brains and libido are both engaged, you have the right ingredients for whipping up a batch of sexual tension!

Ratchet It Up Each Time

Think of sexual tension like a catapult or a bow. When you write the scene in which your hero and heroine first meet, you're settling your arrow against the string of your bow. Then you begin to pull. With each scene, you draw the string tighter and tighter, never rushing or jerking, never applying brute force, just drawing back slowly until the string is taut enough to send the arrow flying. And so you release it, thrusting your characters into one another's arms where they live happily ever after with 2.5 kids and a white picket fence. Well … you get the picture.

Remember, draw back on that bow string and keep it tight. Don't let it go until the time is right to shoot. If you release it too soon, it goes nowhere, falling, uh, impotently to the ground. Even if your first sex scene is written in Chapter 1, your characters will thank you for drawing out the tension. Your readers will thank you, too.

Naughty, Naughty

Be sure to keep your quiver well stocked, because once you've released your first arrow—whether that arrow is a hot and heavy kiss or a hotter and heavier love scene—it's time to reach for the next. If you give up on your tension, your reader will give up on you. And you want her to feel that final Cupid's arrow when it hits.

Pop Quiz

Ready for a pop quiz? You better be!

1. Name your five favorite erotic romance authors.
2. Choose your four favorite books by each one.
3. Pick your three favorite scenes out of each book.
4. Find your two favorite highlighters.
5. Grab your one favorite chair.

Now, sit. Study. Mark up those books within an inch of their lives. Use one color for the male viewpoint and another color for the female viewpoint. Look at how the scenes are written. Highlight the things that make the sexual tension work—the word choices, the internal thoughts, the physical reactions, the emotional responses. Learn what these authors are doing right. Then do it yourself!

The Least You Need to Know

- Telling your story in your character's voice is one of the surest ways to bring your reader close.
- Know the rules of grammar before you break them and then break them only to achieve a desired effect.
- To avoid writing cardboard characters, take time to observe the people around you. A wealth of character traits are in front of you for the taking.
- Never force your story's sexual tension, but let it spring naturally from your characters.

Chapter 20

Getting Wild and Kinky

In This Chapter

- Exploring alternative lifestyles
- Having fun with toys and games
- Understanding the appropriateness of fantasies
- Taking advantage of technology

Erotic romance readers who enjoy a bolder slice of the sexual life have no shortage of books from which to choose, and the subgenre presents the perfect venue for authors who love writing about the same. Whether alternative lifestyles, edgy and daring sexual activity, or even bedroom games played with toys, erotic romance offers everything under the sun.

If writing about a variety of wild kinks and pleasures is what spices up your life, then this is the subgenre for you. Let's look at a few of the offerings and how you can put them to work.

BDSM: It's Not Just About the Alphabet

The term *BDSM* embodies a number of practices and beliefs, but it's primarily a lifestyle of self-exploration. Those who choose to embrace it do so willingly and are intent on pushing themselves to the edge of their personal boundaries. It offers lovers a chance to grow as close as possible while learning more about who they are as individuals. It is also a very popular segment of the erotic romance subgenre.

def•i•ni•tion

BDSM is an acronym for the sexual lifestyle that encompasses the practices of bondage and discipline, domination and submission, and sadism and masochism.

The lifestyle is very erotic, one rife with sexual tension—which is why it fits so well into erotic romance! It is also psychologically stimulating, meeting very specific needs for its participants. In short, if you're going to write BDSM stories, you need to know your subject matter. Getting it right is paramount. If you get it wrong, readers who are involved in the lifestyle will see the error of your ways and may not be forgiving enough to pick up your next book.

While some participants enjoy all aspects, others will find pleasure in only a few, perhaps enjoying the loss of control in being tied up but having no interest in receiving pain. BDSM can be gentle and sensual and focused on sensation play, such as running silk or feathers or even ice cubes over a lover's skin. It can also be about one lover inflicting pain on another for the purpose of arousal. What needs to be stressed here is that BDSM is not abuse. It is a consensual relationship.

Because so much of BDSM is based in psychological needs—a need to control, a need to relinquish control, a desire to experience intensity to the point of pain, or to be at another's mercy, etc.—you have to know what drives your characters, what frightens them, and what need is fulfilled through the exchange of power between a dominant and a submissive.

Naughty, Naughty

Because a BDSM lifestyle is tied deeply into a character's psyche, developing your story people completely is paramount. Don't pair your hero with a heroine who likes the idea of handcuffs because you think it will make your story erotic! Look for the underlying reasons they choose to live their lives this way, and give readers an honest look into who your characters are.

Bondage: Tie Me Up, Tie Me Down

Although much of bondage is about restraint and the exchange of power—along with sensation play, or S&M play (discussed in an upcoming section)—another sort is based in stimulation. Consider a heroine whose hero forces her to wear a body harness beneath her clothing while at work, one that rubs against her breasts and between her legs every time she moves. Although her movements are never restricted, she is still in a submissive position—and he still holds the power, arousing her with no more than the apparatus against her body and the thoughts it brings to her mind.

Slip of the Tongue

When discussing the differences between various bondage scenarios, author Kathryn Anne Dubois says: "While some books 'play' with bondage, it is done in a politically correct way—either role playing or simply consensual. But often in erotic romance, the character is bound against his or her will and gets aroused in spite of being mad as hell. This makes all the difference in keeping that erotic edge. (Notice the 'victim' is mad, rather than afraid.) Whether it's erotic romance or erotica, the woman is never 'abused.' If she is spanked, she's mad rather than hurt and terrified."

The Dom/Sub Relationship: Who's on Top?

In a BDSM relationship, the person who is the submissive yields to the one who is the dominant. While one couple will keep their roles in their relationship constant, another couple will switch. Giving up power, or even any knowledge of what one's partner is going to do, satisfies a psychological need for the submissive participant. The dominant partner takes much of his pleasure from fulfilling the desires of his submissive, always respecting his partner's feelings and the limitations she has set.

Of course, the dominant can just as easily be the female partner and quite often is! How many erotic romances have you read with a dominatrix heroine?

S&M: Pleasure in Pain

Yes, pain can be pleasurable. Think about an excruciating workout that taxes your muscles yet feels so good afterward, or a deep-tissue massage that hurts so bad but feels like heaven at the same time.

Inflicting pain during sex is hardly limited to hard-core S&M floggings. Many romance novel heroines have gouged scratches into their hero's back with their nails or received bruises from bite marks their hero has left on their buttocks and thighs. Sexual pain is very intense and very erotic at the same time. Anyone up for a spanking?

Ménage à Trois: Count to Three

Many erotic romance novels feature protagonists with multiple sexual partners. Two, three, four, … I'm sure there are books featuring more.

As I've mentioned elsewhere, some readers and publishers want their erotic romance couples to remain completely monogamous once they've met. That said, some readers and publishers have no problem with a hero sharing his heroine or vice versa. Often, said sharing takes place before an emotional commitment and is part of the characters pushing their sexual envelopes. In other cases, a third person may be a permanent fixture in the main couple's life. Perhaps one partner—or the couple together—enjoys the fantasy of sex with strangers, or even voyeuristic and exhibitionist scenarios.

If these setups are ones you enjoy writing, you can bet you'll find readers ready to enjoy what you've written!

Sex Toys: It's Time to Play!

From whips and silk scarves to vibrators and feathers—and even on to the more exotic devices used in various lifestyles such as ball gags and butt plugs—sex toys are a perfect addition to an erotic romance starring an adventurous couple. (Need a quick alternative to nipple clamps? Clothespins work in a pinch!)

Scorchers

Sex toys don't have to be … sex toys. A feather from a Mardi Gras mask, an ice cube from a cold drink … just use your imagination!

In one of my books, my heroine used her pearl necklace on the hero when they showered together. In another book, my heroine used candles. And wax. I also had a couple make use of a back vibrator in interesting ways, and another hero who came up with a good use for his silk tie.

There's no end to what your characters can bring to the bedroom to add to their joint pleasure.

Food for the Soul—and the Body

We make love with our mouths by kissing, tasting, licking, etc., so what could be more sensual than sipping champagne from the small of a lover's back … unless it's using whipped cream and honey elsewhere! But don't stop there. That inherent oral sensuality means that, as sexy as it is, seductive eating doesn't have to be done *from* the body. Remember the lobster-eating scene from *Flashdance?* Where Alex sucks on the tender morsels dripping with butter, licking her fingers while using her stocking-foot to caress Nick's crotch beneath the table? A character can also tease her lover by using her tongue on a spoon of crème brûlée or even by wrapping her lips around a banana!

Including food in sexual activity also gives you a chance to use several of the five senses to evoke reader response. She can taste it, smell it, and recognize the sticky or creamy or velvet-soft consistency and know exactly what your characters are experiencing, too!

Scorchers

The only caveat I might mention—and almost hesitate doing so because we're writing fantasies—is to be sure no food gets left behind! But … I *have* heard readers say they've been unable to deal with a sex scene where food products were inserted internally because all they could think about was the possible health hazard!

Water Sports

Sex in the shower is one of my favorite sexual encounters to write; I've probably done it in at least half of my books. Who doesn't love the feel of hot water, rich soapy lather, and hands slick with both on their skin? In fact, I think I've received more reader mail about the shower scene I wrote in my Harlequin Blaze, *The Sweetest Taboo*, with Sebastian and Erin than any other scene I've written!

We've got showers, bathtubs, swimming pools, hot tubs, lakes with waterfalls, rivers … a never-ending selection of places to get wet and wild. I even know of one author, Julie Elizabeth Leto, who wrote a fabulous water hose scene in her 2000 Harlequin Temptation, *Good Girls Do!* And in her 2001 Temptation, *Pure Chance*, Julie let her characters have their fun in a water fountain on an erotic sculpture!

Some authors may eschew locations that might introduce chemicals or bacteria into the body, while others fully embrace the fantasy—and the eroticism. (If you're still not convinced on the eroticism factor, check out the waterfall scene between Viggo Mortensen and Diane Lane in the 1999 movie *A Walk on the Moon!* Ooh-la-la!) Wherever you stand, there will no doubt be a water scenario that works in your story!

Exhibitionism: Look at Me!

When talking about exhibitionism in erotic romance, I'm not talking about any criminal type of indecent exposure. No streakers. No trench-coated flashers. (I might have to take that last one back. A flasher in a role-playing situation …?) Rather, I'm talking about characters who get a sexual charge from being seen in a state of undress and who are discreet, never reckless, when exhibiting. They also do so with specific intent—such as arousing a lover or arousing themselves.

A heroine might enjoy wearing revealing clothing and moving provocatively to show off her body. Her motive? It could be her own sexual gratification. It could also be a game she plays with her lover, teasing him with brief glimpses of her breasts when she leans forward or allowing her short skirt to blow up in a strong wind.

Scorchers

Are your hero and heroine a couple who enjoys both voyeurism and exhibitionism? Have them sign up for speed dating so they can watch one another flirting and making out with other people.

A character who enjoys this extravagant sort of behavior is one worth exploring in an erotic romance. Learning what drives her to expose herself in public and why she gets off to doing so can take your characterization to a level that truly involves your reader in her journey.

Voyeurism: Look at You!

When is a voyeur not a Peeping Tom? How about in an erotic romance when he's watching his partner, who enjoys the risk of showing off her body in public?

Another type of voyeur is one who, by accident, sees what wasn't meant to be seen. Maybe a man catches a glimpse of a woman dressing through a window when walking by her house, or when standing on a ladder making repairs to his roof. Then again, maybe she knows exactly what she's doing in offering him a chance to see her.

Scorchers

Consensual voyeurism provides the character involved a chance to participate visually and from a safe distance while well aware of what lies ahead for the both of them.

Pairing an exhibitionist with a voyeur can provide not only a titillating story for both characters and reader to enjoy, but can give you a chance to develop fully realized story people who will see your plot through to the end. Because voyeurism is often considered a sexual aberration, your challenge is to show it in a sexually charged relationship—and in a positive light!

May the Forced Fantasy Be with You

Politically correct or not, some authors enjoy writing—and readers enjoy reading—scenarios involving forced seduction. While early romance novels occasionally featured characters who fell in love after the hero raped the heroine, similar setups are rarely found in today's releases. (The first historical romance I read, Kathleen E. Woodiwiss's *The Flame and The Flower*, began with just such an encounter between Brandon and Heather.) Forced seductions, however, are not found only in historical settings—or in books, for that matter. *General Hospital*'s Luke and Laura anyone?

Scorchers

Much has been made about the image of the romance genre because of early works that included forced seductions. Such works gave rise to the term "bodice ripper."

That said, many readers refuse to read romances that even hint at a forced seduction that's not part of a BDSM fantasy or role-playing game. On the other hand, many readers can't get enough of the fantasy.

Fantasies involving force can range from an unwilling seduction to a more aggressive rape scenario. A plot of this sort does have an audience, but such a story may not find a home with as many readers as one in which sexual aggression plays no part in the protagonists' relationship. Do a bit of market research if you have an idea that fits in this category—especially if you're concerned about reader reception.

Slip of the Tongue

On the subject of fantasies, author Jaid Black says: "Whether it's politically correct to admit to or not, I know for a fact that many of my female readers love voyeuristic rape fantasies, key word being *fantasies*. They certainly wouldn't want it to happen in real life, but [they] enjoy the escapism and total lack of control provided by *forced seduction* scenes in erotic romance novels."

Stranger on a Train

Another common sexual fantasy is an encounter with a stranger. For many, it's the risk, the loss of inhibitions, the freedom to let go, or even the idea of taking on a new persona while with someone who will never be seen again. (Of course, when such a plot device is used in erotic romance, we know there will be a whole lot of seeing going on!)

There's an inherent eroticism to the danger involved in such activity, especially so if the sexual encounter takes place in a public place—say beneath a table in a dark restaurant, on the dance floor in a club, or in the backseat of a car. There are psychological dangers as well and, again, this is part of the allure.

Do understand that by "strangers," I'm not talking about a couple who have just met, might have spoken a time or two, but are still virtual strangers, agreeing to have sex. I'm talking about a character unexpectedly encountering someone they've never seen before, a someone who turns them on, … and taking it forward from there!

Playing Dress-Up

Role-playing games are a staple of erotic romance. Whether it's the power play between a boss and his secretary, a fantasy scenario acted out as master and slave, or a forbidden tryst engaged in by a teacher and a student, playing dress-up gives two characters the chance to let their imaginations run wild.

These scenarios are also a big part of the BDSM lifestyle. A captive submits to a captor, giving up control over her own body, yielding to her partner's will and allowing him to dictate her actions. Surrendering to another's demands in such a situation allows the captive to relinquish responsibility while comfortably exploring her personal sexual boundaries.

Scorchers

Characters in erotic romance don't have to wait for a Halloween costume party to don that French maid or Catholic schoolgirl outfit. Even those leather chaps will come in handy for a bedroom game of "Ride 'Em Cowboy"! Have a Caribbean pirate fantasy? All you need is a sword at the ready! Not feeling well? How about a little bit of nursing?

Long-Distance Lovin'

In the past, couples separated by career obligations or duty to country or family were able to do no more than exchange letters via the postal service or, reaching way into the past, the Pony Express, slow boat across the Atlantic, etc. Today's couples are fortunate to have technology that enables them to reach out and keep in touch.

Using this technology in an erotic romance where such devices would be available gives you a great plot tool for ramping up sexual tension and exploring a character's sexuality. The distance created by a phone line or an Internet cable allows a character to flirt and safely challenge her own sexual limits by discovering how far she'll go with the man on the other end of the line.

I've seen books written entirely in e-mail exchanges (which may seem like it throws all my Chapter 8 structure advice out the window—but it doesn't!) and others in which instant messaging conversations played a big part. There are any number of electronic communication methods your characters can use not only to keep in touch, but to flirt, seduce, get each other hot and bothered, etc. Here are a few:

- Phone sex
- Instant messaging
- Text messages
- Camera phone pictures
- Chat rooms
- E-mail exchanges
- Web cams

And even more! Think of a couple who meets after having signed up for a dating service that connects members via mobile technology based on their submitted profiles. When two members come within a certain distance from one another, the service sends one's specified information to the other's cell phone or handheld to make a possible match.

Scorchers

My first book for Harlequin Temptation, *Call Me,* featured eight chapters of phone sex before the hero and heroine got together in person for the real thing. Also, the spy guys from my *SG-5* series for Kensington Brava communicate electronically in more than one of the books. Not exactly long-distance lovin', but a device I've employed for communication purposes on more than a few occasions to ramp up both plot and sexual tension!

Can you imagine the plot possibilities should both members want to find someone looking to share their love of exhibitionism? And after they've made contact, imagine the plot possibilities as they text message sexual dares to one another. I feel a sit-down session with the muse coming on!

The Fast and the Furious

Speed dating is another approach to meeting and mating that has roots in a contemporary urban setting. Participants visit for 8 minutes or so with several potential dates, asking questions, checking for compatibility, flirting, playing footsie under the table, making out … oh, wait. That was my muse butting in again! When their 8 minutes are up, they move to the next person in line.

One of the best things about writing erotic romance is taking ordinary situations and finding an extraordinary—and of course, sexual—twist to take. An innocent set of circumstances can provide for an incredible level of eroticism when given just the right punch!

The Practice of Tantric Sex

Tantric sex enables couples to experience intimacy by channeling their sexual energy for the purpose of making a spiritual connection. Many modern practitioners consider sex a sacred act and use it to seek a closer union with a higher power.

def•i•ni•tion

Tantra is a spiritual discipline rooted in various religions and often embracing mystical rituals and rites. **Tantric sex** is a union of a couple focused on using sexual energy for spiritual enlightenment.

The information available on *Tantra* and Tantric sex fills more volumes than I could ever properly synopsize here. If you're interested in writing about characters who embrace this esoteric practice, you'll have no end of research sources! As with BDSM, however, you do need to understand the practitioners' beliefs to accurately portray characters who seek enlightenment through sex.

The Least You Need to Know

- The BDSM lifestyle is, by definition, charged with a high level of eroticism and is very popular with readers of erotic romance.
- Sexual exploration takes many forms—food, toys, lifestyles, etc.—but should always be consensual and fun, and never include abuse.
- Many fantasies, whether politically correct or not, have an inherent element of danger that adds to the eroticism.
- Technology offers many opportunities for characters to stay connected and play sexual games.

Part 6 Satisfy Me: Meeting Your Reader's Expectations

Know your audience. Romance readers know exactly what they'll get when they pick up a book labeled "romance" on the spine. Readers of erotic romance have those same expectations and more. Specifically, readers of erotic romance expect eroticism.

They want their emotional journey, but they want to experience the sexual relationship down to every toe-tingling kiss—no matter how intimate that kiss may be. Part 6 is where I spend some time talking about the fantasy and reality of steamy sexual activity and how to give your readers the emotional—and the physical—ride they're looking for.

Chapter 21

Doors Wide Open

In This Chapter

- Where's the love?
- Understanding degrees of explicitness
- How hot is hot?
- Feeling the heat of emotion
- Getting involved in your writing from the inside out

Readers of erotic romance do not expect the sexual action in their books to take place behind closed doors. They don't want a scene to end with a couple climbing into bed and have the next scene begin the morning after, leaving the hours between to the imagination.

While such is often the expectation for readers of traditional and sweet romances, readers of erotic romance want to be there for the entire ride. Whether the sex scenes are abundant with graphic detail or are more emotionally focused, readers come to the genre for the open-door policy.

How Do I Know If It's Love?

Many authors refer to all scenes of sexual activity between their story's hero and heroine as love scenes or write solely about characters making love. Other authors write scenes of sexual intimacy driven by emotions that have no basis in romance and call such intimate encounters sex. I'd wager a guess that a good portion of erotic romance authors include both types of scenes in most of their books.

Love scenes and sex scenes. Is it all about semantics, or is there really a difference? As with so many other elements of erotic romance, the difference is in the eye of the beholder. Some authors and readers want their characters—even those who have been sexually adventurous early in the story—to be romantically involved before they consummate their relationship, and after that, anything goes. Other authors and readers enjoy witnessing characters becoming romantically involved *through* sexual exploration. How you choose to look at your own work depends on your audience and your characters' individual journeys, as well as your personal view on what makes a romance erotic.

Scorchers

Don't feel you have to tie yourself down or embrace a single definition of the intimate scenes you write in lieu of the other. The genre is plenty big enough for sex scenes and love scenes both!

Turning Up the Heat

Believe it or not, not all erotic romances are created equal in the explicitness department. As much as I've emphasized the importance of bringing the reader into the bedroom with the characters, I haven't yet talked much about how the graphic nature of stories billed as erotic romance can differ from author to author and publisher to publisher.

Many authors enjoy focusing on a love scene's senses and emotions and render their consummations with a more subtle touch. Other authors enjoy focusing on a sex scene's physicality and are subtle about almost nothing.

I currently write for two different publishers, and although I'm given a lot of freedom at both houses, I tend to write less explicitly for one than the other because of audience expectations. One line is marketed as "red-hot romance." The other was initially marketed as "erotic romance," to clue readers into the content yet the books no longer bear the designation on the cover now that the imprint is well established in the genre.

I don't want to put off a reader wanting a tamer level of heat by writing too hot for the "red-hot romance" line. Neither do I want to disappoint a reader who wants the heat turned up by not writing hot enough for the more erotic imprint of publisher number two. It's a tough balance, one I look at closely with each and every book I write.

Scorchers

In every book I write, I try to vary the steam level in the love scenes. A first time could be either tender or rough, depending on the circumstances, while a scene both characters think will be their last time together could be melancholy or even infused with anger. Each situation will require different words to paint the right picture. Alternating in this fashion is only one of many tricks to keep scenes from seeming repetitive and also gives readers a better look at the emotional states of the characters involved.

To demonstrate how I switch things up, here is a scene I wrote for *Kiss & Makeup*, my August 2005 Harlequin Blaze. The first example is a toned-down version of the original. The second is how the scene actually appeared in the book.

> *Example #1:* He shuddered at the constriction and the pull, closed his eyes as she fondled him, as she moistened her fingers to ease her way.
>
> He spread his knees wider, giving her the access she wanted. She played with what she found there, with his flesh, returning to touch him more intimately.
>
> His eyes were still closed, his jaw taut, his hands laced together on top of his head. And so she leaned forward, ran the tip of her tongue around one nipple and then the other before dipping down.
>
> She worked him with her tongue, held him between her lips. With one hand, she explored him, gauging how close he was by his pulse.
>
> It didn't take him long. His hands came down to grip her shoulders, and his hips began to thrust. She continued the pressure of her lips, releasing the leather strap she'd bound around him.
>
> He finished, and she stayed with him, giving him the pleasure of her love in the most intimate way she knew to do.

> *Example #2:* He shuddered at the constriction and the pull, closed his eyes as she fondled his balls, as she wet her fingers with the sticky moisture he'd already released and used it to ease her way farther between his legs.
>
> He spread his knees wider, giving her the access she wanted. She played with the ridged extension of his erection, with the puckered flesh behind, returning to slide a finger between his balls, separating his sac and rolling his jewels in the cup of her palm.

> His eyes were still closed, his jaw taut, his hands laced together on top of his head. And so she leaned forward, ran the tip of her tongue around one nipple and then the other before dipping down and taking his cock into her mouth.
>
> She worked her tongue along the seam beneath the sensitive head, sucked the plump mushroom cap between her lips. Holding him with one hand, she explored between his legs with the other, gauging his release by his pulse and the constriction of the sac around his balls.
>
> It didn't take him long. His hands came down to grip her shoulders, and his hips began to thrust. She continued the pressure and suction of her lips, releasing the leather strap she'd bound around him.
>
> He came in bursts of warmth she caught with the cup of her tongue, and she stayed with him until he was finished, giving him the pleasure of her love in the most intimate way she knew to do.

Look at both and see how the explicit language varies, yet how both convey the same emotional connection between Shandi and Quentin. Because really, the emotional connection is what makes or breaks an explicit scene.

Naughty, Naughty

In addition to considering how a particular publisher might prefer a scene to be written, consider your characters and where they are in their relationship. Characters who are more comfortable with one another may be in a place where emotions play a larger part in their love scenes, while those just getting to know one another may be more focused on their physical connection. Tapping into their circumstances will guide you through writing your scenes.

Is It Hot in Here Yet?

Now let's take a closer look at what might constitute the various levels on the erotic romance heat scale. Be aware, however, that many readers, authors, and review sites or publications use the following terms interchangeably or assign them a completely different meaning—or don't use them at all. One reader's sensual romance will be another reader's sweet while still another will consider the story sizzling!

Scorchers

Most electronic publishers assign sensuality ratings to their e-books. One publisher's website breaks down its releases into three categories of sexual content, and another provides seven different designations of heat levels. The best way to know how hot (or not) you should write is to become familiar with each publisher's way of rating its books.

I've only chosen to describe four levels of heat. You may prefer to break down the subgenre even further—if you break it down at all! These are totally subjective designations based in how I've seen erotic romance develop over the years. Feel free to come up with your own definitions!

Sweet

A "sweet" designation is usually reserved for books in which the hero and heroine share little more than a chaste kiss, so it would seem to be a misnomer in erotic romance. After all, our characters definitely do very little that's chaste and a whole lot more than kiss!

So let's think of sweet erotic romances as the tamest of the lot. Still extremely sexy, but sweetly so! Softer, with a sexuality that's less in-your-face. Perhaps these books have fewer love scenes than others. Maybe the intimate scenes are more emotionally than physically focused, or the detailed descriptions used to bring said scenes to life are less graphic than those found in other books.

Scorchers

Not all erotic romance publishers will be accepting of books falling under my "sweet" definition. These books, however, might find a home with a regular romance publisher looking for a higher level of sexual tension in their releases.

Without relying on purple prose, the author may have eschewed clinical or anatomical detail in favor of metaphor. Perhaps she writes as if through a filter. There's never any question as to what the characters are doing, but the love scenes are rarely drawn out. Basically, these books, while still erotically charged, have less explicit detail.

Steamy

The next step up gives us what I'll refer to as sensual romance. These books keep the bedroom door wide open and describe exactly what's going on between the characters while they're there. Oftentimes, however, readers are allowed to use more of their imagination than would be required in a book with full sexual detail. The love scenes are often numerous—although perhaps not as intense as in spicier works—and much of the time is spent in foreplay, whether it begins over dinner or in bed.

Sensual romances emphasize the senses, making the sexual experience one that's extremely evocative. These stories also devote a lot of attention to emotional detail, and they stress that connection as much as they do the physical.

Sizzling

Between the sensually sexy stories and those that present a no-holds-barred approach to sex are the ones with a spicy sizzle and burn. A large part of erotic romance falls into this category.

These books contain intense, graphic, and even clinical language as well as sexual slang. The stories are still primarily one man/one woman romances, with the main protagonists remaining monogamous after they've met. They might possibly have other partners when the story begins but quickly relegate them to the past. These books might play with kinky subjects, but they're usually not tackled with any hard-core detail.

Scorching

An erotic romance labeled as "scorching" leaves no sexual experience unturned. These stories take physical intimacy to the limit, exploring alternative lifestyles and intense sexual activity. Think multiple partners, forced seductions, BDSM rather than playful bondage, etc.

Slip of the Tongue

Author Jordan Summers looks at the varying levels of explicitness in erotic romance like this: "The levels of heat in erotic romances vary as widely as individuals' definitions for the word *erotic*. Forget the dictionary definition. For some, a love scene that takes place with the door open is considered extremely erotic. For others, the author must use explicit language to describe the sex act and the various body parts involved for them to fully appreciate the romance. Publisher requirements mirror that of readers. Certain publishers expect explicit language and will ask you to correct your manuscript if you've used clinical terms or euphemisms. Other publishers don't put word restrictions on the author, but prefer you use explicit language sparingly. Assumptions aside, erotic romances are as unique and varied as the authors who write them."

Although all erotic romance focuses on the emotional journey of the characters involved, these stories may place more significance on the physical aspects of the relationships and seem more extreme in their sexual content for doing so.

In the Bedroom

The importance of the sexual heat in erotic romance cannot be emphasized enough—even while it doesn't have to steam up every single page. Neither does every scene have to be written with the same level of heat—which is why I hesitated to define the categories as I just did. While many authors tend to write similarly steamy scenes in one single book—or in all their books—other authors switch the tone, depending on the reason for the encounter. And that reason is as vital to the success of the scene as the physical activity itself.

Scorchers

As important as it is to give readers of erotic romance the intimate details they want, it's equally important to include the emotional factor. Don't forget that the emotion involved doesn't have to be love. There does, however, need to be a driving force behind all sex scenes, and readers will better relate to the characters and understand what's at stake if they recognize that motivation.

Giving the necessary attention to the emotional component has the very nice side effect of increasing the sexual heat. Why's that, you ask? Remember Chapter 16's discussion of brain sex? That's why! A body's physical response is only one factor in arousal—at least in erotic romance. Readers want the doors to be wide open on a character's emotions as well.

The thrill of sexual attraction is as much emotional as it is visceral. Beyond the initial flurry of excitement, characters experience an entire range of feelings while making love. They may be so sick with worry about pleasing their partner that they can't relax enough to please themselves. They may be filled with wonder that this person has come into their life. They could even be frightened at the possibility of their illicit encounter being discovered, or maybe they're bold and daring enough to try things they've never tried before. Bringing these feelings into the bedroom is essential to creating meaningful sex scenes, whether they're love scenes or not.

Are You Feeling It?

I've talked a lot about writing for readers, meeting their needs, and fulfilling their expectations, but I haven't talked much about writing for ourselves as authors. I don't necessarily mean writing as an unpaid hobby, or journaling, or telling stories on paper for the pure joy of doing so with no expectation of seeing them in print. Many authors enjoy doing all that, and more power to them! Right now, however, I'm talking about getting as much enjoyment out of the writing process (stop laughing!) as readers get out of reading the finished product.

Scorchers

Deep point of view gives me a sense of being my character and sharing his sensory experiences, his memories … everything.

A craft trick I use to help me feel what I write is deep point of view, which I addressed in Chapter 19. This enables me to immerse myself fully in a character's head and get under his skin so his thoughts are the ones going onto the page—often in a fluid stream of consciousness. To do this, I use sentence fragments, expletives and exclamations, and choppy thoughts rather than full-realized ones.

If my hero is thinking back to his days spent held captive in a pit in the middle of the Thai jungle (*The Bane Affair*, Kensington Brava, 2004), I get just enough of what he wants to remember. I'm then able to put down on the page what's important to him and only what the reader needs to know.

When you're as deep as you can get in a character's head, it's impossible not to have him emote. This is when you stir a reader to tears or to laughter, when you cause a hitch in her chest or an ache in her heart. Because we're writing erotic romance, our ability to feel that first breathless attraction and the physical arousal that follows is paramount—and we don't want to stop there.

Scorchers

Don't limit what you're feeling to your story's sex scenes. The doors to the bedroom are not the only ones you want to leave wide open. You want to bring all your characters' sensory experiences to life.

Not only that, being able to personally experience those feelings gives us a deeper insight into what words are best to use to convey the same to our reader. Here are a few tricks that utilize viewpoint and enable you to get into a character's head to channel him—and feel him—as you write:

- Have a character journal about a particular scene.
- Play the part of a character's psychiatrist, and have him tell you about his fantasies—sexual or otherwise.

- Write a conversation he might have with his best friend (male or female—or both) about sex and relationships.
- Visit him in his dreams—night and day.
- Eavesdrop on his confessions.

The Squirm Factor

I can't remember when I first heard it or even who said it, but I've since read articles or listened to workshop tapes where more than one author has advised that, "If you're not squirming in your seat while you're writing it, how do you expect your reader to be squirming in her seat while she's reading it?" The "it" is obviously your book, and the squirm factor can be based on sexual tension or a fully described sex act.

Readers read to feel alive. Why shouldn't authors feel just as alive while they write? Arousal is part of life and sexuality, and in erotic romance, we're writing about both. It only makes sense that we'd get a bit hot and bothered while writing explicit scenes.

What's interesting is how it happens for each author individually—and oftentimes, it's tied into the individual project. I've written scenes that feel so mechanical during the process that I swear they're pancake flat. Other times, I wonder if my heart could possibly beat any faster before breaking my ribs. In the end, both methods produce workable scenes.

Slip of the Tongue

An author friend told me once that on her first pass through a love scene or sex scene, she is so intent on getting down the necessary emotional component, the conflict, and the character growth, that she doesn't have time to stop and feel the roses, so to speak. It's when she goes back a second time to layer in the senses that she feels the power in what she's put on the page. Makes perfect sense to me!

Born to Be Wild

I mentioned in this book's introduction that the very first manuscript I sold required editing to tone down the heat factor. At that time in publishing history, explicitly steamy scenes weren't a mainstream element in romance, and erotic romance was only a gleam in the industry's eye. The first writing contest I won asked specifically for hot, sexy scenes—and the scene I submitted wasn't even a love scene. It was from the manuscript that would eventually be released in 1993 as *Playing Love's Odds* from Meteor Kismet.

In the snippet I submitted for the contest, the story's hero was naked and swimming off the dregs of a nightmare, while the heroine was sitting on the edge of a fishing pier, talking him through the terror. It was a very sensual and sexually tense scene, but the protagonists never even touched. Those two experiences—the contest win and having to tone down a sex scene in my very first book—proved to me that I couldn't write any other way.

Many of you are probably here because you know the same about yourself. Eroticism and sensuality are inherent to your voice, as well as to the way you see your stories unfolding. Others of you may have taught yourselves to concentrate on these factors to imbue your stories with eroticism. However you came to the genre, I won't be a bit surprised if you find that the freedom inherent to erotic romance enables you to tell your most compelling and fulfilling stories ever!

Slip of the Tongue

Author Saskia Walker says: "I remember my first 'erogenous moment' reading a Mills and Boon novel. Sadly, I can't remember the title or author, but there was a moment where the hero stroked the heroine's inner wrist at length while holding her against her will and telling her something about herself. Reading that caused me to experience something inexplicable, indescribable, well … grown up, *you know!* It also unlocked something else in me: my awareness of senses in both the reader and the writer. My theory is that erotic writers are made early in life. What intrigues me is whether reading books with behind-the-closed-door or cut-to-the-fireplace love scenes might have forged in them the possibility to be an erotica/erotic romance writer."

The Least You Need to Know

- Even within erotic romance there are different levels of explicit and graphic detail.
- Leaving the door wide open on the emotional component of sex scenes is as important as giving readers a bird's-eye view of the physical activity.
- Many authors have a natural inclination to write at a highly explicit level, while others need to give their love scenes more focus to infuse them with eroticism.
- Use deep point of view to immerse yourself fully in a scene in order to feel everything a character is feeling and understand his thoughts.
- The more you squirm when writing a love scene, the more your readers will squirm, too!

Chapter 22

The Marriage of Fantasy and Reality

In This Chapter

- Determining how much reality is too much
- Playing safe with sex
- Dealing with sex's little inconveniences
- When fantasy becomes a bad thing
- Understanding the multi-faceted role of sex
- Revealing the truth about hopes and dreams

The romance genre often receives the short shrift when it comes to literary respect. Detractors argue that romance novels present an unrealistic view of relationships—especially sexual and romantic relationships.

No matter how much fantasy our books include, we also show a hero and a heroine working realistically as a team to make their romantic partnership work. Romance readers, of course, know the truth, just as authors of erotic romance know it's not always easy balancing the reality with the fantasy.

In this chapter, I discuss ways to manage that, as well as looking at whether or not there's a need to do so—or if fantasy and reality can exist side by side on the bookshelf and between the pages of a book.

Dealing With the Reality

Romance authors often walk a fine line between fantasy and reality when writing. Many readers read romance for the fantasy escape. These readers don't want their books to include their same problems or to reflect anything about their lives. They get enough of that on a daily basis.

Many choose to read about a different time or place, finding their escapism in historical and paranormal romances. Others may prefer to read contemporaries set in exotic locations, or ones featuring suspense elements that add a fantasy twist. Whatever they choose to read, they are driven there by the promise of being taken away.

Others identify more with novels that reflect their personal experiences. These readers are often empowered by reading about a heroine tackling problems similar to their own and emerging triumphant in the end. Still others find they need to be totally grounded in a story by familiar landmarks or pop culture references. They may even see these stories as ones that could happen to them—and that's their version of fantasy.

What's great about this demand for variety in our genre is that we authors aren't limited in what we write. We can write to the market, or we can even write to please ourselves, knowing we'll find other readers who share our wants and needs. And so many authors write for themselves anyway, it's the perfect win-win situation.

Scorchers

In addition to considering your personal preferences along with those of your readers, don't forget to look to your characters to tell you *their* feelings on dealing with safe sex and contraception. Staying true to your characters is as important as staying true to your audience and yourself!

One of the fantasy-versus-reality issues all authors have to address at some point or another is the sex in our books. As with the story line, many readers are looking for a total escape in the sex scenes. They don't want to deal with precautions taken against sexually transmitted diseases or consider the possibility of pregnancy unless it's part of the story's plot. Other readers won't read books that *don't* address these subjects in a realistic fashion—fantasy or not—citing as the reason their inability to respect characters who ignore the issue of safe sex.

Making the call on how to approach these issues is one each author has to do for herself and often depends primarily on the type of story she's writing and the audience she's writing for.

Making Babies

The discovery or revelation of a "secret baby" is a long-time staple in romance novel plots, as is the unplanned pregnancy that acts as conflict between the story's hero and heroine. In the context of erotic romance (contemporaries primarily), pregnancy is one of life's little realities that is addressed with a condom or a mention of another method of contraception, if mentioned at all.

Because we expect our characters to be sexually active, reading about a heroine taking birth control pills won't come as a shock. In fact, we'll admire her for being responsible and protecting herself. (We also won't be waiting for a pregnancy twist to the plot!) Neither will we look at her askance if she has a stash of condoms in her purse. And a hero who is always prepared is, well, a hero—even if that hero is a heroine!

Slip of the Tongue

When discussing the subject of condom use in erotic romance, author Alyssa Brooks says: "Much of erotica is about readers fantasizing about sexual things they wouldn't do. In the heat of the moment, stopping to roll on a condom is a hindrance to the eroticism. However, in today's world, protection is very important. That is why I often like to include a forward/disclaimer about safe sex, reminding folks that this story is fiction, but in real life, use protection!"

Staying Safe

The issue of safe sex in contemporary romance is not limited to the erotic subgenre, but because our characters are more sexually active, it's one many authors feel compelled to address. They may go about it with a quick one-liner such as, "He rolled on a condom as she climbed on top," or they make condom application part of their characters' sexual fun and games. Doing so can add even more eroticism to their love scene.

Slip of the Tongue

Author Cheyenne McCray says: "I believe in including safe sex in my books. When I create a paranormal world, I have a little more leeway because I can make up new rules for that world. When I write contemporary erotic romances, I have the hero using a condom. A couple of times I've had the heroine on birth control, but they talk briefly about being vetted as far as diseases go. It's such a small part and keeps the story flowing, but I think it is necessary."

Yet even authors whose characters discuss their sexual histories and contraception may have them use condoms anyway. In my Harlequin Blaze *Bound to Happen*, my hero and heroine, Ray and Sydney, were high school sweethearts reunited. Even though they weren't strangers and were comfortable discussing their sexual pasts, in one scene, Ray chose to find his satisfaction outside Sydney's body because he didn't have a condom at hand. Being an emergency responder and having been witness to the devastating effects of sexually transmitted diseases, this decision was perfectly in character for Ray.

Slip of the Tongue

On safe sex, author Shiloh Walker chimes in: "If I'm writing fantasy, I don't worry about it much. If I'm writing contemporary, suspense, that sort of thing, I do try to bring it up at some point. Safe sex is something the vast majority of the population is aware of. It's taught in middle school, high school, and has been for years. Safe sex is a topic of discussion in the news, magazines, … the information is out there, and the average person who is going to be reading my stuff should be aware of that. Plus, I write *fiction*. Fiction and reality are two different things; what's acceptable in fiction isn't safe in reality. As adults, the people reading my books have to be responsible enough to see the difference."

Wet Spots and Condom Wrappers

Your characters have done *it*. *It* was fantastic. *It* rocked their world. *It* caused the earth to move. But now the sheets are messy and there are leftovers to deal with, dispose of, clean up … Do you write about it? Or is this one of those things we ignore in lieu of the fantasy?

This is totally your call as the author. I've written scenes and never mentioned condom disposal. In other scenes, I have. I've also had characters end up giggling and wrestling each other in and out of the wet spot(s)! Don't think you have to ignore this sticky reality, but don't think that dealing with it has to be gross!

Aches and Pains

Similar to tackling the cleanup of a love scene's leftover bodily fluids is the matter of dealing with the aching muscles and tender skin that follows a particularly intense encounter. It's going to happen; all those scratches and bite marks and bruises and abrasions that are so much fun at the time aren't so great postcoitus. But even that reality is too much information for many readers.

Lots of times, giving page time to any of this takes away from the fantasy—even for readers who like to be grounded in reality. But any situation can have an upside. Aching muscles deserve a long, slow massage, don't they? And tender skin? How about a nice warm relaxing bath while held in a lover's arms. See? Turning what might be a negative into a positive can bring your lovers closer together.

Morning Breath and Bed Head

Again, how much reality do you want to include? When thinking about how much reality to add to my own work, I'm always reminded of the movie and television characters who seem to wake up looking as if makeup artist and hair stylist fairies visited while they slept! That's a bit too unrealistic for me; how about you?

It all boils down to context, characters, and plot development. Tell your reader everything she needs to know. Give her a good look at your characters reacting to the mundane details of sexual intimacy if it will help her know them better. If the disposal of a condom plays into a plot point, don't leave it out. If it doesn't, you can write the scene anyway you choose!

Dealing With the Fantasy

Erotic romance isn't alone in taking heat from critics who accuse the genre of being unrealistic in how it portrays romantic relationships; traditional romances get hit by the same accusations. For some reason, boy meeting girl and losing girl and getting girl turns off a portion of the reading public as idealistic.

Anyone writing in the genre, whether published or not, has no doubt taken a few hits from friends or co-workers or even family members over the genre's happily-ever-after requirement. After all, they say, that's an incredibly misleading representation of life. Relationships are never guaranteed to have a happy ending. Neither are they guaranteed to be so perfect—not the romance, not the life after commitment, and definitely not the sex.

Hmm. I don't think they're reading the same books we're writing or else they'd know how completely both traditional and erotic romances explore the conflict—a.k.a. the problems—between couples coming together for the first time, as well as the conflict between couples who've already experienced the blush of first love. Even authors who write full-blown erotic romance fantasies don't write perfect people with perfect lives. Now, about the sex …

The characters in erotic romance have sex for any number of reasons, as I described in Chapter 12. Does the idea of good sex make our books unrealistic? I hope not! Does the idea of a lot of sex mean our books have no basis in reality? Say it isn't so!

Of course our books are works of fiction, but they also portray characters experiencing the universal desire to find a lifelong mate—and that includes discovering sexual compatibility. How can anyone argue that we're presenting pure fantasy when we're writing about the human condition? That said, let's address a few elements that detractors of erotic romance often toss our way.

Slip of the Tongue

Author Saskia Walker shares: "Dr. Lonnie Barbach …, a psychologist practicing with non-orgasmic women, found that reading erotica helped women lead more fulfilling sex lives, promoting health and happiness. …

"When Lonnie bought my story, 'The Welcome Home,' … she praised it richly and said it was unique and educational. … Nowadays, if I ever feel the moral brigade breathing down my neck or I am made to feel uncomfortable about what I do by people who don't relate to erotica, I think of Lonnie, her work with women and her words about my … writing. Working with Lonnie put me on an even footing right from the start, and since then, I've worked with some fabulous editors who use pleasure, sexual health, fun and fantasy as their benchmarks."

Surely Sex Isn't Always So Perfect

The sex in erotic romance runs the gamut from tender and sweet to rough and sweaty. The act can be an expression of love or the fulfillment of physical need with no emotion but relief involved. However it's written, sex is a requirement of erotic romance. There's a high level of reader expectation for sex done well—not only written well, but depicted as a pleasurable and satisfying encounter for the participants. Does that mean readers will toss books that feature imperfect sex?

Of course not. I've talked several times about how to use unsuccessful sexual encounters to increase story conflict and sexual tension, as well as to initiate character growth and plot momentum. Our readers, however, do want the good stuff, a lot of it, and often. It's a staple of our genre. In fact, all that good, hot sex defines our genre. And if that's an unrealistic fantasy, I'd rather not know!

"Not Tonight, Dear, I've Got a Headache ..."

It's true. Sometimes we're just not in the mood. We don't feel well. We're tired, stressed, busy. Even knowing how much better we would feel after making love and that accompanying release of endorphins, finding the energy to do so is an effort in itself.

Such situations present perfect opportunities for characters to go to bed, cuddle close, and relax together without feeling the need to perform. This intimacy increases the bond between them. They might even talk quietly, sharing secrets and dreams, revealing bits and pieces of who they are.

Not every night a couple climbs into bed together will result in orgasmic bliss. That doesn't mean those nights can't be used—and ruthlessly so—to show character growth and the developing emotional connection between your story's couple.

Orgasm or Bust

There are times it just doesn't happen. No matter how much we want it to, or how much attention we pay to the process, sometimes our minds just won't let go. Maybe we try too hard, or are under too much stress, or just aren't feeling it.

We want to write about sex that's mind-blowing. We want to give our characters that pleasure and evoke the same enjoyment in our readers. Once in a while, however, it doesn't hurt to have things go awry. But, but … this is escapist fantasy, you say. You're right—and the whole idea of bad sex may not fit with how you see your story. All I'm saying is that having your characters experience simultaneous orgasms every time they're together is not a requirement of the erotic romance genre!

Scorchers

If you've ever wondered what would happen if you added a disastrous sexual encounter to your book, why not give it a try? It's a great way to build character, and commiserating through the failure can bring characters close—maybe just close enough to relax and let the fireworks fly!

It Seems Everyone's an Expert

The fantasy element of erotic romance—all those sexy people having all that hot sex—can make it seem like every character we write is sexually adept and skilled beyond all imagination. Even our inexperienced characters may seem like experts because of their enthusiasm.

Sure, some of our characters may be connoisseurs of the art of love, but for the most part, we write about characters who know what they like, go after it, and get better with practice!

Do Romance Novels Foster False Hope?

In addition to presenting unrealistic relationships, erotic romance novels are also said to foster the false hope that there's someone out there for everyone and that everyone will spend their courtship boinking like bunnies, find a happy ending, ride off into the sunset, and live their lives in a state of sexual bliss. There are those who do, and there are those who don't, and if you ask me, our books are totally reflective of that reality.

Scorchers

Because the erotic romance genre's explicit and copious sexual content does take a lot of heat, as an erotic romance writer, a thick skin comes in handy! Authors take different approaches to dealing with detractors, and finding your own comfort zone can only help!

We show characters going up against great odds—external and personal—and persevering. They may not always win, but they grow as individuals and together as a couple. We show them confronting relationship issues such as lies and deception or external life issues such as natural disasters or job loss or even death.

No, not every true-life situation will result in triumph, but many times, as clichéd as it sounds, it's not the destination but the journey that proves a person's worth—the same as it does with our characters. Even the sexual journeys our characters take are about more than the physical pleasure their encounters bring. False hope? I say hope. True hope.

It's Raining Men

In an earlier chapter, I described the biological differences between women and men that result in a gender-specific way of approaching relationships and sex. I tried then to make clear that I was not writing in absolutes. I know quite well that men come in all shapes, sizes, and psyches just as women do!

Now, however, I'm talking about the concept that our books feature unrealistic heroes because of how our story men are portrayed—gorgeous, sexy beyond belief, perfect bodies, incredibly talented lovers who know all the right buttons to push so sex is always earth-shattering, etc.

Yes, many of our books do feature perfect paragons of masculinity! That's a part of the genre's fantasy appeal for its readers. As readers know, however, our books also feature introverted scientists and freckled boys next door and men whose beauty is held only in the eyes of their heroines. I'd say that's pretty realistic, wouldn't you?

In a Perfect World

What sort of relationships do erotic romances portray? Well, two characters who are there for each other and who are there for more than the sex, through thick and thin, good times and bad. We write about support systems and best friends and, yes, about great sex. I have a hard time believing anyone could consider a relationship emphasizing the positive while facing and dealing with the negatives of conflict unrealistic!

What sort of expectations do our novels foster, and are we doing readers a disservice? Is it wrong to show characters working to make a loving relationship last? Should we not write about characters looking for love or wanting another person to accept them for who they are, one with whom they can share a fabulous sex life? I'm thinking those are fairly universal expectations, and we should be thrilled to be writing in a venue in which we can showcase characters who want the same!

Scorchers

I heard an argument recently that erotic novels portray unrealistic relationships partially by depicting men who are always there for their women. Quite frankly, that makes me wonder more about the debater's view of relationships than any of the content in our books!

The Least You Need to Know

- While many authors enjoy writing straight sexual fantasies, others prefer to dose their books liberally with realism, giving readers a wide variety to choose from.
- How an author deals with the issue of safe sex depends on what type of story she is writing as much as her personal philosophy.
- The readers of erotic romance have certain expectations when it comes to the sexual content of the stories, but that doesn't mean every character is a sexual expert or that every sexual encounter ends perfectly.
- Romance novels feature characters facing and conquering seemly insurmountable odds, empowering readers and giving them hope for doing the same.

Chapter 23

How Steamy Is Too Steamy?

In This Chapter

- Remembering the romance
- Taking journeys of self-discovery
- Covering more emotions than love
- Understanding how personal tastes drive definitions

Is there such a thing as too steamy? As long as you follow the tenets of the genre, absolutely not! Remember, in the end, an erotic romance is a novel about love and commitment.

However, there *is* a lot of controversy about what constitutes an erotic romance vs. a story of erotica vs. straight pornography. Can the sexual envelope be pushed too far?

Let's take a look at some of the differences between the sexual and emotional components of the three story types, as well as the expectations held by the readers of each genre.

In Erotic Romance ...

In Appendix E, I've gathered thoughts from several authors on what differentiates erotic romance from erotica. Many of the genre's detractors—those who claim there's no difference between the two and that erotic romance is pornography in sheep's clothing—are overlooking a major point.

Erotic romance is *romance*. Period.

That one single word draws a clear line of demarcation between erotic romance, erotica, and pornography. Yes, the content of the stories that fall under the erotic romance umbrella includes a wide range of sexual topics and sexual activity, but the same can be said for traditional romance.

Many romance review magazines and websites rate the level of sexual heat in traditional romances from sweet to sensual to sexy, for example, saving the steamier designations for erotic romance, but still making it clear that erotic romances are not the only ones to come in a variety of sexual flavors.

Slip of the Tongue

When looking at the array of erotic romances available and the level of sexuality in each, author Emma Holly says, "From a strictly practical standpoint, erotic romance is whatever readers are willing to buy that has the 'erotic romance' label on the spine. Currently, this covers a huge range of stories, from almost sweet to extremely explicit."

What makes a romance novel an erotic romance is often nothing more than a reader's perception or a publisher's decision to put said designation on the spine. Then again, not all readers will agree with a publisher's designation—even finding it misleading because it doesn't match their idea of what content merits the label.

In the end, what is erotic is subjective and can only be determined by the reader reading the book. One girl's sweet is another girl's sizzle.

The romance part, however, is not subjective.

As I said in Chapter 1, a romance novel contains the same elements found in any good work of fiction—with a few add-ons specific to the genre. Erotic romance is then a romance novel that's tweaked—not as an afterthought but during the planning stages—to fit the parameters of the subgenre, just as a paranormal romance is tweaked to fit that subgenre's parameters. It really *is* that simple!

A plot, a hero and heroine—both with clearly defined and motivated goals—believable conflict, graphically detailed sex scenes (whether they're love scenes or not), and, most important … a romance! Those are the elements that make erotic romance work and define it for readers.

Sex Drives the Relationship

I find that the number-one telling difference between traditional romance and erotic romance (beyond the inclusion of graphic sexual detail and all that entails) is that characters in erotic romance tend to fall into bed and *then* fall in love.

In traditional romances, most couples move more slowly through the various stages of intimacy. They meet (or if they've already met, they acknowledge the spark between them), date, get to know one another, discover shared interests, meet friends, meet family—basically, they go through a period of courtship. Physically, this period includes a lot of kissing and touching but stops short of consummation until the couple is ready to commit to spending their lives together.

In an erotic romance, there's no stopping, and the consummation—or other sexually intimate activity—can occur anytime. In fact, much of the getting to know one another and discovering shared interests and outlooks on life is done during and after sex. Where a traditional romance couple might sit on the porch and talk about their lives, the couple in an erotic romance will do the same while spooned together in bed.

This is what separates romance from other genres and erotic from traditional romance. That's not to say that only erotic romances use sexual intimacy to develop plot and character, but it is a requirement of erotic romance, where it may be an added bonus elsewhere!

Scorchers

Many of the fictional couples I've written have shared their deepest, darkest secrets after sex. Lying naked together, all barriers down, they've been unable to hold back and have revealed everything from dreams to fears. When you think about it, the quiet time after sexual intimacy is often when we're most vulnerable. Being so close to another person makes it hard to be anything but honest—and makes for a great time to write tell-all conversations!

Sex Scenes Are Love Scenes, Right?

Believe it or not, even erotic romance authors look at the subgenre and its requirements in different ways. When interviewing the authors who participated in the roundtable discussion in Appendix E, more than a few talked about the importance of the first consummation scene in establishing a couple's romantic relationship.

When writing, they involve their characters in other sexual activity but save the consummation until more is at stake—a *more* that is usually emotional although might also spring from conflict related to the external plot. Other authors use consummation as a *source* of conflict, a *source* of increased sexual tension (as described in Chapter 14), a *source* for challenging characters and spurring them into emotional growth and change extraneous to the romance.

So no, not all sex scenes in erotic romance are love scenes. That doesn't mean they aren't rife with emotion, or that they're gratuitous, or that they aren't vital to the forward motion of your plot. In fact, they had better be all those things or else they have no reason to exist!

Slip of the Tongue

In discussing whether or not they plan out the sex scenes in their work, authors Cheyenne McCray and Jaid Black responded as follows: Cheyenne—"Sex scenes must be a natural part of the progression of the hero's and heroine's relationship. I do tend to keep the sexual tension going before I write the consummation scene, but that scene must belong there and not just be thrown in for the sake of sex." Jaid—"The consummation scene is all important. It's probably the only sex scene I end up reworking, revising, and generally agonizing over. The first penetration is everything in an erotic romance. If it comes too soon, you don't have enough sexual tension to work with from there on out; if it comes too late, it's anti-climatic."

Sex Is Monogamous, Isn't It?

This one's a toughie and is a major objection many detractors have to the concept of erotic romance. I've heard said that no book with a hero or heroine engaging in sexual activity with another character can possibly be a romance. Again, subjectivity. The sales of erotic romance prove that readers *do* buy into the idea of multiple partners in love stories.

You don't get it, you say. How could a romance protagonist have sex with someone who's not his or her partner? First of all, remember that the characters in erotic romance often fall in love after they've fallen into bed. They've made no commitment to a partner, so there's no issue of infidelity to deal with. Secondly, many erotic romances explore fantasies and alternative lifestyles in which monogamy is not required.

This doesn't mean erotic romance readers will accept a promiscuous protagonist. Then again, promiscuity is hardly a heroic trait, and not one an author would assign to a hero or heroine in the first place! That said, here are a handful of reasons a hero or heroine might be intimately involved with another party:

- One member of a couple gets a voyeuristic thrill at seeing his or her partner seducing a stranger.
- The story is a fantasy in an alternative world where sexual activity is not restricted by contemporary expectations.
- The couple has not yet agreed to make their relationship exclusive, and each character continues to see other people.
- The hero and heroine are involved as a couple in a polyamorous relationship with a third person.

A Final Caveat

As I've said before, eroticism is in the eye of the beholder. What turns on one reader won't give another a tingle, while the same thing may cause a third to cringe in disgust. Additionally, we each have personal comfort zones delineating what we'll believe as romantic. Many readers define erotic romance as traditional romance taken to a graphically explicit extreme. They want a straight one man/one woman love story, but they want the doors left wide open. Other readers want all the kinky frills of toys and multiple partners and politically incorrect fantasies.

The beauty of erotic romance is that it offers an expansive range of sexual content. All a reader has to do is find an author who works for her. And all an author has to do is write what she loves to write!

In Erotica ...

At its most basic, erotica is literature (or art) designed to sexually excite. The fact that it *is* often depicted as literary or artistic sets it apart from pornography for those wishing to avoid the taint of sleaze while still enjoying the intrinsic worth of the work. For many others, however, there is no distinction. They feel anything that sets out to purposefully produce sexual arousal—and that includes erotic romance—is morally repugnant and to be avoided!

The primary reason I'm pointing out the differences is to explain that erotica does not require a romance and erotic romance does. That doesn't mean erotica has no literary merit. It's mainstream acceptance shows otherwise!

Many erotic romance authors also write short stories or vignettes for erotica publications. There's a crossover audience, and branching out enables these authors to find new readers. In Appendix C, I've included a section of online resources with information on submitting to erotica anthologies and editors. If you're interested, check it out!

Slip of the Tongue

When defining erotica, author Sasha White says: "Erotica is all about the main character's journey. The sexual acts and scenes that take place in an erotica story propel the character on a journey. Most often it is one that involves a lot of looking inside oneself and acceptance. The sex scenes are explicit, but not gratuitous. They are part of the story and key to the evolving relationships within the story." Author Shannon McKenna adds: "Porn doesn't move me, or if it does manage to do so, it does on a much simpler, clumsier, baser level. It doesn't get my higher cognitive functions involved at all, or my heart or imagination, and so the payoff is so so so much less. Good erotica gets everything inside me jazzed up."

Sex Drives the Plot

When it comes to fitting sex into the plot, erotica and erotic romance are closely linked, but because erotica does not require a romance or a happy ending, it allows for more leeway in a story's climax as well as its overall structure.

There are literary erotica stories in which little or no external action occurs beyond the protagonist's sexual encounters, and her (or his) internal journey drives the narrative. The one I read that stands out most in my mind was a wife's personal journey through her sexual relationship with her husband and another woman from her past. There was no sense of rising tension and no defined plot, but it worked as a character study—which is what much of erotica is.

Sex Scenes Explore Multiple Emotions

Although erotic romance can also explore multiple emotions, as I've said many times, those books will end with a romantic and loving commitment. The characters in erotica are not bound by the same constraints. Neither are readers of erotica necessarily expecting a romance, ergo, the authors don't have specific reader expectations to live up to.

In the story I mentioned in the "Sex Drives the Plot" section, the primary emotions were a sense of melancholy and regret while the protagonist examined her sexual dissatisfaction. It was an illuminating story and was definitely emotional, but no, it was not a romance!

Sex Isn't Always Monogamous

In erotica, there is no expectation of a committed romantic relationship at the end of the book. It's a possibility, of course, but not a requirement. Because of that, the concept of monogamy is irrelevant.

Not only that, the very idea of erotica lends itself to sexual exploration and sexual fulfillment for any number of reasons—emotional and physical both. A female protagonist on a quest to find the one man who meets both her physical and spiritual needs would definitely be playing the field. Readers would then follow her on her journey to do just that!

Love Is in the House

Can a story of erotica contain a romance? Certainly. Any genre of fiction can contain a romance! And that's all I have to say about that!

In Pornography ...

Two romance publishers currently publish my books. My single-title releases say *romance* on the spine. That makes no difference to anyone whose definition of pornography encompasses the content my books include. I've been told more than once that I write pornography. I define what I write as erotic romance. My own thesaurus includes the word *erotica* as a synonym for pornography, while my dictionary says that erotica is intended to cause sexual desire and pornography to stimulate erotic feelings. How's that for showing the interchangeable nature of the words? I think this is yet another of those situations where "eye of the beholder" comes into play!

Slip of the Tongue

On the subject of defining pornography, author Jaid Black says, "*Pornography* is a dangerous word … one person's porn is another person's pleasure. … What is pornography? I don't know. If there aren't children, dead people, animals, etc. involved, then it pretty much boils down to a matter of personal taste."

No Plot Required

Anyone who has ever watched a porn movie or read a work of stroke fiction knows there's little going on besides sex. There may be a hint that something external has brought all the characters together to do their thing, but there's no requirement for story that demands a true plot or well-developed characters … or at least characters who are well developed beyond their physical attributes!

No Emotion Needed

Because pornography's main purpose is sexual stimulation, there's also no requirement for the stories to have an emotional component. This gets a bit trickier when using *erotica* and *pornography* as synonyms because erotica is often about self-realization and discovery—both of which involve emotional growth.

That said, because character arcs are not universally considered an element of pornography, there will usually be little—if anything—in the way of emotion or growth required.

Make It Wet, and Make It Hard

Whereas readers of erotic romance want a relationship with their sex, readers or viewers of pornography simply want their sex. They want it graphically, explicitly written. They want it often. They want it a lot. If anything defines pornography, it's the abundance of sexual content!

A Place for Each Genre, and Each Genre in Its Place

Many readers don't differentiate between erotic romance, erotica, and pornography simply because they have no reason to. They know what they want and know what content a book needs to have to meet that need.

In the end, they may call it nothing more than fiction!

On labeling and segregating by content, author Saskia Walker says: "I don't think there is any need to say what the difference is between *erotica* and *erotic romance*. The clue is that the word *romance* is missing in one. However, I've seen people define *erotica* as 'sex without emotion.' I think what they mean is portraying sex outside of the sphere of love and affection. Emotion as a definition includes such things as joy, happiness, delight and reverence. These things are found in erotica. But the gist of it is that erotica may not necessarily be focused on sex within a romantic relationship—although, having said that, many of my erotic shorts are about committed couples who are deeply in love. In my opinion, there are just not enough committed couples in erotica, and I'm doing my little bit to help change that.

"So what about the difference between *erotica* and *porn*. Many people seem to have an issue with this. Can I just point out that I don't! In dictionary terms, the words are almost interchangeable, and that's increasingly accepted in the mainstream, especially so in these days when the porn culture seems commonplace. For me, *porn* is sex devoid of story, where *erotica* does more than just depict sex. It's a literary endeavor, an experiment with words to stimulate the senses through the imagination. I want my readers to turn the pages through a combination of compelling story and arousing content. I dislike labels in general, because they hamper as much as they reveal, but it seems we must be labeled. I write erotica and erotic romance. To me *porn* has a much wider trawl net—and *sensual romance* doesn't say enough—but I'm not in the least offended if someone says I write porn, simply because it's their take on what I do. My take is that I write erotica."

> **Scorchers**
>
> While erotic romance, erotica, and pornography each have an audience, some readers readily move among the three genres, depending on their mood and what they're looking for in a book at any given time.

The Least You Need to Know

- Erotic romance novels include all the elements the romance genre requires in its books, including the promise of a happily-ever-after ending for the main protagonists.
- Erotica can include a romance or romantic elements but is primarily a work of sexual discovery through a range of emotions.
- Pornography concentrates primarily on physical activity between characters rather than their emotions.
- The differences between erotic romance, erotica, and pornography are most often defined by the individual consumer, based on his or her views and beliefs.

Chapter 24

Getting a Rise Out of Readers

In This Chapter

- Evoking a physical response in readers
- Writing to a reader's emotions
- Crafting reader reactions with word choices
- Why readers choose to read erotic romance

Just as characters don't exist in a vacuum, neither do readers. They read to be involved and to respond, whether that response is emotional, spiritual, mental, or physical. Erotic romance is not stroke fiction, but if you fail to raise your reader's temperature while she's experiencing your love story's emotional high, you may not have met her expectations. Meeting your reader's expectations is your number-one goal. It's also the first stop on the road to success.

Readers read to participate in the journey your characters take. They read to feel. They want to share your hero and heroine's experiences down to every pounding pulse and drop of sweat. And yes, they want to feel all the good stuff going on between the sheets, too. Let's take a look at what your readers want and how to give it to them.

Make Your Body Talk

Reading is a visceral experience. Readers are caught up in your story's events via your use of the five senses when you write. They smell the scent of fear in a character's sweat or taste the whipped chocolate icing that brings a joyous sparkle to a character's eyes as she licks it from her lover's fingertip. They understand why a character is panicking over a decision because they, too, feel the gnawing, roiling sensation in their stomachs.

Scorchers

Your characters aren't the only ones you want to physically appreciate your story. You want your readers to undergo the same responses, whether prompted by fear, joy, panic, lethargy, or arousal.

I have an amazingly vivid memory of reading Penelope Williamson's brilliant historical novel *Heart of the West* and wondering if my heart was going to burst out of my chest or if I would ever again be able to draw enough breath to fill my lungs. Not to mention thinking if I didn't stop sobbing that the next morning my co-workers would wonder who in my family had died. And all that over nothing more than two characters finally getting together after pages and pages and years and years spent apart.

That sort of reaction is what you as an author want to evoke in your readers. You want them to be so involved with your characters' individual journeys and their story as a couple that they feel every one of the physical sensations your characters do. Let's look at a few of those.

Slip of the Tongue

Author Shannon McKenna has this to say about the visceral experience of reading love scenes: "For me, the litmus test for a love scene is that it has to be incredibly important to both of the characters. Absolutely charged with urgency and significance. A huge, huge big deal to them. I'm repeating myself, I know, but for me, that's what works, and that's what's essential. If I don't feel it, I usually not only skip the love scene, I stop reading the book. But if I do feel it, I love delicious love scenes."

Racing Hearts

Ever feel as if your heart is going to beat its way straight out of your chest? Whether brought on by a sudden fright or a burst of excitement, that pounding, thudding, exploding, on-the-verge-of-a-heart-attack sensation is one universally shared and understood. You can play to that response in many situations, using sharp evocative words and short sentences to give a scene a sense of urgency. Remember, a fast-pace scene will result in a reader response that reflects the same intense exigency.

While an increased heart rate can signal fear or panic, it's also a sign of arousal. Your love scenes are not only about the bodily sensations going on down below. A rapid pulse and the sense of blood rushing through one's veins is equally evocative! Don't lose any opportunity to get your reader—and her heart—involved!

Goose Bumps

You know the feeling. The hairs on your arms stand on end. Your skin pebbles with gooseflesh as if you, too, have been plucked. The nape of your neck tingles, and you shiver in response, the sensation tickling its way down your spine. Such a reaction can be evoked by cold or fear but can also be the result of anticipation.

Think about your female protagonist hoping to run into her male counterpart in the same location where they've previously crossed paths, growing anxious while she waits, wondering if he'll show. The telling details you add to the scene—what thoughts are going through her mind, what she remembers about him, his scent, the timbre of his voice, the light touch of his fingertips as he reached for the door handle at the same time she did—will evoke the same quivering response in your reader, and that's exactly what you want to do!

I Can't Breathe!

There's nothing to match shortness of breath as a recognizable physical reaction to a situation full of emotional conflict. You know the feeling—it seems you'll never again be able to fill your lungs, that your chest is being crushed by a monstrous weight. The reaction can come at the end of a long run, or an even longer sweaty marathon in bed!

Scorchers

Being able to evoke physical sensations in a reader with nothing more than the words you use to paint your scenes means you've done your job as an author well!

It's Called Arousal ...

Arousal is a wonderful, perfectly normal response to reading an erotically charged scene. Why wouldn't a reader feel the same things the characters are feeling when she's living and breathing their story?

I've heard more than a few authors say that they know an erotic scene is working when they find themselves squirming in their seat as they write it. Do you squirm when you're writing? If not, how do you expect your readers to feel it?

Let go! Write true and write pure, and write with 100 percent honest involvement, without censors or critics reading over your shoulder. That's the only way to grab your readers by the throats—or by other body parts—the way you want to!

Scorchers

You can control the mood and pace of your scene through the words you use. Short sentences and sharp evocative words will convey a sense of urgency in an action sequence, while longer, descriptive sentences that employ more adjectives or metaphors will give a languorous quality to a dreamy or sensual scene.

Tingles and Tickles and Shivers

As an author, you want to involve your audience by making the most of your characters' bodily reactions. Doing so allows your readers to experience the same things. Leave no response unexplored. If your heroine steps barefoot into mud, let your reader feel it squish between her toes, too. If your heroine is exhausted and sweat-drenched after an hour spent searching for the path she followed into the woods, let your reader feel the perspiration burning her own eyes as well.

When your heroine cuddles down beneath her sheets and blankets, give your reader the full experience of being wrapped in a cool cocoon that quickly warms with her body's heat. Should your heroine have cause to stand on the edge of a wind-swept moor awaiting her hero, be sure your reader knows the same sensation of her hair whipping around her face and the heavy fabric of her skirts slapping her legs.

That's all well and good, but how do you do this? It's all about how you choose your words, how they give the verisimilitude I discussed in Chapter 8 to the scene, and how you construct your sentences.

Here, let's do a quick compare and contrast using one of the previous examples:

> *Example #1:* Rachel stopped, braced one hand on the tree beside her, struggled to pull air into her burning lungs. The bark was sharp and scraped her palm when she doubled forward and heaved. Minutes later, she straightened, flinging back her hair. Strawlike tips of a cluster of strands scratched the corner of one eye, and she squinted against the sting of salty sweat.

Example #2: Rachel stopped next to the tree at her side to catch her breath. She leaned forward to pull herself together, waiting until the nausea passed before standing up and pushing her hair from her face.

The first example shows Rachel in action by using many evocative words: *struggled, burning, sharp, scraped, heaved, flinging, scratched, squinted, sting*. The second example simply tells the reader that Rachel stopped and took a break. There's nothing in this example for the reader to feel, while in the first example, myriad physical sensations are described. Using specific words to suggest specific sensations allows your reader to feel what Rachel feels, and that connection is what brings her fully into the scene.

I Get So Emotional!

Physical responses aren't the only ones you want to wring from your reader. You want her emotions completely involved. You want her to weep when your characters weep, to laugh when they laugh. You want her to feel their depression and despair, their excitement, and their emotional exhaustion.

What you don't want to do, however, is manipulate your reader unfairly, whether by using an *unreliable narrator* or any other trick of authorial intrusion. Nothing will have a reader throwing a book at the wall faster than feeling as if she's been duped. Don't jerk your reader around. Send her on a true and vivid emotional roller coaster with sweeping ups and downs!

def•i•ni•tion

An **unreliable narrator** is a point of view character whose bias, inexperience, or ignorance colors a story's narration or provides a compromised look at the truth. This narrator often appears blind to things that are obvious to the reader, rendering himself unbelievable. After all, if the reader can figure out what's going on, why can't the narrator?

Buckets o' Tears

Tears come in so many flavors: joy, anger, sadness, humor. While one character may find a situation so comical that she laughs until she cries, another may weep with relief when she's let off with a warning instead of being issued a traffic ticket.

What does this means to you as an author? You have almost infinite opportunities for your characters to emote and draw readers into their emotional condition—whatever it might be. Think of how many times you've heard readers talk about sobbing through a particular scene in a book, or how many times you've done the same. As long as you're honest with your characters and with your readers, bringing both to tears without playing games with either's emotions, you're doing everything right!

Oh, the Agony!

Oh, those curve balls. You know, the ones life throws at your characters, one after another, never letting up. We suffer right along with them at every turn, sharing their desperation, buying into their angst, understanding when they think about abandoning their quest for true love because of the pain. Kudos to an author who can push us to the edge of frustration, irritation, disappointment, exasperation, and then know exactly when to bring us back!

Naughty, Naughty

No matter what craft elements you employ to evoke an emotional response from your reader, one thing you don't want to do is "cry wolf" or write to evoke an over-the-top response. Be sure you're writing true to your scene and aren't influencing your reader with dishonest intent into feeling false emotions.

Think about your favorite romance novels. How many of them were pure torture to read because it seemed as if the hero and heroine would never reach their happily-ever-after? That agonizing wait for the ending payoff is a large part of why romance readers choose to read romance novels. They can experience a wide range of emotions and still know the ending of the book will be satisfying—no matter how painful the trip!

Shiny Happy Endings

As a reader, there's nothing more satisfying than to reach the end of a book having experienced two characters meant for each other falling in love. We get to vicariously experience every one of the ups and downs associated with the event. We feel the thrill of excitement at the possibilities ahead, the "he loves me, he loves me not" anxiety … even the toe-tingling bliss of the first kiss and the awe of the arousal and first consummation that follows. It's a beautiful thing, this falling in love business. Give your reader the full emotional ride!

Readers and authors of romance know that outsiders unfamiliar with the appeal of the genre often scoff at our requisite happy endings. But that very genre requirement—that we'll reach the last page without having to worry that we won't get the payoff we're looking for, that we'll never have to regret the investment of time or emotions in a story that leaves us wanting something more or something else—is exactly the reason we've chosen this genre to fulfill our entertainment needs. Nothing there to scoff at that I can see!

Slip of the Tongue

On describing that all-important connection with the reader, author Jo Leigh says, "The things that move us as readers are the things we connect with. The broader the experience, and the more specific the event, the stronger the emotional experience of the reader is going to be. That seems a little contradictory, but it's not really. What you're shooting for is a broad experience, say lust, disappointment, or embarrassment—one that you can be reasonably sure every reader will have experienced for themselves, and at the same time, making that event so singular, so specific, that the reader becomes the protagonist."

The Reasons We Read—and *Need*—Erotic Romance

Readers choose to read erotic romance for so many reasons, I won't possibly be able to do justice to the many by exploring the few I've chosen, but I'll give it a try.

The romance part is obvious. Reading romance addresses the primal and fundamental need we all have to spend our lives in love as part of a mated pair rather than spending our lives alone.

The erotic part is equally obvious to those of us who prefer to experience every aspect of a story couple's romantic journey. We delight in eroticism. It's an exhilarating rush, a delicious celebration of our sexuality and of life. It makes us feel alive because it cuts so close to the bone.

But that's only one of the reasons we enjoy the subgenre. Let's take a look at a handful of others.

Slip of the Tongue

The beauty of the romance genre is that it truly offers something for everyone. As author Shiloh Walker says, "Erotic romance is romance. Period. The difference between a good erotic romance and a good nonerotic romance is simply the erotic romance books tend to be more graphic, more basic, and I think, more honest. Not everybody is going to think in the terms that are used in erotic romance, but then again, I don't think in the flowery terms that are often used in more traditional romances. Sex is a pleasure, meant to be enjoyed by two people who love each other."

For the Validation of Female Sexuality

Sexual equality or not, the idea that "good girls don't" still lingers in some circles. Those of us reading and writing erotic romance know that good girls most definitely do. Reading stories that mirror our own sexual experiences—both physically and emotionally—and celebrate the enjoyment and fulfillment offered by romantic relationships helps validate our own feelings. There's nothing more enjoyable than to have that identification; even if the characters are fictional, the authors behind the stories are not!

For the Connection with the Characters

For the most part, romance readers read more for a book's characters than they do for the plot. Of course, we love a good story, but because we're reading for the romance, the characters are the important part of the story equation and are a primary consideration. In fact, many authors agree that the romance *is* the story, and anything else is secondary.

However you as an author view the genre, for your reader, it's a specific choice of entertainment and escapism. If she doesn't feel a connection with the characters, then for her, the book has lost its value. Readers want to connect with these story people on every level. Witnessing their intimacy and the pleasure it brings them gives us joy at the love they've found as well as hope for their continued happy ending.

For the Emotional Journey

Readers of romance love a good love story. We are big fans of seeing couples falling in love, of feeling everything from that first rush of attraction to the sizzling completion of that first consummation.

Emotions are what bond us as human beings who live and love. We laugh together, cry together, rejoice and mourn together. Why wouldn't we want to feel the same sense of attachment to the characters with whom we spend so much time? After all, we are along for one of the most emotionally intense rides of their lives. Feeling what they feel creates a tie of closeness. Witnessing the unfolding of their romance fulfills us on so many levels, giving us hope and a satisfied sense of all being right with the world. This is why erotic romance is our chosen form of entertainment. Nothing else brings the same satisfaction to the table!

For the Bond Made with Other Readers

C. S. Lewis said, "We read to know we are not alone." Any romance reader who has spent any amount of time online can't help but be amazed at the reading community spread out across the web's message boards, chat loops, blogs, review sites, etc. The Internet has given those unable to meet with others in homes, bookstores, and libraries, etc., a place to come together to discuss their favorite books.

Whether in person or online, readers who share common interests know the value of these friendships, and readers of erotic romance are no different. Knowing others also enjoy these intensely intimate stories gives us an opportunity to openly explore our shared love of the characters, their emotional journey, and, yes, their physical exploits in a supportive atmosphere.

For the Feeling of Empowerment

We may turn to books for entertainment, but they also provide food for thought. How many of us have finished reading a book, a chapter, or a scene and found ourselves identifying with a character because her situation reminds us of our own? Watching her struggle with her problems and emerge triumphant can authenticate our own feelings and give us a sense that we, too, have power over what life throws our way.

Our stories are peopled with intelligent, confident, and mature characters who find themselves in situations—sexual and otherwise—similar to ones we've gone through. Finding personal validation through their journeys proves how fulfilling and necessary these stories can be.

For the Sexual Instruction

Who among us hasn't learned something about sex while reading erotica or an erotic romance? Maybe we came away from reading a scene thinking we'd like to try that at home. Maybe we received an eye-opening lesson about the workings of the male—or the female—body. Maybe the author so skillfully described an act that it appealed to us at a visceral level when it never had in the past. It could even have been a case of thinking, *Yeah, that didn't work so well for me either!*

Scorchers

Whether or not we pick up an erotic romance expecting a sexual education, that's often the end result. As a reader, enjoy! As an author, rejoice!

The Least You Need to Know

- Eliciting physical responses in readers is sure proof that you've drawn them into your characters' world.
- Readers love to be emotionally involved in our stories as long as they don't feel manipulated.
- Words are powerful tools for evoking the same reactions in your reader that your characters experience.
- Readers of erotic romance enjoy these stories for reasons ranging from personal fulfillment to solely entertainment.

Appendix A

Glossary

advance A dollar amount paid up front to an author that is later deducted from earned royalties.

antagonist A character at odds with a story's protagonist, or main character, and who is causing him conflict.

author intrusion Any language or story content that reminds the reader he is reading by showing the author's hand.

BDSM A sexual lifestyle encompassing one or more of the practices of bondage and discipline, domination and submission, and sadism and masochism.

category romances Love stories published in a line requiring specific content. Each book has a shelf life of one month, and all are numbered and priced the same. (These are also called series romances.)

character arc The emotional growth or change—usually though not always for the better—a character undergoes during the course of a work of fiction.

chick lit A genre of fiction most often aimed at young women and usually featuring a female protagonist in an urban setting dealing with friends, career, family, and men.

deep point of view Writing done from a place of penetrated immersion deep inside a character's head that relates his thoughts and feelings.

deus ex machina A plot device where a solution to a problem seems to magically drop out of the sky, as did the gods lowered onstage by machinery in early Greek and Roman plays.

double entendre Words or a phrases with two possible meanings, one of which is suggestive.

e-book reader An electronic device used to read electronically published books.

exposition A story narrative that provides background information the reader needs to understand what is happening.

head-hopping Changing a story's narrating viewpoint so often that a reader feels bounced between characters' heads.

larger-than-life The condition of being impressive or commanding attention due to one's presence.

mass market A standard size paperback book often sold in airports and grocery chains in addition to bookstores.

over the transom A submission to a publisher made without being solicited.

pantsers Authors who do very little or no preplanning before starting a story and who write by the "seat of their pants."

protagonists The main characters whose stories are told in a work of fiction.

purple prose Heavily ornate and overwrought prose intended to evoke an emotional response in a reader.

reserves against returns A portion of an author's earnings held back until bookstores have returned unsold copies of his or her book.

reversal A plot device where a twist causes a story's forward motion to stop or reverse course and turn in a new direction.

romance genre A fiction genre that tells stories of couples falling in love and finding a happy ending.

royalties A prenegotiated percentage of a book's sales dollars paid to an author at specific intervals.

sexual tension A strong sexual desire between two characters that draws them together.

stream of consciousness A continuous flow of thoughts and feelings recorded as they occur.

subgenres Any number of categories within a main genre.

subtext The implied or underlying meaning of a story's content or of spoken dialogue.

suspension of disbelief The willingness of a reader to overlook a story's inconsistencies to enjoy the reading experience.

synopsis A brief narrative outline of a novel explaining the main points of the plot as well as introducing the characters.

Tantra Teachings of spiritual enlightenment based primarily in Hindu or Buddhist text.

Tantric sex The practice of using sex to make a spiritual connection with one's partner.

trade paperbacks A paperback book that is larger than the mass market size yet smaller than a hardcover book.

unreliable narrator A narrator whose credibility is prejudiced or compromised due to his stake in the story.

verisimilitude The state of being "very similar" or appearing to be real or true.

Appendix B

Erotica and Erotic Romance Publishers

This list of publishers is divided into two sections: print and electronic—though several of the e-publishers do offer paperback versions of their books. At the time of this writing, all these publishers provide contact information or submission guidelines on their websites.

Word of warning: Many of the publishers listed here publish straight erotica as well as erotic romance. In addition to featuring their books and submission guidelines, they may also provide external links to sexually oriented websites or include sexually graphic advertising banners on their pages.

Additionally, several print publishers only consider agented material. Check out *The Literary Marketplace* or *The Writer's Market* (available at most bookstores or libraries) for listings of literary agencies.

Print Publishers

Avalon Publishing Group
Blue Moon Books
Caroll & Graf Publishers
Thunder's Mouth Press
245 West 17th Street, 11th Floor
New York, NY 10011-5300
www.avalonpub.com

Bantam Books
Random House, Inc.
1745 Broadway
New York, NY 10019
www.randomhouse.com/about/contact.html

Avon Red
10 East 53 Street
New York, NY 10022
avonromance@harpercollins.com
www.harpercollins.com
Avon *strongly* recommends e-queries. No attachments, just a query. Please use the word *Query* as the subject of your e-mail.

Berkley Heat/NAL HEAT
Penguin Group (USA) Inc.
345 Hudson Street, 5th Floor
New York, NY 10014
www.penguinputnam.com

Black Lace Books
Virgin Books Ltd
Thames Wharf Studios
London
W6 9HA
www.virginbooks.com

Harlequin Blaze and Spice
Harlequin Enterprises Limited
225 Duncan Mill Road
Toronto, Ontario
M3B 3K9 Canada
www.eharlequin.com

Kensington Aphrodisia and Brava
Kensington Publishing Corp.
850 Third Avenue
New York, NY 10022
www.kensingtonbooks.com

Red Sage Publishing, Inc.
PO Box 4844
Seminole, FL 33775
www.redsagepub.com

Pocket Books
Simon & Schuster
1230 Avenue of the Americas
New York, NY 10020
www.simonsays.com/content/
feature.cfm?sid=33&feature_id=1627

Tor/Forge
Tom Doherty Associates, LLC
175 Fifth Avenue
New York, NY 10010
www.tor.com

Electronic Publishers

Allure Books
www.allurebooks.com

Amatory Ink
www.amatory-ink.co.uk

Amber Quill Press
www.amberquill.com

Aphrodite Unlaced
www.aphroditeunlaced.com

Black Velvet Seductions
www.blackvelvetseductions.com

Changeling Press
www.changelingpress.com

Chimera Books
www.chimerabooks.co.uk

Chippewa Publishing, LLC
www.chippewapublishing.com

Circlet Press
www.circlet.com

Diverse Publications Ltd.
www.diversepublications.co.uk

Ellora's Cave Romantic Publishing
www.ellorascave.com

Erotique Press
www.erotiquepress.com

Extasy Books
www.extasybooks.com

Freya's Bower
www.freyasbower.com

Fictionwise
www.fictionwise.com

Heat Wave Romance
www.heatwaveromance.com

Liquid Silver Books
www.liquidsilverbooks.com

Loose Id, LLC
www.loose-id.com

Magic Carpet Books
www.erotica-readers.com/ERA/G/MagicCarpet.htm

Midnight Showcase
www.midnightshowcase.com

New Concepts Publishing
www.newconceptspublishing.com

Ocean's Mist Press
www.oceansmistpress.com

Phaze Romantic and Women's Erotica
www.phaze.com

Pink Flamingo
www.pinkflamingo.com

Renaissance E-Books
www.renebooks.com

Romance At Heart Publications
www.rahpubs.com

Sensorotika
sensorotika.neptunemediagroup.com

Silk's Vault Publishing
www.silksvault.com

Silver Moon
www.coyotemoonpublications.com/?q=node/10

Tantalizing Tales
www.tantalizingtales.com

Torquere Press
www.torquerepress.com

Triskelion Publishing
www.triskelionpublishing.com

Venus Press
www.venuspress.com

Whiskey Creek Press Torrid Romance
www.whiskeycreekpresstorrid.com

Wicked Velvet
www.wickedvelvet.com

Appendix C

Further Resources

In this appendix, you'll find several publications and organizations to explore—all of which offer additional information on the erotic romance industry and market.

Word of warning: Many of the online sources listed here feature erotic content as well as that specifically related to erotic romance. They may also provide external links to sexually oriented websites or include sexually graphic advertising banners on their pages.

Publications

Amatory Thesaurus
www.amatory-ink.co.uk/thesaurus/thesindex.htm
An online thesaurus specifically for sexual words.

Erotic Quills
www.darkerotica.net/EroticQuills.html
On writing erotica by Morgan Hawke.

JERR—Just Erotic Romance Reviews
www.justeroticromancereviews.com/
The sensual side of romance—reviews, contests, interviews, articles, and more.

Lady Jaided
www.ladyjaided.com
The premier magazine for today's sensual woman.

Romantic Times Bookclub
www.romantictimes.com
A magazine for lovers of romance, mystery, and women's fiction.

Steaming Up Your Love Scenes
www.mninter.net/~emmah/Workshop.htm
A workshop by Emma Holly.

The Erotic Reader
www.theeroticreader.com/writer.html
Writing resources.

Organizations

EPIC
www.epicauthors.org
A professional organization for published and contracted e-book and print authors.

Erotic Authors Association
www.eroticauthorsassociation.com
Honoring Literary Merit and Achievement in the Writing and Publishing of Erotic Literature.

Erotica Readers and Writers Association
www.erotica-readers.com
An international community of women and men interested in the provocative world of erotica.

Erotica Romance Writers
www.eroticaromancewriters.com
An online erotic romance community.

Passionate Ink
www.passionateink.org
A special interest chapter of RWA for erotic romance writers.

Romance Writers of America, Inc.
16000 Stuebner Airline Road,
Suite 140
Spring, TX 77379
www.rwanational.org
Advances the professional interests of career-focused romance writers through networking and advocacy.

Appendix D

Recommended Reading

During the writing of this book, I asked a number of erotic romance authors to tell me what books they felt best represented the subgenre and what books had drawn them to the subgenre as readers or as authors.

As I've said elsewhere in this text, I've always favored steamy romances over sweet, but the book I read that showed me how beautifully eroticism and romance could be when combined was Emma Holly's *Top of Her Game*, published originally by Virgin Book's Black Lace imprint and released again in 2004 by Cheek.

Here are the rest of the responses:

Jami Alden: *Take Me* by Bella Andre. It had such an emotionally charged, romantic love story along with amazingly hot sex.

Jaid Black: *Prisoner Of My Desire* by Johanna Lindsay. It was the book that hooked me on the romance genre and set the standard for what I expected to get out of them, erotically speaking. It was through reading this book that I discovered what made me tick sexually. Specifically, a circumstance where a strong heroine is forced into a situation of submission by an alpha male. Very hot!

Sunny Chen: *The Lover* by Robin Schone. She writes a story that touches a deep chord about a plain-looking woman who hides a deeply passionate soul, yearning to spark a man's sexual passion and tender love.

Portia Da Costa: I can't quote a favourite erotic romance, but my favourite erotic novels of all time are *The Domino Trilogy* by Cyrian Amberlake. They're written as erotica, or even porn, but there is a dark romance within them.

Sylvia Day: *Kiss or Kill*, which is actually a novella (in Red Sage Publishing's *Secrets, Volume 8*) not a book, and it's by Liz Maverick. It was my first erotic romance, and it's a futuristic. With just that one story, I was hooked on both futuristics and erotic romances. It changed everything for me as a writer by opening doors for my imagination.

Emma Holly: My favorite erotic romance is Laurell K. Hamilton's *Kiss of Shadows*, the first in her Merry Gentry fey series. Part of why I love it is because there's one heroine and a lotta heroes, but I also admire Hamilton's knack for creating sexual suspense. She gives her characters really good reasons to really want to have sex, and the reasons exist on many levels: emotional, physical, and even political! She has a wonderful way with words as well—very original and evocative. When you read her sex scenes, you feel like you're there.

Lydia Joyce: Alison Kent's *Indiscreet*. Or anything by Judith Ivory. She is not usually labeled "erotic," but her writing is incredibly sensuous and sexy. So that's one book but two authors. Not cheating too much, yes?

Angela Knight: *Victorious Star* by Morgan Hawke. It was so intense, so hypnotic, that it set the bar for me for erotic romance. Morgan writes with utter honesty and fierceness, and I've read it several times. Plus, it's DAMNED hot.

Cheyenne McCray: There are two books that stand out to me, and it's because of the authors' voices more than the territory they explore: *A Fine Work of Art* by Shelby Reed and *Holding the Cards* by Joey Hill.

Jordan Summers: *Tempting the Beast* by Lora Leigh. Leigh combines all the elements of a good story: action-adventure, emotional complexity, and heightened eroticism. You follow her two main characters through uncharted emotional and physical waters, hoping all the while that they beat the odds and end up together.

Karin Tabke: *Exit to Eden* by Ann Rice. Wow, did that book open my sheltered eyes. Not only was it intense, passionate, and down right sexy, it was a true love story with a happily-ever-after.

Saskia Walker: *Pure Sin* by Susan Johnson, maybe because it was the first *true* erotic romance I read. It was 1996/1997. At the time, I was dabbling with writing and finding I had to read across many genres to get everything I wanted as reader. In the UK, there was no erotic romance. On the one hand we had Black Lace books that included erotic content, but the romance angle often didn't go as deep as I wanted it to. On the other hand we had romances that lacked the sexual aspect; it either wasn't there at all or was so fleeting and devoid of meaning/character growth as to be redundant. I was actually reading fantasy more than anything, writers like Storm Constantine, who embraces both romance and sexuality in the characters and relationships she creates in her fantasy worlds.

I struck up a chance online friendship with an American woman who was also a writer and soon after became my closest friend and critique partner. She told me the kind of books I dreamed of writing were being published in the US and posted me *Pure Sin*. The impact it had on me was profound, life changing. Susan Johnson did everything I wanted to read as a reader, and write as a writer. She had a fully realized romantic relationship that included its sexual aspect. Her stories break all the rules of traditional romance, yet they are grounded in fully realized, realistic settings. She doesn't shy away from real life truths, like the fact we often have sex for the wrong reason or with the wrong person, before the right one comes along. This was everything I wanted. I started to look to the States for my reading, and for my possible home as an erotic romance author.

Shiloh Walker: It's a toss-up between *Elizabeth's Wolf* by Lora Leigh and *Dream Specter* by Mary Wine. They are two of my all time favorites, and that includes all the genres that I read. And I read everything from s/f, to fantasy, to mainstream suspense, to most of the genres within romance. These two books just have everything I want from a romance, whether it's erotic or not. They have steaming hot sex, but there's such emotion in these stories, a lot of suspense … and they are paranormal. I love paranormal.

Sasha White: *The Ninety Days of Genevieve* by Lucinda Carrington. It's a Black Lace erotica novel, but has a romance in it. The heroine goes on a journey and learns some hard truths about her life, and herself, and ends up in love. It's my favorite probably because it was the first real erotica novel I ever read, but also because it shows that erotica can have romance in it. The book is ten years old, but if it came out today it would be classified as an erotic romance.

Appendix E

Author Roundtable Discussion

The following is a Q&A with 18 authors published in the erotic romance genre.

How Do You Define Erotic Romance? Erotica? Pornography?

Jaid Black: Erotic romance is a symbiotic relationship between the erotica and romance genres; there cannot be one without the other. Erotica is sex without love and/or sex without rhyme or reason to it (i.e., little to no plot!). Pornography is a dangerous word … one person's porn is another person's pleasure. For instance, whether it's politically correct to admit to or not, I know for a fact that many of my female readers love voyeuristic rape fantasies, key word being *fantasies*. They certainly wouldn't want it to happen in real life, but enjoy the escapism and total lack of control provided by "forced seduction" scenes in erotic romance novels. What is pornography? I don't know. If there aren't children, dead people, animals, etc. involved, then it pretty much boils down to a matter of personal taste.

Pamela Clare: Erotic romance to me is a story that pushes sexual boundaries but remains focused on a romantic plot; the sexuality is merely a part of the overall romance plot. Erotica is more about sexual experimentation or exploring sexual boundaries. Sexuality is in the foreground for its own sake, not to further a love story. Erotica can have wonderful literary merits, but it's not romance. Pornography is f*cking for the sake of f*cking. There's not art or any attempt at literary quality. The purpose is to show people getting off, nothing more.

Emma Holly: Trying to define the lines between those genres feels a bit like handcuffing myself—and not in a good way! I would rather just write the story than worry about someone slapping a label they consider derogatory on it because I have or haven't included a certain act or situation. From a strictly practical standpoint, erotic romance is whatever readers are willing to buy that has the "erotic romance" label on the spine. Currently, this covers a huge range of stories, from almost sweet to extremely explicit.

Jordan Summers: Erotic romance is a romance that develops into a deeper emotional connection through the characters' physical relationship. Sex comes before the emotional development as opposed to traditional romances, which has the sexual relationship developing after the emotional connection. A happily-ever-after ending is expected in an erotic romance.

Erotica stories are based around sexual discovery and are specifically written to evoke particular emotions like fear, love, anger, frustration, etc. They do not need to have a relationship or a happily-ever-after in them for the story to be complete, but a change of some kind must occur. Pornography is a series of written or visual events meant for no other purpose than to titillate. In-depth plots and emotional connections are not necessary ingredients for these stories, nor do they require a happily-ever-after ending or a change of any kind to take place.

Saskia Walker: Pornography depicts sex devoid of story. Erotica is a literary experiment with words to stimulate the senses through the imagination, a combination of compelling story and arousing content. Erotica may or may not be about a monogamous ongoing relationship. It can include the myriad emotions of having sex, but may not include love. As the genre grows, it includes not only erotica aimed at women but also at couples. Violet Blue's *Sweet Life* series, for example. Many of my erotica shorts are about couples in committed, loving, ongoing relationships, defying many authors' definition of erotica having no emotional content. It is the least easy to define precisely, because of the way it has changed over the last thirty or so years. Erotic romance is a love story that embraces the whole relationship including the physical side. It does not leave the reader outside a closed door.

Sasha White: Erotic romance is a *romance*. It's a story about a relationship between people where sex often happens *before* romantic feelings evolve. But the focus *is* the relationship, and love is the result. Erotica is all about the main character's journey. The sexual acts and scenes that take place in an erotica story propel the character on a journey. Most often it is one that involves a lot of looking inside oneself and acceptance. The sex scenes are explicit, but not gratuitous. They are part of the story and key to the evolving relationships within the story. Porn is sex. It's body parts rubbing together for the reader's (or viewer's) titillation. There's not often much of a storyline; it's stroke material. And nothing is wrong with it. It's just different.

What Attracted You to Writing Erotic Romance?

Bella Andre: Honestly, I had heard that writers were doing well in this genre. I did some research, read some "romantica" and told my husband, "I don't think I can write this." He said, "You'll never know until you try." So I sat down on that Saturday afternoon and wrote the best, fastest, most fun three chapters. I sold the book (*Authors in Ecstasy*) a week later to Ellora's Cave, and the rest is history.

Pamela Clare: Sensual equality for women. Ever since I was a teenager, I've been aware that the sexual world is primarily organized around male desires and interests. Even books like *The Joy of Sex* seem to me to be written for a male audience. I feel so many women have defined themselves and their own sexuality through "the male gaze," basing their expectations for what sex is and what their sexual experience is supposed to be about on what they see men enjoying and desiring. But women are different. We're a different species. We're every bit as sexual as men (contrary to what many of us were raised to believe), but we're sexual in a different way. I was in high school when it seemed to me that part of what I needed to do when I got older was to create a space in which women could experiment with what true female sexuality is. What are *our* fantasies? What do we want from men? If we were able to demand anything, what would it be? Having said all that, I never really set out to write erotic romance. I just wanted to push the boundaries of sexuality depicted in romance to make it more real.

Emma Holly: Writing erotic romance allows me to explore stuff that's always fascinated me: sex and longing, love and power, the differences between men and women, the incredible variety of human desires, and how all these things shape our lives. When you write about what excites you, that's a wonderful source of creative energy—and that's true no matter what genre you end up deciding on.

Lydia Joyce: The kind of stories I write demand explicitness in the love scenes because that is where so much character development takes place since that is often where my characters are the most honest and defenseless. Therefore, the border between "pretty hot" and "really hot to burning" was simply an issue of quantity for me. I chose to go with stories that provide opportunities for more love scenes because writing sex is a strength for me and it sells well.

Cheyenne McCray: When I read traditional romances, I kept wanting more when it came to the sex scenes. More emotion, more feeling, more reality. When I discovered my publisher, I felt like I'd been given a new set of wings. I was free to write whatever I wanted to write, and push the boundaries, especially my boundaries, as far as I could go.

Does Writing Hot Come Naturally or Did You Decide to Try to Write Sexier for Marketing Reasons?

Jaid Black: For me it's a natural gift—or curse—depending on one's vantage point! Back when I started writing, before erotic romance caught on, publishers were telling me to tone the sexual content and situations in my books down significantly and then resubmit my work to them. I got sick of the rejections, eventually started my own company so I could publish my work the way I wanted to write it, and have never been happier. In retrospect, I'm glad I received all those rejection letters. I'm also glad I'm stubborn and unwilling to cave in when something matters to me! Otherwise, without those two variables, there would be no Ellora's Cave and thereby many undiscovered authors of impeccable talent.

Sunny Chen: Well, I started out writing a romance. But it was when I hit the love scenes that my writing really took off in terms of ease and quality of writing. Words and emotions just flew out of me, detailed and explicit. It was the best part of my writing, according to my husband, who is a bestselling literary author, so I had to keep it. The Kensington editor who eventually read it agreed with him, calling it "literary erotica," which was the pitch that eventually got my *Mona Lisa* paranormal series read and bought by Berkley. I still remember blushing redder than a beet when editors, agents, and other ladies attending the Romance Writers of America conference where I was pitching my book, would ask me what I write, and I had to answer, "Erotic paranormal and contemporary romance." Writing hot, I'd have to say, came very, very naturally for me. Fortunately or unfortunately, I don't know yet.

Lydia Joyce: I naturally have a strength in writing "sexy," and I naturally write high sexual tension and explicit sex scenes. I chose to go with a relatively high *quantity* of sex scenes per book for marketing reasons. Though my sex scenes set me apart from many authors, they are very, very difficult for me to write because they are so psychologically complicated—and because there is a very fine line between sexy and silly, and if I cross it, I want it to be on purpose.

Angela Knight: I've always written hot. Marketing is not a good reason to write anything, because I think it you try to write something you don't love, it shows.

Shiloh Walker: Naturally. Writing the hotter stuff for marketing reasons isn't something that will work for everybody. I've read some and thought it was more like a kid sister playing dress up in big bad sister's clothes. If it feels awkward, chances are that's just not what that writer was meant to write.

Have You Ever Been Embarrassed by Anything You've Written for Any Reason?

Alyssa Brooks: I think every erotic writer has occasional embarrassing moments. After all, your fingers are spilling your inner thoughts onto paper, revealing to everyone what you find hot. I'm proud of what I write, but sure, when I tell the dentist that my day job is writing love stories with spankings, my face does turn a little red.

Sunny Chen: Oh, definitely. By all of my romances, which are very hot, very detailed, and very explicit. I was raised in a very conservative religious background, and was always a bit of an oddball in my family. I was the only one to read "sinful" Harlequin and Silhouette romance books (not to mention the steamier romances I've moved onto since) in not just my family circle, but also among my friends. My proper and professional Chinese American family still doesn't understand why I would rather write romances than practice medicine; I'm a family practice physician and a graduate of Vassar College. I was the typical nerdy straight-A student who always had her nose buried in a book. But instead of a textbook, they were hot and steamy romance books.

Emma Holly: Occasionally I feel self-conscious about a sex scene, but it's usually because what I've written came a bit too close to the bone, so to speak, and I feel like I've exposed something personal that I maybe didn't even know was there. More often I'm self-conscious because I'm not sure I pulled off what I was trying to do. Now and then, some little voice will tell me what I've written doesn't fit the general consensus for what's PC, but I tend to ignore that one.

Angela Knight: People are going to judge a woman who writes erotic fiction. That's particularly true for those who live in the Bible Belt, as I do. I've learned to downplay the sexual content of my books to those who aren't erotic romance readers, because I'm well aware they may not approve.

Karin Tabke: No, and if I did, I would delete it. If it embarrasses me then it would embarrass my readers, and who wants that?

Are You Concerned Over Complaints About the Genre's Electronic Cover Art, Over-the-Top Sex, Borderline Pornography, Etc.?

Pamela Clare: As a journalist, I'm a staunch supporter of the First Amendment. I don't want to see any junta of writers ban anything from any group of which I'm a member. At the same time, some of the electronic art I've seen is just plain *bad*. Some of the writing is bad, too. This is true for any genre. I'm certain the market will sort it out eventually.

Portia Da Costa: Yes, in a way. I don't think it's necessary to put acres of bare flesh on covers. The art of suggestion is far sexier. If I see a bare body on a cover, it puts me off, and I think it puts a lot of people off, even if they like strong erotic content. Hence my concern. Regards content, I'm only concerned about substandard writing getting published in print or e-books and giving the rest of us a bad name.

Sylvia Day: Definitely. I think most of the electronic cover art is dreadful and embarrassing. I think some of the sexual content is disturbing and not well written. Some will say that poor cover art and bad writing exists in every facet of the publishing industry, and I agree. But either erotic romance has a higher profile so the faults are more glaring, or the genre has a higher proportion of the negatives. Either way it's a problem and it needs to be addressed. Passing the buck with "everyone is doing it" is a sorry excuse.

Jordan Summers: I do admit that when someone calls an erotic romance 'borderline pornography' it bothers me. I don't think pornography requires a plot or an emotional connection to exist. Erotic romance needs an emotional connection and a solid plot. As for the covers, the publishers are simply responding to reader demand. If readers weren't buying the books with the racy covers, then the publishers would change them. As an author, I have little to no control over the cover art.

Shiloh Walker: I don't concern myself with other people's books. I write what's true to me. I think some people have started doing the over-the-top sex for various reasons—seeing how far they can push it, for money, to snub their nose at the people who look down on it. But a lot of these books, well, in my opinion, the quality is lacking. The sex is gratuitous, it's crammed into every nook and cranny, and the story is substandard. That's not a good erotic romance. In order to write a good erotic romance, you have to start with the romance, not the sex. If you're just putting sex in for sex's sake, you're slutting up the book and you are part of the problem some people have with erotic romance. As to [the] cover art issue, I may be in the minority, but I think some of the covers are just plain ridiculous. A book can have a wonderful, sensual cover without showing a guy's butt or a scene where you can all but see the penetration. We're writers; we're supposed to be professional. A lot of people are going to have a hard time being seen as professionals by others in the industry if they have a gang bang on their cover. Again, I think a lot of these covers are designed to thumb noses at the people who are down on erotic romances, particularly cover art. That's not a particularly professional way to handle it.

Do You Find You Often Have to Defend Your Work to Others Who Accuse You of Writing Nothing but Sex?

Jaid Black: Not often, but it does happen every once in a while. Mostly from straight romance authors who eat a steady diet of sour grapes. Why? I don't know. Maybe they are jealous because many of us make more money than they do and putting us down makes them feel better or whatever. For the most part, I consider the source and shrug it off.

Pamela Clare: Yes. I see this as a chance to educate people. I tell them that if people are reading my 400-page novels for sex, they're working hard for minimal pay-off, because I average only about 40 to 60 pages of outright sex in any given book. That's a lot of reading just to read sex scenes.

Lydia Joyce: Rarely. I'm a "scary person," and so few people dare accuse me of anything. I eat the few who do for breakfast. They taste good with orange juice. Virtually everyone who wants to think I write nothing but sex has a prurient interest in the matter, but most often, I am asked about relationship advice, as if my occupation made me into a combination of Dr. Phil and a sexual therapist. Now, *that* is embarrassing.

Cheyenne McCray: In the past, I felt the need to, but I now feel comfortable enough in my skin, in what my readers want, that I don't worry about that any longer. And if anyone accuses me of writing nothing but sex, then they haven't read my books. I write *romances* with intricate subplots, and the sex is a natural part of the hero and heroine's relationship. Out of the twenty-plus books that I've written, I would say that only three come close to erotica, but they also either have a happily-ever-after ending, or a "hopeful" ending, where the hero and heroine find a bonding where they want to continue seeing one another.

Karin Tabke: I never *ever* defend what I write. I write what I write and you can read what you read. I believe in a person's right to have an opinion and would never argue that someone's opinion of erotic romance was wrong, just as I would not want anyone to argue my view. To each his own. I do find that romance writers for the most part, and erotic romance authors big time, feel they have to defend what they write. I say, bull. Don't waste your time or energy defending yourself against a person or persons who don't get you and never will. Go write.

Does Your Family Support Your Career Choice? Are Any of Them Embarrassed by What You Do?

Bella Andre: My family is overwhelmingly supportive of my career choice. In fact, my father works with several Nobel Prize winners and he gave each of them a copy of my debut novel, *Take Me*, for Christmas. And he cried with joy when I told him Simon & Schuster bought three novels from me. My mother-in-law is a huge fan, reads everything I write, and also gives a copy of my books to any- and everyone. No one has ever made so much as one judgmental comment. And my husband is the one who encouraged me to try writing in this genre in the first place! He's very proud.

Jaid Black: My immediate family is totally proud. My dad refers to me as "my daughter, the porn pusher," but I know he's just joking so my panties don't get in a wad over it! The only people in my family who put down what I do for a living are distant relatives who have other axes to grind with me. Again, I consider the source. You know how they say "familiarity breeds contempt"? Well, sad as it is, I've also found that "success breeds contempt." It happens amongst family, friends, and colleagues alike. People accuse you of changing, when in reality, it's their perception of you that has changed. I'm the same person I was a decade ago, minus the failure part. I don't lord my accomplishments over anyone's head—hell, I rarely even talk of them unless something major happens, like I hit a bestseller list—so I found out pretty quickly who the true loves in my life are.

Sunny Chen: My religious and conservative mom, dad, and older brother are all proud that I'm a published author, but at the same time, hugely uncomfortable at what I write. But my eminently respectable husband, an acclaimed bestselling literary author, is thrilled that I'm published. He, of all people, knows just how hard that is to achieve. And my young son and daughter are also very proud. "Mommy's an author, too."

Lydia Joyce: All my close relatives support me and understand what my message is, but I have some more distant relatives who are censorious. I mostly nod and smile and say, "It's interesting that you would think that," until they go away. You aren't supposed to eat relatives for breakfast.

Karin Tabke: Absolutely. And nope. When I contracted with Kensington for their erotic romance line Aphrodisia, I asked my family (I have four kids ranging from ages 15–25) and my in-laws one night at Sunday dinner if they were okay with my real name going on the cover. I added that if they were uncomfortable with my subject matter I would be happy to use a pen name. A resounding, "No way, go for it. We're proud of you," followed.

Do You Find Yourself Ever Second-Guessing What You Do Because of Controversy Over the Genre in Publishing or Reading Circles?

Jami Alden: I only second-guess myself in the sense that I worry that my books aren't "edgy" enough or don't "push the envelope" in terms of the sex scenes, that in the future I might get pressured to put my characters in situations I'm not comfortable with. And I guess I do worry about someone reading something in another book that was maybe too out-there or a turnoff and doesn't pick up my book as a result.

Bella Andre: No. I do, however, spend time assessing what it is that I want out of my writing career. Plus, I'm keeping my eye on the market.

Larissa Lyons: No. If I ever second-guess this career choice, it's because I think it is one of the most difficult mentally. You have to be extremely strong and believe in yourself completely in order to withstand the criticisms of others and the extremely competitive field of publishing.

Cheyenne McCray: Never. I write what works for the story. I might be a little nervous about what the readers will think when I break new ground with a certain audience, but I don't let any controversy affect my writing in any way, and I never will.

Do You Worry About Your Explicit Writing Falling into the Wrong Hands, i.e., a Too-Young Audience?

Jami Alden: Ideally, no one under the age of eighteen would read my books. That being said, I was reading Susan Johnson by the time I was fifteen, and I turned out okay. Not to be cavalier about it, but in a weird way I think reading romance novels at what some might call an inappropriately young age actually made me more conservative about sex. Think about what romance—even erotic romance—promotes: sex between people who love each other and are committed to each other.

Alyssa Brooks: Yes, I do, and unfortunately, in reality it will happen. I hope that bookstores, parents, and such will be good enough to censor the availability of explicit reading material. But on the other hand, I remember what I read, and even did, at sixteen and realize that you'll never keep everything from the hands of a teen. Whether it's erotic romance, or *Playboy*, teens are interested in sex, and where there's a will, there's a way. As a parent, I don't like it, but bottom line—it's my job to protect my kids.

Pamela Clare: No. I think violence is worse than sexuality. Sex is a natural human activity; killing isn't. I think we have that formula backward in the United States. Kids can watch the most graphic violence at a young age—cartoon violence, videogame violence, movie violence—but we keep sex at a distance. Our culture is still suffering from a Puritan hangover, and open expressions of sexuality, particularly those that focus on sex in the context of healthy, healing relationships, can only help society as a whole. I started reading romances when I was about fourteen. I didn't understand everything that was going on in the love scenes, but I enjoyed them. I think young people just skip over what they don't understand. And, hey, they might learn something. I encourage men to read romance for that reason. My sons, 19 and 16, read my books with my blessing.

Emma Holly: I don't encourage people under eighteen to read my books, but I know some of them do. Sometimes I hear from mothers that their daughters are reading me, but since neither the mothers nor the girls seem traumatized, I've lost any worry I might have felt over that. I suspect if the kids are really too young, a lot of what I write will simply go over their heads and they'll be bored. In any case, it's not my job to be the reading police. My mother gave me an amazing amount of freedom in what I read when I was young. Now that she's passed on, it's one of the things I most admire about the way she raised me.

Angela Knight: Now, that does concern me. However, you don't see kids shopping the romance aisles very often. And too, the relationships I depict are positive and loving, so I don't see my work as damaging.

Cheyenne McCray: Yes, I do. I can only hope that parents are vigilant about what their children read and that only adults eighteen and older read my books.

Sasha White: No I don't. I think maybe because I read it when I was way underage, it doesn't bother me. And kids are going to get their hands on sexy material no matter what we do. That's not to say I support kids finding it. I'm just saying it's going to happen, and we can't control everything for everyone. Plus, the characters in erotica are real.

They're not always the tiny beautiful blonde. They're overweight, they're stressed, they have doubts. I'd rather have young minds read an erotica story where sex is portrayed in an honest, positive light, where women can have as much control, pleasure, and satisfaction as a man, instead of something that completely objectifies women and makes them feel they are only sexually attractive when they are airbrushed and perfect.

What Responsibility Do You Feel to Include Safe Sex in Your Books?

Jami Alden: I don't know if it's so much responsibility as my own personal hang-ups. Personally, I worry about safe sex. If a man and a woman in a contemporary romance don't at least have a discussion—even after the fact if they got too "caught up in the moment"—about safe sex and/or birth control, I get pulled out of the story. A little voice in the back of my head will say, "Is she worried about getting pregnant? Is she on the pill? What about chlamydia?" I also use the choice to use or not use a condom as a device to show commitment between the hero and heroine or to make sex that much more special.

Jaid Black: I don't feel any sense of responsibility. I write for adults who, one would hope, can separate fantasy from reality. If they can't make that distinction, they've got more problems than I could ever create for them. I think it's very clear that I write fantasies … and condoms aren't a part of any sexual fantasy I've ever had. They are distracting to me as a reader, so as an author I don't write them into my sex scenes.

Pamela Clare: In contemporaries, I make certain we know how the heroine is preventing pregnancy and, in new relationships, make sure the hero *of his own accord* brings condoms. I would *not* be able to respect a heroine who had unsafe sex in this day and age. I would not find a man heroic who placed a woman at risk for disease or unplanned pregnancy. It just offends me. Passion is passion, but HIV is forever. I know some readers don't want that level of realism. They argue that romance is fantasy and shouldn't have to carry the same burdens as the real world. And yet so many women don't take care of themselves sexually, so this desire to ignore the harsh realities of modern life isn't something women are doing just when they read. I know educated college women who got pregnant unintentionally because they were using nothing; I know women who've had cervical cancer and herpes because they failed to protect themselves. For whatever reason, they're too timid to ask a guy to wear a condom or too hesitant to be put on the pill. I want my novels to model heroic, responsible sexuality—even if it is scorching hot. And, really, there's nothing less sexy than a guy who doesn't care about a woman enough to protect her or a women who's self-esteem is so low she won't take care of herself.

Sylvia Day: All of my contemporary stories feature the use of condoms. However, this isn't because of a feeling of responsibility on my part, but due to my own threshold of believability. I simply cannot believe an adult contemporary couple who is just beginning a sexual relationship would not protect themselves from disease or pregnancy. I have set aside books I was reading where the contemporary protagonists failed to use condoms. That lack of realistic detail ruined the plausibility of the entire book for me.

Larissa Lyons: After giving this a lot of thought, I decided not to include condoms in my stories, unless they are directly part of the plotline. Reading is recreation. When I pick up a book, I want to escape from life's stresses, not be reminded of them. When someone picks up an erotic romance, they expect to be entertained *and* aroused, so interrupting a hot scene to slap a rubber on a penis doesn't make sense. I do think including a disclaimer at the beginning of each story, reminding readers to always practice safe sex is a good idea.

Jordan Summers: I feel very responsible, if the book is a straight contemporary novel. If the book is from a different genre such as historical, paranormal, or fantasy, then I don't worry about it. The rules for those 'worlds' very rarely apply.

Saskia Walker: I take guidance from the publisher I'm submitting to. I stared writing shorts for Black Lace, where the fantasy angle is pushed up front and there is a foreword about safe sex. It doesn't bother me whether condoms are used or not, this is fiction and fantasy we're dealing with. Some readers don't like the awkward interruption of real life concerns; others are shocked if those things aren't included. Ultimately we aren't delivering sex manuals, we are writing fiction. I'm happy either way, though.

How Do You Research Your Sex Scenes If You're Writing About Something Unfamiliar to You? Do You Have Any Favorite Sources, Websites, or Books?

Portia Da Costa: By reading nonfiction books about various sexualities, and watching relevant video or television. Too many sources to mention. Also, and probably most usefully, I just fantasise.

Lydia Joyce: My two favorite sources for information about the Victorian sexual underworld (though not directly about sex) are *My Secret Life* by Walter and *London Labour and the London Poor* by Henry Mayhew. About sex itself, I rely on "girl talk" and insight into the nature of people.

Larissa Lyons: I simply imagine myself in that situation and start to write. It is only after completing a story that I do any detailed research on a specific sexual act or prop. This way, I can correct anything I may have written wrong and add in any details that will enhance the scene or story. But by not researching things like this in the beginning, I find that I'm able to remain truer to the character's emotions, which I consider paramount.

Cheyenne McCray: It does depend. A lot of what I write comes from a very vivid imagination! However, when I wrote several 'playful' BDSM books, I read a lot of books by other authors in that subgenre that helped me to understand the lifestyle. I also had people in the lifestyle read my books to make sure that what I was writing fell in line with what that lifestyle is all about. In regards to writing sex scenes, BDSM is the subject that I've had to do the most amount of research on because I had no knowledge of the lifestyle and I didn't understand it.

Do You Ever Plan Out Sex Scenes as Part of the Plot and Character Advancement, or Do You Let Them Fall Where They May?

Bella Andre: Yes, sex scenes are an integral part of my plot. In fact, they are often what drives the story forward.

Sunny Chen: Yes, often as plot and character advancement. How a person makes love, resists it or embraces it, selfishly or unselfishly, reveals much. But usually the love scenes come about naturally on their own as the story unfolds and the characters are brought together.

Angela Knight: I definitely plot sex scenes as a means of character advancement or plot development. They shouldn't be inserted just because it's time for nookie.

Larissa Lyons: I've done both, depending on the overall story arc. For me, planning the sex scenes is no different [from] planning the story. As a seat-of-the-pants writer, I usually have only a vague idea of where my story is going until I get there. Sometimes, though, the idea of a specific sex scene will provide impetus for an entire story.

Sasha White: I rarely plan anything in my stories. I'm not a plotter. I try to get my know my characters as best I can, and then I start them on a path, and they take me, and hopefully the reader, on their journey with them.

Are You Afraid of Going Too Far Sexually? Of Skirting a Reader's Ick Factor?

Alyssa Brooks: I don't think it matters how far sexually you go, but how you write it. I have a friend who can take an anal sex scene and make it the most romantic, sensual piece of work. Anal sex can also be written as a very dirty, gritty act. It's all in how you display it! That said, how your characters think of sex is of huge importance. It isn't just about their physical reactions, but also their mental and emotional responses to the sexual act.

Sunny Chen: Actually, I have to push myself to always go more edgy. Toward areas that make me a little uncomfortable. I grew up conservative. It's more a matter of me having to shed fear and inhibitions than going too far. And I try to never repeat a love scene. So far I've written twenty of them and they're all different.

Karin Tabke: No, in fact, I have recently read a few things that I thought would ick me out, but were so beautifully written it had the opposite effect. So, if it does ick me out, then I won't keep it, but if I've done my job as a writer, then by all means I'll keep the scene.

Saskia Walker: I think we have to live with the fact we might hit somebody's ick factor, no matter what we do. You can't please all the people all the time. For me, it's about how things are done. If the author handles it in a way that is credible and entertaining, even the oddest of practices can work. We have to get real though—what we are dealing with is a "take it or leave it" entertainment product, not something we force on people who might not like it. If I read a passage in a book I don't particularly enjoy, I skim past it.

Has Your Publisher Ever Asked You to Add Sex Scenes to Spice Up Your Work?

Alyssa Brooks: Oh yes … a few times! One editor specifically told me "sexy *all* the way through" is what they wanted for their erotic romance line. She requested I cut quite a bit of really good stuff to get to the action already. I've learned it's important to remember that the attraction and, ultimately, the sex drives the plot in an erotic romance. You can't just take any traditionally written romance novel and fluff up the sex scenes to make an erotic romance. It doesn't work that way, and when you try it, you end up with a book that's simply not hot enough. You might call it a sensual romance, but it's not an erotic romance.

Sunny Chen: No. Actually, I'm surprised they haven't asked me to tone it down. In my paranormal *Mona Lisa* series, I have the heroine with two lovers, and as the series progresses, even more. Very nontraditional. I thought they were going to make me take out one of her lovers, to make it more traditional one guy–one girl, but they love it as it is.

Portia Da Costa: No. Writing hot is second nature to me, and I've never had to write any sexier than I already do. I've always been asked to tone down rather than spice up.

Sylvia Day: Yes. And I've been asked by publishers to make my sex less graphic. Each publisher has a target audience, and they want to tailor their stories to appeal to that demographic.

Karin Tabke: No, although one editor expressed concern when she learned my characters didn't actually get into bed until page 220 of a 380-page single title. I assured her it wasn't time before page 220, but the pages leading up to it were sizzling.

Do You Think Readers of E-Books and Those of Print Books Look for Different Things, i.e., Have You Found One Group of Readers to Be More Open-Minded or Adventurous in Their Reading Material Than the Other?

Angela Knight: It seems to me that e-book readers are more adventurous. I think they start reading e-books looking for edgier stuff to begin with; I know I did. Print readers, however, include a sizeable population who are not into kink. A writer has to take that into consideration, because you can definitely turn readers off.

Larissa Lyons: Undoubtedly. I think anyone unfamiliar with e-books may not be aware of the true caliber and variety available online. Coming from a print reading background only, I have been shocked and amazed at the amount and types of stories available online. As a confessed s/f junkie, I was thrilled to see romances that actually take place at s/f conventions! There is a tremendous amount of freedom available with e-published books. Print markets are definitely more traditionally oriented, although I do see the print market adapting and changing as e-books command a larger and larger share of readers' time and money.

Jordan Summers: I believe e-book readers are far more adventurous than their print counterparts. In my opinion, this is due to a heightened sense of anonymity that frees them to explore subjects they wouldn't dream of touching in a brick-and-mortar store.

Karin Tabke: I think e-books opened the door for the new open book attitude prevailing now in print erotic romance. Definitely the e-readers are more open-minded, and I'm glad it's finally coming across to the print publishers. I think also that traditional print book readers will stay the course with what they read and what they won't read, but e-readers will now be able to buy in print what they have only been able to find in electronic form.

Are There Similarities or Differences in Writing for the Two Mediums (Print vs. Electronic) in What Your Readers Want and the Respect You Get?

Bella Andre: Certainly writing for one of the big New York publishers gets more respect from most people, but it depends who you talk to. Booksellers at Borders and Waldenbooks are very thrilled by Ellora's Cave books because they sell so well in print. The main difference in writing for e-publishers is that you generally write a much shorter book—novella length, or sometimes even as small as [10,000] words. But even print publishers now often print anthologies, so that seems to have changed as well. The short format does well for erotic romance.

Alyssa Brooks: I cannot tell you the number of times as an e-published author that I was asked when I would 'really' be published by various people, even my husband! Most do not see e-books as real books, and many never will. But you know something? I didn't see much of a change in the reactions when I received my first print contract. Now people just ask when I'll be famous, because until I become a household name, I'm still not a 'real' writer, don't you know! But who am I to complain? I'm never satisfied either!

Jordan Summers: The differences seem to be diminishing rapidly. Both require a decent plot and storytelling ability. You have more freedom to explore mixed genres and controversial subject matters in electronic format. There are very few taboos in electronic publishing. The readers of electronic books seem to be more vocal than print readers.

My readers are very specific when it comes to their needs and wants. The strange thing is that the only lack of respect I've ever received did not come from readers. It came from other writers.

Karin Tabke: I'm only published in print, but I know several authors who publish in both formats and their reader base is solid on both fronts. As far as the respect I get as a print published author compared to an e-published author? Amongst the choir, there is that group of print published authors who will never see those who are electronically published as their equal, but I think that wall is slowly coming down. There are just too many damn good e-published authors out there.

Saskia Walker: The thing I've noticed is that e-book readers are more actively communicative on the net, so you're more likely to see someone commenting about a book in an informal setting like a chat list. It kind of goes with the territory. If they are technically savvy enough to be reading online, they are also active online.

What Do You Enjoy Most About Writing Erotic Romance?

Jaid Black: The legitimacy it lends to female sexuality as an entity distinct from that of male sexuality. Our fantasies are different, our sensual needs are different, and erotic romance lets us cater to the female experience.

Pamela Clare: The realism. Life is X-rated. We're all sexual people. If we were to film every moment of our lives, we'd end up with a very erotic movie. By depicting my characters' sexuality, along with the rest of their personalities, we (readers and I) get to know them very well. I never liked the soft-pedaled approach to sex scenes where the door slams in your face after the first kiss. I want to watch and see how these people express their love for each other sexually.

Lydia Joyce: I can get away with more in every other area than most writers at my level—plot, setting, characters, etc. By having the "spice" hook, I win wiggle room elsewhere. My publisher did not freak out when I said, "Yeah, and this book is about an ex-streetwalker," or "This book is set in the Ottoman Empire; isn't that *cool?*" By stepping out of one set of restraints, it seems that I am also less constrained by others.

Cheyenne McCray: The freedom. The ability to push the envelope, to push my own boundaries as far as I possibly can. I find it fun to experiment and try new things in my writing.

Sasha White: That I can be true to the way things happen in the real world. That I can write about that fact that one-night stands happen, and women don't happen to remain virgins until they fall in love, in order to find love.

What Do You Enjoy Least About Writing Erotic Romance?

Jamie Alden: I find it incredibly challenging to balance the emotional and physical aspects of a sex scene. I often worry that I'm getting too mechanical or play-by-play and losing that elusive emotional intensity that I strive for.

Jaid Black: I feel somewhat branded, pigeon-holed. There are times when I don't feel like writing about sex, but I know if my readers pick up a G-rated Jaid Black book, they will be pissed. I'm considering taking on another pen name just so I can write romantic comedies without an expectation of eroticism in the novels.

Sylvia Day: Reviewers [who] concentrate their reviews so much on the sexual content and "heat level" and don't spend enough time talking about the story and characters. I think most review sites offer a "heat rating." That should be enough of an indication. The volume of sex and specific sexual content shouldn't be the focus of any review.

Larissa Lyons: The competition! If only I had realized five years ago when I started learning how to write traditional romance that these so-called e-published erotic romances weren't just a bunch of skanky, poorly written porn novels masquerading as romances, I'd have a lot more stories written! Until meeting my critique partner, I had never visited an e-publisher's website, and I truly had no idea that so many of these stories are written with such care and talent.

Shiloh Walker: I'd like to hear more about the stories I write, instead of about all the hot sex and the hot men. I put my heart and soul into the book and sometimes, all I hear is, "Oh, man, that guy was soooooo hot!" What about the heroine—her courage, her heart? It's not a romance without the two characters. If you just have a hero, it's mainstream. What about the story? I'd like to hear more about that, because the story itself is more important to me than how hot the guy was or how hot the sex was.

What Single Piece of Advice Has Helped You Most or Would You Like to Pass On to Others?

Bella Andre: Obviously, write the stories you want to write. But most important, join a great writers group. I've gotten all my leads about publishers and agents and editors from other women writers. They really are my best friends.

Jaid Black: Write what you love to write even if every agent and publisher you encounter says it won't sell. Facts are, they don't know everything, or even close to it. That said, if you want to play the game, you need to know how to find your way around the playground. The publishing houses *say* they are looking for cutting-edge work, but really they're just looking for a new spin on the tried and true. You need to decide going into it if you will follow the leader or be one. Carving your own path is difficult, sometimes seemingly impossible, but it can be done.

Alyssa Brooks: If you are going to write erotic romance, be bold, be different, experiment. But don't hold back! And by all means, in this genre, you must be strong enough to stand up to other's harsh opinions.

Sunny Chen: You must be fearless in writing romance. And you must write what moves you most. All else might be good, but you have to be more than good to be published. You have to do at least one thing extraordinarily well. For me, that happened to be my love scenes.

Pamela Clare: Write as hot as you want to write. Your editor can always tone it down.

Portia Da Costa: The advice I give for writing erotica is to always start with a "bang"! It's a sure way to grab your readers' interest. Try [to] have your characters erotically involved on the first page, or even in the first paragraph. I've sometimes even managed it in the first sentence! In the case of erotic romance though, where you have to have a romantic relationship, too, I'd recommend a prologue in order to use this technique.

Sylvia Day: If you can cut a sex scene out and the story would still work, cut it out. Every sex scene should further the character arcs.

Emma Holly: Set your own standards and honor them. You are the person whose values should be embodied in your work. You are the person who most needs to be proud of you.

Lydia Joyce: Be yourself, completely irreplaceable and as big as you can possibly be.

Angela Knight: *Don't give up*. Keep writing. Write what you love. Submit it. Then submit it some more, if it gets rejected. Look for ways to improve, and be ruthless with yourself. Don't accept less than the best you're capable of.

Larissa Lyons: What has helped me the most is something I read on Morgan Hawke's website: "It's all about the delayed f*ck." This little phrase has stuck in my mind more than anything and made me realize how very important sexual tension is, even more so than the actual sex. Ms. Hawke's website is a gold mine of articles and links, and I'd recommend any aspiring erotic author take the time to check it out. What would I like to share with others? If writing is your passion, take the time to learn how to do it right, and don't let anyone stop you from achieving your dream.

Cheyenne McCray: Don't be afraid or timid when you write your sex scenes. *Do not* think about what your mother, neighbor, or anyone else will think about what you're writing. At the same time, write what's comfortable for you, and you can always up the heat factor the second time around.

Jordan Summers: Be true to your vision. Write what makes *you* happy.

Karin Tabke: Stay the course, *do not give up*, and just as important, be true to yourself.

Saskia Walker: Ignore the naysayers!

Shiloh Walker: Keep your head down and write. Don't let yourself get pulled into some of the drama that happens inside the writing world. I've been exposed to a lot of catfights, lies, bullshit, petty jealousy and politics that did nothing but irritate. I'm happier when I'm just writing and not worrying about how this writer thinks or what that writer feels or what she said about this one … etc. … etc. … etc. …

Sasha White: Perseverance is the key to success.

Thank you to the following authors:

Jami Alden (www.jamialden.com)

Bella Andre (www.bellaandre.com)

Jaid Black (www.jaidblack.com)

Alyssa Brooks (www.alyssabrooks.com)

Sunny Chen (www.sunnyhotromance.com)

Pamela Clare (www.pamelaclare.com)

Portia Da Costa (www.planetportia.com)

Sylvia Day (www.sylviaday.com)

Emma Holly (www.emmaholly.com)

Lydia Joyce (www.lydiajoyce.com)

Angela Knight (www.angelasknights.com)

Larissa Lyons (www.larissalyons.com)

Cheyenne McCray (www.cheyennemccray.com)

Jordan Summers (www.jordansummers.com/js)

Karin Tabke (www.karintabke.com)

Saskia Walker (www.saskiawalker.co.uk)

Shiloh Walker (www.shilohwalker.com)

Sasha White (www.sashawhite.net)

Index

Numbers

A

B

C

E

F

I

J-K-L

P

Q–R

S

T

U-V

W-X-Y-Z

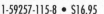

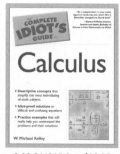

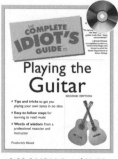